WORKERS' COMPENSATION AND EMPLOYEE PROTECTION LAWS

IN A NUTSHELL

Third Edition

JACK B. HOOD
Adjunct Professor of Law
University of Georgia School of Law

BENJAMIN A. HARDY, Jr.
Adjunct Professor of Law
University of Mississippi School of Law

HAROLD S. LEWIS, Jr.
Walter F. George Professor of Law
Mercer University School of Law

**WEST
GROUP**

A THOMSON COMPANY
ST. PAUL, MINN.
1999

2nd Reprint — 2001

TO
Pat, Sara, and Laura
Linda and Andy
Leslie, Harold, and Marianne

*

PREFACE

Our purpose in writing this Nutshell is to provide an overview of the laws affecting employees in the workplace. It is our hope that the sections on workers' compensation and employment discrimination will provide both students and lawyers with insight into the most common questions in the field. Only summaries have been attempted in the sections dealing with other employee protection legislation, because the subject areas were too large for detailed explanations.

An excellent and comprehensive treatment of workers' compensation is to be found in Larson's multi-volume treatise on the subject, and we have given useful citations to that work at relevant points. In the areas of employment discrimination, one may find useful Lewis' hornbook, Civil Rights and Employment Discrimination Law (West 1997) and Lewis' practitioner's handbook, Litigating Civil Rights and Employment Discrimination Laws (West 1996 with 1997–98 Supplement). The Nutshell by Professor Leslie on Labor Law (West 1992) is also useful, along with Rothstein, Craver, Schroeder, Shoben, and Vander Velde's hornbook, Employment Law (West 1994).

We would like to acknowledge and thank the Mercer University Law School, and our research assistants and Mercer Law School student, Martin L. Kent, and University of Alabama Law School student, Joshua M. Alford. We also express our appreciation to the law libraries at Mercer University, Samford University, the University of Mississippi, the University of Alabama, and the University of Georgia.

JACK B. HOOD
BENJAMIN A. HARDY, JR.
HAROLD S. LEWIS, JR.

August, 1998
Macon, Georgia

OUTLINE

PART 1. HISTORICAL BACKGROUND OF COMPENSATION LEGISLATION

OUTLINE

OUTLINE

OUTLINE

Page

TABLE OF CASES

References are to Pages

A

C

TABLE OF CASES

D

TABLE OF CASES

E

TABLE OF CASES

F

H

I

J

K

L

M

N

O

TABLE OF CASES

LIII

Q

R

S

T

U

*

WORKERS' COMPENSATION AND EMPLOYEE PROTECTION LAWS

Third Edition

*

PART 1

HISTORICAL BACKGROUND OF COMPENSATION LEGISLATION

CHAPTER 1

EMPLOYMENT RELATED ACTIONS AND LEGISLATION

A. EMPLOYEE'S COMMON–LAW REMEDIES

The common-law imposed a number of duties on employers for the protection of their employees, and an action existed for the breach of these duties, however, as a practical matter the common-law failed to provide adequate remedies for such injuries and deaths. The common-law duties imposed upon the master were as follows:

(1) to provide a safe place to work;

(2) to provide safe appliances, tools and equipment;

(3) to give warnings of dangers of which the employee might reasonably be expected to remain in ignorance;

(4) to provide a sufficient number of fit, trained, or suitable fellow servants to perform assigned tasks; and

(5) to promulgate and enforce rules relating to employee conduct which would make the work safe.

Employee remedies based upon a breach of the foregoing duties were restricted by the "unholy trinity" of common-law defenses: (1) fellow-servant doctrine; (2) contributory negligence; and (3) assumption of risk. See Prosser and Keeton on Torts § 80 (5th ed. 1984).

1. FELLOW–SERVANT DOCTRINE

Unless there was an express contract the rule at common law was that a master was not liable to a servant for injuries due to the negligence of a fellow servant. Priestly v. Fowler (1837); see Murray v. South Carolina Railroad Co. (1841). The doctrine provided that the negligence of a co-employee was not to be imputed to the master; of course, the injured employee, for what it was worth, could still sue a co-employee. The fellow-servant rule was not founded in abstract or natural justice, and the rule was an exception to the rule of agency and the general rule that a master was responsible for injuries caused to third persons by the negligence of servants who were acting within the scope of their employment. In support of the fellow-servant doctrine it was said that the negligence of a fellow-servant was one of the risks incident to employment, and the risk was assumed by the servant as an implied term of the employment contract. Public policy in support of the doctrine was to the effect that the rule would make servants careful and watchful with regard to each other, thus promoting greater care in the performance of their duties.

The harshness of the fellow-servant doctrine was lessened by the recognition of certain exceptions. For example, servants who did not have a common master and who were not engaged in the same enterprise, were not barred from recovery by the fellow-servant rules. Furthermore, if they were employed in different departments of the same enterprise, the employees were not generally to be treated as fellow-servants. The most important exception involved the negligence of a "vice-principal" because the fellow-servant bar did not apply to the vice-principal. One approach required that the vice-principal be a supervisory employee, representing the employer in his duty toward the employee. The vice-principal exception has been held to apply to any servant, as opposed to just superior servants. The key inquiry aimed at an employer's liability was whether a servant (alleged vice-principal) owed an obligation to the injured employee to meet the common-law duties of the employer. In order for the master to be liable, these duties were viewed as being non-delegable. The vice-principal exception was subject to an important qualification. It was not applicable to those incidental dangers which arose out of the operational details of a fellow-servant's work. No duty was owed by the master with regard to these risks.

2. CONTRIBUTORY NEGLIGENCE

An employee or servant was required to exercise reasonable care for his own safety, and his failure to use the precautions that ordinary prudence required, barred any recovery under the contributory negligence defense. Exceptions existed on the basis of the last clear chance doctrine and in situations in which the master's conduct was willful or wanton. As a result of the doctrine's harshness, statutes sometimes abrogated the defense and statutorily imposed requirements for worker safety, placing certain servants in a special, protected category. In some jurisdictions comparative negligence statutes aided employees.

3. ASSUMPTION OF RISK

The assumption of risk defense was grounded in the notion that the servant or employee had voluntarily agreed to assume the dangers normally and ordinarily incident to the work. Risks were covered which a mature worker was presumed to know, regardless of whether one had actual knowledge. The employee further assumed such extraordinary and abnormal risks of which he had knowledge and appreciation. Assumption of risk was customarily based upon contract theory, as opposed to contributory negligence which was based upon tort theory. Contributory negligence involved the notion of fault and a breach of duty to one's self, whereas assumption of risk could exist in the absence of fault because of its contractual nature. Employees or servants did not assume those risks growing out of the negligence of the master, or a vice principal. Generally risks arising out of the non-delegable duties doctrine were not viewed as the ordinary sort of risks which one could assume; these were treated as extraordinary risks which one did not assume. It should be kept in mind that recovery could still be barred by one's contributory negligence.

In summary, the foregoing "unholy trinity" may be explained in large part on the basis of the highly individualistic attitude of the common-law courts and society's desire to encourage industrial expansion and development by lessening the financial costs upon industry for industrial injuries and deaths. See generally Dodd, Administration of Workmen's Compensation, § 7 (1936); Horovitz, Injury and Death Under Workmen's Compensation Laws (1944); Prosser and Keeton on Torts § 80 (5th ed. 1984).

B. EMPLOYERS' LIABILITY ACTS

Employers' liability acts came into being in response to rising industrial injury and death rates in the 19th Century, and in response to dissatisfaction with the common-law remedies available to employees. For example, in 1855, the State of Georgia enacted a statute making railroads liable to employees and others for negligence in situations previously barred by the fellow-servant defense. By 1908, almost every American jurisdiction had passed similar legislation. Congress, in 1908, placed interstate railroad employees under an employers' liability act system and later extended this same coverage to seamen. The state and federal acts generally barred the use of the fellow-servant rule, substituted comparative negligence for pure contributory negligence, and later barred the use of the assumption of risk defense. These employers' liability laws were, however, soon found to be unsatisfactory for several reasons: workers or their survivors had to bring law suits for damages; the employers' defenses, while considerably weakened, still made it difficult for workers to prosecute their cases; the outcome of the cases were always uncertain; actions were costly to bring and were lengthy; cases produced ill-will between the employers and employees and posed a constant threat to job security.

C. EUROPEAN COMPENSATION LEGISLATION

The historical origins of modern workers' compensation legislation may be found first in Germany and then in England. Philosophers and politicians, especially socialists, were of great influence in the development of European compensation legislation which later influenced the development of similar compensation legislation in the United States.

1. GERMANY

The German influence began in 1838 with the enactment of an employers' liability act that was applicable to railroads. In 1873 Germany extended coverage to workers in factories, mines and quarries. In 1884, Germany enacted a compulsory system of accident insurance which is regarded as the first true workers' compensation act, and it covered all employees engaged in manufacturing, mining and transportation. Similar workers' compensation laws were enacted in Austria in 1887, Norway in 1894, Finland in 1895, and Great Britain in 1897.

2. GREAT BRITAIN

The Workmen's Compensation Act of 1897 provided the prototype, and was the forerunner of the majority of compensation acts passed in the early 1900's in the United States. The Act contained important limitations: only hazardous employments were covered; there were no insurance provisions; and the employer bore the complete burden of compensation benefit costs. The statute also gave rise to the key phrase, "arising out of and in the course of employment," which is generally found today in compensation statutes in the United States. The British legislation differed from the German. Germany attempted to provide broader coverage in the area of social insurance and to provide a more complete compensation system. The British Act gave a workman only moderate recovery, with the cost being borne by the employer as an expense of doing business.

D. STATE COMPENSATION ACTS

There was a gradual recognition after the turn of the century that the common-law remedies of employees injured or killed on the job, were filled with inequities. The states were slow, however, to adopt workers' compensation laws, and initial attempts to do so faced legal and political opposition. Early compensation legislation was very limited and legislators exercised great caution in replacing the common-law recovery system. While it is beyond the scope of this work to address the various attempts of the states to enact compensation legislation, a sampling is necessary for historical appreciation of workers' compensation legislation in the United States.

1. MARYLAND

In 1902, Maryland passed the first workers' compensation act in the United States. It applied to death cases only, and provided coverage to a limited number of workers. This act was declared unconstitutional in Franklin v. United Railways and Electric Co. (1904), because it was held to deprive the parties of the right to jury trial and said to be violative of the separation of powers doctrine (an insurance commissioner, under the executive branch, was performing judicial functions). In 1910, Maryland enacted a voluntary workers' compensation statute, but apathy on behalf of employers and employees rendered the legislation ineffective.

2. MONTANA

In 1909, Montana enacted a compulsory workers' compensation statute, which was designed for employees in the coal industry. The employer and employee were both required to contribute to a state fund, and a covered employee or his beneficiaries could elect to sue at law or receive compensation from the fund; however, workers could not receive the benefits of both. This legislation was declared unconstitutional in Cunningham v. Northwestern Improvement Co. (1911), because it was held that employers were denied equal protection of the laws, in that there was the potential for double liability (employers had to contribute to the state compensation fund and additionally were open to suit if an employee or beneficiary so elected).

3. MASSACHUSETTS

Massachusetts, in 1908, passed a voluntary workers' compensation statute. The voluntary nature of the act was designed to avoid some of the theoretical constitutional problems concerning compensation acts. As a result of the voluntary nature of the act, both employers and employees had no incentive to commit themselves to the scheme. Thus, the Massachusetts act proved to be ineffective.

4. NEW YORK

In 1909, in New York, a commission on Employers' Liability was created (popularly known as the

"Wainwright Commission"). It was to inquire into the liabilities of employers to employees for industrial accidents, and to compare and study: efficiencies, costs, justice, merits and defects in the laws of the other industrial states and countries. The Commission reported that the current common-law system with its employers' liability act exceptions provided insufficient compensation; was wasteful in terms of resources; caused unsatisfactory delays and was essentially antagonistic in nature. The Commission proposed two statutes in light of constitutional problems. One proposal was aimed at employers and employees when especially dangerous employments were involved. The other statute was designed as an elective statute to cover employments outside of the especially dangerous work categories. In 1910, both compulsory and voluntary acts were passed. Predictably, the voluntary statute suffered from employer indifference, and the compulsory statute was declared unconstitutional in Ives v. South Buffalo Railway (1911). Employers were viewed as having been denied due process under both the state and federal constitutions in that employers' property, i.e., money, was taken without consent and without fault.

In 1913, New York amended its constitution to permit the enactment of a compulsory workers' compensation statute and in 1914 the New York legislature passed a compulsory workers' compensation law that applied only to hazardous employments. In Jensen v. Southern Pacific Co. (1915), the New York Court of Appeals upheld the statute as a valid exercise of police power. As might be expected, thereafter mandatory coverage was extended and broadened in New York.

5. FLORIDA

By 1920, most states had adopted some form of workers' compensation legislation. The last state to adopt a compensation act was Mississippi in 1949. In 1935 the State of Florida enacted its first workers' compensation act which was elective in theory. The development of the law in this area in Florida is typical of its development in the United States. For example, from 1935 forward, practically every session of the Florida legislature amended the compensation act. It must be pointed out, however, that the Florida legislature in 1978, because of its concern over excessive awards and a backlog of claims, initiated a study of the problems. In 1979 the legislature enacted a Workers' Compensation Reform Act which "re-established the centrality of the wage-loss principle," and represented a departure from the development in many other jurisdictions. The current theory in Florida is that awards should not be based on the medical nature of the injury alone but should focus on the economic impact of the injury. Florida's wage-loss approach is designed to avoid compensating a worker for an injury per se, or basing an award on conjecture as to the future course of a specific injury; instead, its goal is to provide compensation for an employee's economic losses as they arise. See Abinger & Granoff, Legislative Overview: The Florida Workers' Compensation

Act, 1979, 4 Nova L.J. 91 (1980). This approach has been used by Florida in an advertising effort to attract new industry. Florida may not have the most progressive and acceptable of workers' compensation programs, however its innovations will no doubt influence other jurisdictions. The Florida experience exemplifies the continuing political battles fought in legislatures between employees in the work force and employers and insurance carriers.

E. FEDERAL LEGISLATION

There are a variety of federal acts designed to provide compensation or recovery for certain employees injured or killed on the job. Additionally, there has been federal legislation aimed at regulation of safety practices, labor standards, discrimination, social security benefits, etc. and which may affect employees' rights in the workplace. Provided below is a brief history and introduction of the more important federal acts providing compensation or recovery; other employee protection laws will be addressed in Part III.

1. FEDERAL EMPLOYEES' COMPENSATION ACT

In 1908, Congress enacted a workers' compensation act for a limited group of federal employees, and, in 1916, it expanded the coverage to all civil employees of the United States government without regard to the hazards of their employment. An extensive revision of the FECA was undertaken in

1949, and today, the FECA, 5 U.S.C.A. § 8101 et seq., is considered to be one of the most liberal workers' compensation acts in existence, and provides coverage for federal employees and their dependents for death or disability resulting from personal injury "sustained while in the performance of duty." Congressional appropriations finance all administrative and benefit costs, thus making the government a self-insurer. The Secretary of Labor supervises administrative claims procedures through the Office of Workers' Compensation Programs. The Employees' Compensation Appeals Board reviews appeals from final decisions. When an employee is covered by the FECA, all other rights against the government are barred. Third party actions may be commenced when appropriate, and there may be an election of civil service retirement benefits (assuming eligibility), as opposed to compensation benefits. The Supreme Court, in Westfall v. Erwin (1988), indicated that co-employee liability was possible in FECA situations; however, Congress legislatively overruled Westfall by enacting the Federal Employees Liability Reform and Tort Compensation Act of 1988 (28 U.S.C.A. § 2679). The FECA's exclusive liability provision does not directly preclude third-party indemnity actions against the United States. Lockheed Aircraft Corp. v. United States (1983).

Members of the armed forces of the United States are not covered by the FECA, however, analogous legislation does provide them with disability compensation and death benefits. 10 U.S.C.A. Ch. 61 &

75; 38 U.S.C.A. § 301 et seq. Coverage is allowed in cases of service-connected disability or death. The military scheme requires a "line of duty" determination to be made in each case, and either the particular branch of service and/or the Veterans Administration provides the machinery for the claims process and supervision. See Federal Benefits for Veterans and Dependents, VA Pamphlet 80–92–1.

It should be noted that the Feres doctrine precludes servicemen's recoveries under the Federal Tort Claims Act against the United States for injury, death, or loss "incident to service." Feres v. United States (1950). Furthermore, service personnel cannot generally maintain damage actions against superior officers for violation of constitutional rights. Chappell v. Wallace (1983).

2. FEDERAL EMPLOYERS' LIABILITY ACT

In 1906, Congress passed the first Federal Employers' Liability Act, but the United States Supreme Court held the Act unconstitutional because it infringed upon state rights in that the Act applied to intrastate as well as interstate commerce. Howard v. Illinois Central Railroad (1908). This first FELA was held constitutional, however, as far as the District of Columbia and the territories of the United States were concerned. El Paso & Northeastern Railway v. Gutierrez (1909). In 1908, Congress enacted a second FELA which applied to common carriers engaged in interstate commerce only. It is this second FELA statute which remains effective to this day and is codified at 45 U.S.C.A. §§ 51–60. The FELA is not a true workers' compensation act for it requires an employee to prove negligence even though the burden of proving that negligence has been greatly liberalized by the courts. The FELA at the time of its passage was considered the most progressive of the various employers' liability acts that existed at the time. Comparative fault replaced contributory negligence and the fellow-servant rule was abolished completely. In 1939, Congress amended the act with an eye toward the elimination of the assumption of risk defense. Subsequent court decisions make it clear that there is no assumption of inherent risks based upon the risk of ordinary railroading; nor can there be assumption of risk for obvious dangers knowingly encountered by the railroad employee, but of course, comparative fault may come into play.

One should note that the Safety Appliance Act and the Boiler Inspection Act impose absolute and mandatory duties upon the defendant carriers, which can provide the basis for liability under the FELA. The traditional common-law tort compensatory approach is taken toward personal injury damages under the FELA, but the Supreme Court has remained receptive to new claims, especially in the emotional distress area. Atchison, Topeka & Santa Fe Ry. Co. v. Buell (1987); see also, Consolidated Rail Corp. v. Gottshall (1994) (fear of cancer). In death cases, a pecuniary loss approach is employed for beneficiaries. Most courts have held that punitive damages are not recoverable. Actions may be filed in state or federal courts; if filed in state court the action cannot be removed to federal court.

3. THE JONES ACT

Historically, under the general maritime law, seamen were allowed maintenance and cure which consisted of subsistence, medical care and unearned wages, but they had no effective negligence remedy. At the turn of the Twentieth Century, the Supreme Court began fashioning the doctrine of unseaworthiness, which provided a proper cause of action, but a limited remedy for seamen. See The Osceola (1903). Because of concern for the welfare of seamen, Congress enacted the Seamen's Act of 1915, which abolished the fellow-servant defense, but this legislation was effectively nullified in Chelentis v. Luckenbach Steamship Co. (1918). In 1920, Congress passed the Merchant Marine Act of 1920, commonly known as the Jones Act. It provided seamen with the same negligence remedy that is available to railroad employees under the Federal Employers Liability Act. 46 U.S.C.A. § 688 et seq. Both state and federal courts may entertain these actions and comparative negligence applies. In the 1940's, the Supreme Court transformed the unseaworthiness doctrine into an effective liability basis for recoveries by seamen. The unseaworthiness doctrine essentially imposes liability without fault on the part of a shipowner who fails to provide a safe and seaworthy vessel. The determination of a worker's status as a seaman is of critical importance. Chandris, Inc. v. Latsis (1995); see Harbor Tug & Barge Co. v. Papai (1997). Thus, today once a person is classified as a seaman he may join actions for maintenance and cure, Jones Act negligence and unseaworthiness in order to obtain compensation for his personal injuries. Fitzgerald v. United States Lines Co. (1963). Punitive damages appear to be unavailable to seamen in actions against their employers or vessels. See generally, Guevara v. Maritime Overseas Corp. (5th Cir.1995).

Sometimes there can be an overlap between seamen's rights to recovery under the aforementioned theories and the various state workers' compensation laws. This area is sometimes called a "twilight zone" of coverage. See Ch. 9, C., infra.

In Miles v. Apex Marine Corp. (1990), the Supreme Court recognized that seamen have a general maritime law cause of action for wrongful death. This action is generally limited to pecuniary damages. Beyond one marine league from shore the Death on the High Seas Act of 1920, 46 U.S.C.A. §§ 761–767, is generally applicable, but seamen's damages are pecuniary in nature regardless of whether they are sought under the Jones Act, general maritime law, or the Death on the High Seas Act. See also, Dooley v. Korean Air Lines Co. (1998). As a result of the Miles decision, the lower courts have generally held that seamen can only recover for general and special damages in claims for personal injuries. See generally, Hood, Hardy &

Shea, Seamen's Damages, §§ 8–1 & 9–1 (2d ed. 1995).

It should be noted that the penalty wage statute, 46 U.S.C.A. §§ 10313(f)–(i), 10501(b)–(d), permits an action for delayed payment of wages. In appropriate circumstances, this action may be joined with other seamen's remedies. Griffin v. Oceanic Contractors, Inc. (1982).

4. LONGSHORE AND HARBOR WORKERS' COMPENSATION ACT

In 1927, Congress enacted a national workers' compensation statute for the benefit of longshoremen and other persons engaged in maritime employment on navigable waters. The Longshoremen's and Harbor Workers' Compensation Act (hereinafter "LHWCA") was prompted by the case of Southern Pacific Co. v. Jensen (1917), which had nullified a New York workers' compensation statute as applied to longshoremen. Coverage under the 1927 legislation was said to exist only if the accident occurred on navigable waters; Nacirema Operating Co. v. Johnson (1969); and the fact that a worker's employment was maritime in nature, was not a coverage issue. Calbeck v. Travelers Insurance Co. (1962). By decisions of the Supreme Court, covered workers were also given an unseaworthiness remedy against a vessel, Seas Shipping Co. v. Sieracki (1946), and the vessel owner was given an indemnity action against the stevedore employer, Ryan Stevedoring Co. v. Pan-Atlantic Steamship Corp. (1956).

In 1972, Congress significantly amended the LHWCA. In summary, the amendments increased benefits, eliminated the unseaworthiness remedy against vessels, abolished the vessel owner's right of indemnity against stevedore employers, and instituted needed administrative changes. Most importantly the 1972 amendments broadened coverage, by using both "situs" and "status" for coverage. The situs test is no longer confined to navigable waters, but it includes dockside workers on adjoining shore areas. See Northeast Marine Terminal Co. v. Caputo (1977). The status test is met if a worker is engaged in "maritime employment." 33 U.S.C.A. § 902(3). See Chesapeake & Ohio Railway Co. v. Schwalb (1989).

In 1984, Congress amended the LHWCA, restricting coverage and changing the name of the act to the Longshore and Harbor Workers' Compensation Act; 33 U.S.C.A. § 901 et seq. All private maritime employments upon navigable waters or adjoining land areas are generally covered by the LHWCA. Specifically excluded are seamen and government employees. Also excluded are clerical employees, recreation employees, temporary employees not engaged in longshore or harbor work, agricultural employees, employees on certain small commercial vessels, and employees who repair or break recreational vessels under 65 feet in length, so long as there is state workers' compensation coverage for these employees.

As might be expected, jurisdictional battles arise because claimants wish to assert seaman status, and while employers prefer to claim immunity from suit under the LHWCA. Seaman status is usually a jury question. Southwest Marine, Inc. v. Gizoni (1991).

When there is an overlap of coverage due to state workers' compensation law, the LHWCA does not necessarily pre-empt. The Supreme Court's concurrent jurisdiction doctrines (sometimes applied in twilight zone cases) indicate that generally, an employee covered by both has an option. See Sun Ship, Inc. v. Pennsylvania (1980). See Ch. 9, C., infra.

It should be pointed out that the receipt of LHWCA benefits does not preclude the initiation of a third-party action based upon traditional negligence concepts. 33 U.S.C.A. § 905(b); see Scindia Steam Navigation Co. Limited v. De Los Santos (1981). Furthermore, a longshoreman can pursue a negligence remedy under the LHWCA against a vessel owner who acts as his own stevedore, despite the fact that the longshoreman has received compensation under the LHWCA from the stevedore-vessel owner. Jones & Laughlin Steel Corp. v. Pfeifer (1983). But ship repairers' actions are barred by § 905(b).

The LHWCA has been applied by Congress to employees other than longshoremen and maritime workers. The Defense Base Act applies the LHWCA to injuries on deaths of certain persons engaged in public works contracts outside the continental United States and to certain persons employed at military bases outside the United States. 42 U.S.C.A. § 1651 et seq. The War Hazards Compensation Act (42 U.S.C.A. § 1701 et seq.) provides a compensation remedy for death, injury, or detention of certain persons employed overseas by U.S. government contractors or by the United States government; benefits, disability, etc., are determined by reference to the LHWCA. Administration of these claims is accomplished under the Federal Employees' Compensation Act. Subject to certain criteria, employees of nonappropriated fund instrumentalities of the United States are also entitled to the benefits of the LHWCA. 5 U.S.C.A. §§ 8171, 8172.

In 1928, Congress extended the substantive and procedural provisions of the LHWCA to employees in the District of Columbia (D.C. Code §§ 36–501, 36–502 (1973)). These provisions have now been replaced by the District of Columbia Workers' Compensation Act. D.C. Code 1981, § 1–233; See Greater Washington Board of Trade v. District of Columbia (1982).

Finally, the Outer Continental Shelf Lands Act (43 U.S.C.A. §§ 1331–1343) incorporates the provisions of the LHWCA for the benefit of certain employees engaged in natural resources exploration, development, transportation, etc., outside the states' seaward boundaries on the continental shelves. See Herb's Welding, Inc. v. Gray (1985); Mills v. Director (1989). See generally, Schoenbaum, Admiralty and Maritime Law (2d ed. 1994).

5. FEDERAL BLACK LUNG BENEFITS LEGISLATION

As an incident to the Federal Coal Mine Health and Safety Act of 1969, a basic income maintenance program was established for certain coal miners and their dependents. 30 U.S.C.A. § 801 et seq. The program was designed to provide compensation benefits in certain cases in which coal miners had suffered or died from pneumoconiosis ("black lung"). In 1972, Congress passed the Black Lung Benefits Act, and thereby authorized a national workers' compensation program to be administered under the U.S. Department of Labor. Since that time several important amendments have occurred. In 1978, Congress passed the Black Lung Benefits Reform Act of 1977 and the Black Lung Benefits Review Act of 1977. Later, Congress enacted the Black Lung Benefits Revenue Act of 1981, the Black Lung Benefits Amendments of 1981 and the Consolidated Omnibus Budget Reconciliation Act of 1985. Because of the controversial and political nature of this federal workers' compensation legislation, there is no doubt that future amendments and revisions will occur. For a more detailed description of the black lung compensation legislation, see Chapter 15, infra.

PART 2

THE LAW OF WORKERS' COMPENSATION

CHAPTER 2

THEORIES AND POLICIES OF WORKERS' COMPENSATION

A. CONSTITUTIONAL THEORIES

Traditionally there have been several key constitutional objections to workers' compensation legislation. Most of these objections have centered on the following constitutional issues: due process of law, equal protection, impairment of contract obligations, trial by jury, and the privileges and immunities of the citizens of the different states. Initially, many of these constitutional objections were sustained; however, most constitutional problems have fallen by the wayside, particularly with the adoption by most states of specific constitutional amendments that authorize workers' compensation legislation. These constitutional problems are not always of just historical interest. They can be of importance to a modern day analysis of a particular compensation scheme; for example, see State ex rel. Doersam v. Industrial Commission (1988); Reed v. Brunson (1988).

1.   FREEDOM OF CONTRACT

The U.S. Constitution prohibits the states from enacting laws that impair contract obligations. U.S. Const. Art. 1, § 10. As a result of this general prohibition and the parallel provisions sometimes found within state constitutions, some workers' compensation acts were held at one time to be violative of these provisions. However, the general view is to the effect that even if a workers' compensation act impairs an existing contract obligation between an employer and employee, the impairment may nevertheless be valid because a proper exercise of the police power has occurred. The health, safety and welfare of the people are of overriding importance.

2.   ELECTION

Many of the original workers' compensation acts were said to be "elective" in order to avoid the constitutional difficulties imposed by the impairment of contract clause. An elective compensation act could thus be said to be a part of or to be "read into" every contract of employment, and the act contained provisions for employers or employees to opt in or out. There were usually penalty provisions that encouraged coverage. Later, most elective acts were said to be presumptive, that is, the employer and employee were presumed to be covered unless they had taken specific steps in accordance with the act to avoid coverage. Many acts appear to retain their elective and contractual character because of the manner in which they were written, despite the fact that today most state workers' compensation acts are compulsory.

The majority of states have enacted constitutional amendments that eliminate the constitutional difficulties originally posed in this area. Virtually all states today have compulsory coverage. Any system other than a compulsory one appears to be at odds with the purposes and policies of workers' compensation. It should be recalled that when coverage fails for one reason or another, the employee must then rely upon the common law remedies, or those remedies provided by the employers' liability acts.

3.   PRESUMPTIVE COVERAGE

As previously mentioned, many compensation acts were elective, thus affording the employer and employee the right to accept or reject coverage. While most acts today are compulsory in character, the few remaining elective acts can pose coverage problems. For example, an employer could refuse on the basis of costs to carry workers' compensation insurance, and some employees may not be sufficiently knowledgeable of their rights to make intelligent elections. Consequently, some of the elective acts contain presumptive coverage provisions. In other words, the acts may provide for an election, but, coverage is presumed unless specific steps are taken by the employee or employer to preclude coverage.

4.   COMPULSORY COVERAGE

A majority of states employ a compulsory coverage system of workers' compensation. This has generally been accomplished by state constitutional amendments authorizing workers' compensation statutes; see Schmidt v. Wolf Contracting Co. (1945). These state amendments grant the necessary legislative power for the enactment of workers' compensation laws. These grants include the power to enact all reasonable and proper provisions necessary to effectuate the law and to fulfill the objectives of the constitutional provisions. Needless to say, the legislation cannot exceed whatever limitations exist in the constitutional provision.

5.   EXCLUSIVENESS OF REMEDY

Regardless of whether a workers' compensation act is compulsory or elective, it generally affords the exclusive remedy for employees or dependents against employers for personal injuries, diseases, or deaths arising out of and in the course of employment. The exclusivity provision of workers' compensation acts is the keystone of all such legislation. The employee or dependents recover without regard to fault, and the employer is spared the possibility of large tort verdicts. Initial assaults on the exclusive remedy provided by workers' compensation were based on allegations of denial of due process of law. Common law and statutory actions were being abrogated along with common law defenses. There was strong early resistance (just as there is today) to the adoption of no-fault statutory systems of compensation. Needless to say, constitutional controversies surrounded meanings of employment, requirements to secure payment of compensation, and the hazardous employment classifications. Additionally, equal protection arguments were made. For a discussion of constitutional issues see generally Cudahy Packing Co. v. Parramore (1923); Arizona Employers' Liability Cases (1919); Jensen v. Southern Pacific Co. (1915). Most constitutional issues have been laid to rest by state constitutional amendments and by more liberal and realistic judicial decisions.

B. SOCIAL AND ECONOMIC POLICIES

1. EMPLOYEE–EMPLOYER "BARGAIN"

It is sometimes said that the employee and employer have entered into an "industrial bargain." The employee has given up his right to sue his employer for negligence and possibly receive a potentially greater damage award, and the employer has surrendered the common law defenses available in negligence actions. In exchange the employee is entitled to prompt but modest compensation for injuries, (or one's dependents for death) arising out of the employment relationship regardless of fault. The employer avoids costly litigation, and faces fixed and limited liability that can be covered by insurance.

2.   INDUSTRIAL BURDEN FOR INJURIES AND DEATH

An important economic and social theory underlying the workers' compensation idea is that the cost of employment related injuries, diseases and deaths ultimately should be borne by the purchasers' and consumers' products and services. In other words, built into the cost of any product is the employer's insurance premium for the cost of workers' compensation or the cost of self-insurance. Thus, the costs of employment related injuries, diseases and deaths are properly distributed throughout society.

3.   MEDICAL LOSS AND WAGE LOSS

The benefits payable vary from jurisdiction to jurisdiction. An essential inquiry to be made in each jurisdiction is whether the particular statute is based upon a medical loss theory, a wage loss theory, or both. A medical loss theory dictates, for example, that in the case of one who has lost an arm, compensation is required for the loss of that limb regardless of whether there has been an adverse impact upon earning capacity or lost wages. On the other hand, the wage loss theory is based upon the idea that a person should be compensated for loss of wages or diminished earning capacity and not for any pure medical losses that have occurred. Many jurisdictions mix the two theories and provide compensation based upon wage and medical losses. One may find in a purportedly wage loss jurisdiction the utilization of an injury schedule which provides compensation for pure medical losses enumerated in the schedule. For example, one would be entitled a specific amount of compensation for the loss of an arm regardless of any diminution in earning capacity.

It is worthy of note that the State of Florida in recent years has attempted to employ an almost pure wage loss theory. As a result, Florida has reduced the costs to employers of its workers' compensation system. Regardless of the theory chosen, it should be kept in mind that generally workers' compensation benefits remain modest and have failed to keep abreast of inflation.

4. SOCIAL INSURANCE

It must be emphasized that workers' compensation in the United States is privately funded with an insurance base, whereas, in some countries, as for example, in Great Britain, a comprehensive social insurance system encompassing workers' compensation exists. There have been reform proposals in the United States aimed at establishing a more comprehensive national system, however, the American system remains a private one grounded in insurance. Certainly, a legitimate criticism of the current system can be made because compensation allocations are made regardless of need. It would at first appear that the general public bears the costs of workers' compensation, however, the actual costs are probably borne by limited groups of consumers of particular products and services. As a result of

the fact that workers' compensation is a statutory
no-fault scheme, many lose sight of the relevance of
tort law and its notions of culpability and fault. For
example, intoxication on the job and intentional
self-injuries can prevent the recovery of compensation despite the no-fault theory of the system. For a
further discussion of compensation as social insurance, see 1 A. Larson, The Law of Workmen's
Compensation §§ 3.10–3.40. [hereinafter cited as
Larson].

5. ECONOMIC APPRAISAL

In comparison with the tort compensation system, workers' compensation provides a more efficient economic model. For example, in the case of
automobile accidents the tort system provides recovery to victims and families of only 44% of the
sums provided by the system, with the remainder of
the costs consumed by the inefficiency of the system
itself, i.e., court costs, lawyers fees, insurance administration, etc. Workers' compensation ordinarily
does not require lengthy and costly hearings; attorney's fees are regulated by statute; and while issues
of fault do creep into compensation decisions, ordinarily compensation is assured when a work related
injury or death is demonstrated, as opposed to the
perils of the tort system.

In evaluating the workers' compensation system
one must consider, however, the economic status of
today's industrial worker. Wages generally have not
kept up with inflation and workers' compensation

payments do not reflect current costs of living; further the system fails to provide the amounts necessary for effective educational retraining and vocational rehabilitation. Compensation benefits simply do not reflect the degree of economic harm suffered by a worker and his family; all persons are treated in a uniform manner by the particular workers' compensation act. Additionally, there is generally no provision allowing for increases and escalations due to inflation. As a final criticism, workers' compensation benefits vary a great deal from state to state. Because of this disparity a National Workers' Compensation Standards Act has been proposed.

The U.S. Chamber of Commerce compiles annual surveys of state and federal compensation law changes which are useful in evaluating policy changes from jurisdiction to jurisdiction. Its website address is: http://www.uschamber.com. A complete legal survey is compiled each year by the American Insurance Association, whose website is: http://www.aiadc.org. An abbreviated annual survey of workers' compensation and unemployment insurance laws is available from the AFL–CIO, Department of Occupational Safety and Health. Its website is http://www.aflcio.org.

C. LIBERAL CONSTRUCTION OF COMPENSATION ACTS

It is generally said that there is to be a liberal construction of all workers' compensation acts because such legislation is remedial in nature. In fact, many workers' compensation acts have an express provision requiring liberal construction. The humane and beneficent purposes of workers' compensation legislation are certainly taken to heart by judges and compensation commissions. For example, see Pacific Employers Insurance Co. v. Industrial Accident Commission (1945). While as a general rule workers' compensation acts are to be liberally construed, liberality of construction should not rise to the level of judicial legislation.

CHAPTER 3

WORKERS' COMPENSATION AND THE LAW OF TORTS

A. COMMON LAW AND STATUTORY ACTIONS

The common law remedies, and the statutory actions provided by the various employers' liability acts, form the underlying layer of law upon which a remedy can be based when the applicable workers' compensation act fails to provide coverage. Thus, common law and statutory actions still remain important. Common law and statutory actions are also extremely important when there is third party involvement and recovery is sought against them. Third parties are not covered by the act and are not allowed to limit their liability in the same manner as an employer.

B. THE STRUGGLE FOR COVERAGE AND NON–COVERAGE

Workers are constantly searching for greater compensation than that provided by the applicable workers' compensation system. Whenever possible, and certainly in situations in which there has been no fault on the part of the worker, attempts will be

33

made to obtain increased recoveries through the utilization of traditional tort theories. Attorneys have certainly been creative in this area and there have been many attempts to circumvent the limitations on tort recovery imposed by workers' compensation legislation. Needless to say, because of the potential economic harm posed by large tort damages awards, employers want to insure that workers' compensation remains as a viable shield to tort recoveries. The more important areas in which the struggle for coverage and non-coverage exists are: co-employee suits, dual capacity situations, property damages, negligent inspectors; bad faith liability, products liability, negligent physicians, intentional torts, nonphysical torts and retaliatory discharge.

1. CO–EMPLOYEES

The majority of states provide co-employees with immunity from ordinary tort liability in connection with the employer immunity provisions found in the workers' compensation acts. In a few states, however, common law or statutory actions may be brought against all persons other than one's employer, and this would include a right against a co-employee who may have negligently injured or killed a fellow employee. The co-employee immunity which exists in the majority of states can be found both in statutes and in judicial decisions. For an example of a statutory provision creating co-employee immunity, see New York-McKinney's Workers' Compensation Law § 64.29; for an example of a judicial decision in favor of co-employee immunity which was grounded on public policy, see Miller v. Scott (1960). Even when immunity exists, it will not be available to a co-employee in most intentional tort situations. Immunity does not extend to all acts of persons who happen to be co-employees. See Sauve v. Winfree (1995).

2. DUAL CAPACITY EMPLOYERS

Despite the fact that the employer is generally immune from tort liability, the dual capacity doctrine may place an employer in a position to be sued in an alternative capacity, thus avoiding the immunity provided by a workers' compensation act. The majority of courts are reluctant to find a dual capacity on the part of an employer. See Wilder v. United States (1989) (noting the doctrine to be disfavored). There have been rare instances of success on the basis of dual capacity theories. See 2A. Larson § 72.80.

3. PROPERTY ACTIONS

It should always be remembered that the exclusive remedy provisions granting immunity to employers do not deny a worker's tort claim for any property damage. See Superb Carpet Mills, Inc. v. Thomason (1987) (property action allowed but no punitive damages permitted); Haddad v. Justice (1975). Liberal and modern views of what constitute property interests raise questions with regard to what types of actions might be maintainable against employers.

4.   NEGLIGENT INSPECTORS

Some jurisdictions extend the employer's immunity to insurance carriers and others that may conduct safety inspections. In other jurisdictions, however, an insurance carrier or, for example, a union or union inspector, may be held liable under traditional tort concepts for the negligent performance of such an inspection. Compare Bryant v. Old Republic Insurance Co. (1970) with Unruh v. Truck Insurance Exchange (1972).

5.   BAD FAITH

The possibility exists of a successful bad faith action against either the employer or the insurance compensation carrier based upon the manner in which an employee's claim for workers' compensation benefits is administered. See Simkins v. Great West Cas. Co. (1987). A strong argument for bad faith on the part of an insurance company can be made when it fails to process an employee's legitimate claim for workers' compensation in a manner which demonstrates good faith. Thus, the potential exists for a large tort recovery even if a simple or fairly minor injury has occurred.

6. PRODUCTS LIABILITY

Perhaps the area of greatest interest for third party consideration is that of products liability. In practically every workers' compensation case when an employee has been injured by a particular product or instrumentality, attorneys should consider that deeper pocket provided by the product manufacturer. This is especially true today in light of the impact of Section 402A of the Restatement (Second) of Torts, and its strict liability approach.

Furthermore, the possibility exists for a products liability action by a worker against his employer through a dual capacity theory. For example, an employee of a company manufacturing a product may be injured in the normal course of his employment through the use of that particular product. See generally, Schump v. Firestone Tire and Rubber Co. (1989).

7. PHYSICIANS

Ordinarily a physician who commits malpractice on an injured employee who is covered by workers' compensation is liable in tort to the employee just as the physician would be to any other patient in the particular jurisdiction. However, workers' compensation acts providing co-employees with immunity may provide protection to a physician employed by the employer. See, e.g., Hayes v. Marshall Field & Co. (1953). It should be noted that the dual capacity theory could be used to impose tort liability on an employer for the negligence of a physician employee which causes additional harm to a worker. Furthermore, a physician employee could be viewed as an independent contractor and thus subject to tort liability as a third person.

8. INTENTIONAL TORTS OF EMPLOYERS

Generally there is tort liability on the part of an employer for intentional torts committed against a worker. See generally, Smolarek v. Chrysler Corp. (1989) (retaliation and discrimination); Paroline v. Unisys Corp. (1989) (sexual assault); Childers v. Chesapeake & Potomac Tel. Co. (1989) (intentional infliction of emotional distress). Problems are posed by those difficult cases in which an employer has knowledge of a continuing dangerous condition to a worker and then knowingly fails to take appropriate action to eliminate the hazard. It is possible for the employer's conduct to be characterized as an "intentional tort" which is outside the coverage of the act. For example, see Johns–Manville Products Corp. v. Contra Costa Superior Court (1980); Blankenship v. Cincinnati Milacron Chemicals, Inc. (1982); but see, Kofron v. Amoco Chemicals Corp. (1982).

It should be noted that there is a growing trend in some states to provide enhanced workers' compensation awards for intentional torts in the workplace. These provisions punish the employer while providing a more efficient remedy to the employee who would otherwise have to resort to a traditional tort action with its cost, delay and uncertainty.

Further, there is a recent trend to impose criminal responsibility for certain employer conduct that injures or kills employees. See Illinois v. Chicago Magnet Wire Corp. (1989) (aggravated battery charged for exposing employees to hazardous substances in the workplace; no federal preemption by OSHA). These criminal proceedings can be of assistance to claimants pursuing compensation and other civil remedies.

9. NONPHYSICAL TORTS

The exclusive remedy provisions of workers' compensation acts generally do not bar what are sometimes referred to as nonphysical torts. These would include actions for false arrest or imprisonment, libel and slander. Additionally, actions for sex, race and handicap discrimination, etc., would not be excluded. See generally, Cole v. Fair Oaks Fire Protection District (1987); Boscaglia v. Michigan Bell Tel. Co. (1984); Dorr v. C.B. Johnson, Inc. (1983) (slander).

10. RETALIATORY DISCHARGE

Retaliatory discharge actions are permitted in most states when an employer discharges an employee for filing a workers' compensation claim. See e.g., City of Moorpark v. Superior Court, (1998) (disability discrimination arising out of a workers' compensation claim could form the basis for a common-law wrongful discharge claim). Griess v. Consolidated Freightways Corp. (1989) (public policy supports retaliatory discharge claim). See also Lingle v. Norge Div. of Magic Chef, Inc. (1988) (retaliatory discharge action arising out of the filing of a workers' compensation claim is not preempted by 301 of the Labor Management Relations Act).

CHAPTER 4

THE EMPLOYEE–EMPLOYER RELATIONSHIP

A. EMPLOYEES AND EMPLOYERS GENERALLY

The common law defined a master as one who employed another to perform services and who controls or has a right of control over the other's conduct in performing such services. The master had to have not only the power to control, choose, and direct the servant with regard to the object to be accomplished but also had to possess the power to control the details of the work. The common law definitions are still of importance in establishing who is an employer and employee, however, definitions provided in workers' compensation legislation are controlling. Typically, an employee for workers' compensation coverage purposes is defined as one who works for, and under the control of, another for hire. A liberal construction should be given to the definitions of employer and employee because of the objectives of workers' compensation and the need to make coverage as expansive as possible. The Restatement (Second) of Agency § 220 relating to master and servant provides the basic definitions of employee and employer. The Restatement places primary emphasis on the employer's right to control the details of the work in order for a sufficient employment relationship to exist. Professor Larson has criticized this test and advocates in its place that an inquiry be directed at the nature of the claimant's work in relation to the employer's regular business. He argues that if the particular work has become a part of the cost of the product or services, then the particular work and thus the employee should be covered by compensation. Professor Larson indicates that the right of control test is a false one and that the independent contractor-employee classification issue can lead to unsatisfactory results. See 1 C. Larson § 43.30. Despite this criticism, the traditional test of the employer/employee relationship continues, and the following factors, inter alia, are to be considered: who has assumed the direction and control of the employee; who possesses the power to hire and fire or recall; who bears responsibility for wages and compensation; in whose work was the employee engaged and for whose benefit was the work primarily being done; who furnished any equipment to be used by the employee; and who bore responsibility for the employee's working conditions.

B. EMPLOYEES

On the basis of statutes and judicial decisions, particular classes of employees are sometimes specifically included in or excluded from workers' compensation coverage. Typical employee classifications are provided hereinafter.

1. CASUAL EMPLOYEES

Casual employees are sometimes excluded from workers' compensation coverage. Real difficulties exist in determining who is a casual employee because of a failure to distinguish properly between casual and non-casual employments. Determinations may be based upon the following issues: the contract of hire; the nature of the service or work to be rendered; the scope and purpose of the employment; and the duration and regularity of the service. Ordinarily employment may be casual if it is temporary in nature and limited in purpose, or if it is incidental, accidental or irregular. The casual classification is not determined solely by a lack of frequency or length. As might be expected, the law in this area varies greatly from jurisdiction to jurisdiction, but the majority view may well be to exclude an employment from compensation coverage only if the employment is both casual and outside of the course of the employer's business.

2. AGRICULTURAL EMPLOYEES

The majority of workers' compensation acts specifically exclude agricultural and farm laborers from coverage. Difficulties in this area exist with regard to the appropriate label; for example, one who trained a race horse was not an agricultural employee. See Tuma v. Kosterman (1984). The focus ordinarily is upon the substance of the employee's work as opposed to the employer's class of business. Because of the great number of workers employed in activities incidental to farm enterprises, the line between compensation coverage for ordinary employment and non-coverage for agricultural workers can be a perplexing one. For example, one employed as an agricultural worker, whose duties also include the repair of farm buildings, might not be covered; while one specially employed to repair a farm building would receive the benefits of workers' compensation coverage. See Cannon v. Industrial Accident Commission (1959).

3. DOMESTIC EMPLOYEES

Most compensation acts exempt domestic and household employment from coverage. The test for domestic or household employment is generally whether or not the duties performed are directed at the maintenance of the home. Some jurisdictions treat domestic employees as "casual" employees; others exclude them from coverage because of the "non-business" nature of their employment; and they are excluded in other jurisdictions because of the coverage exception applicable to employers who have less than the statutory requisite number of employees.

4. LOANED EMPLOYEES

The case law addressing the issue of loaned employees is confusing and conflicting. The common law rules are relevant to a determination of who is a lent employee and who occupies the status of the employee's general or special employer. The traditional test of special employment focuses on whether the employee has moved out of the control of the general employer and into the direction and control of the special employer. The inquiry is frequently made in tort cases in an effort to establish the proper employer for purposes of vicarious liability. It must be stressed that the issue in workers' compensation cases is simply the need to find an employer who can provide coverage. While in some states lent employee issues are resolved by statute, other states address the questions through case law which may impose compensation liability on the general or special employer, or both.

5. STATE AND MUNICIPAL EMPLOYEES

State, municipal and public agency employees may be covered by the provisions of state workers' compensation acts, or by some alternative state compensation system. Workers' compensation statutes vary considerably and each state's act must be consulted individually in an effort to learn if a particular public employee is covered. Some of the more common issues are: whether municipal corporations are "employers" under the act; whether one is a state officer or official and thus outside coverage or is an employee. Generally, individuals exercising some portion of a state's sovereign power are considered officials. Police officers and firemen, in particular, have posed problems with regard to workers' compensation coverage. Generally, they are not viewed as "workmen" or "employees," and thus, are not covered; however, many workers' compensation acts have special provisions covering for these occupations.

6.   FEDERAL EMPLOYEES

Employees and civil officers of the various branches of the United States Government or any of its wholly owned instrumentalities who are injured or killed in the performance of their duties are provided compensation under the Federal Employee's Compensation Act, 5 U.S.C.A. § 8101 et seq. The FECA is liberally construed, administered by the Secretary of Labor, and provides federal employees with their exclusive remedy against the United States for injuries or deaths sustained in the performance of their duties. Traditional third-party liability is not disturbed. The term "employee" under the Act is defined by statute and various classes of employees are specifically covered and others are specifically excluded. See 5 U.S.C.A. § 8101. The amounts and duration of compensation payable under the Act are among the most liberal in the United States. The amount of compensation payable under the FECA is generally based on the employee's monthly pay. Disputed claims for compensation are handled administratively under the Department of Labor. Hearings may be had and final decisions of the Secretary of Labor are subject to review by the Employees' Compensation Appeals Board within the U.S. Department of Labor.

Active duty members of the military services are not covered by state compensation acts or the

FECA. They are subject to special federal statutory provisions that cover injury and death sustained in the line of duty. See Chapter 1, E, supra.

7. PARTICIPATION OF EMPLOYEES IN ENTERPRISE

Originally, workers' compensation acts excluded executives, partners, corporate officers and the like, from coverage because they did not fall under the definition of a workman. Additionally, it was felt that workers' compensation legislation was not intended to apply to these groups. Today, the fact that a claimant is a corporate officer does not generally preclude coverage. Even if an injury occurs while one is acting in a managerial capacity, one may still be considered an employee under an act. It is possible, however, because of stock ownership and a controlling interest for one, in effect, to be the business. In these instances there would be no coverage, unless perhaps one could be classified as an employee on the basis of the activities one was engaged in at the time of injury (i.e., non-executive activities). This result is reached on the basis of the dual capacity doctrine (not to be confused here with the dual capacity doctrine concerning an employer's potential tort liability; see Chapter 3, B., 2.), which makes it possible for an executive, who at the time of injury was acting as an employee rather than as an executive, to recover compensation. See Hirsch v. Hirsch Brothers, Inc. (1952).

Partners are treated differently because there is no separate employer entity; partners share equal liability and possess comparable rights in management. In the absence of special legislation, partners are not considered to be employees within compensation coverage even if they have been injured in situations in which they would have been entitled to compensation had they been employees.

8. VOLUNTEERS

One who works for another as a volunteer is not generally entitled to the benefits of workers' compensation because one is not deemed to be an employee. Under most acts only those persons who perform a service for hire are employees and, therefore, volunteers are excluded.

9. ALIENS

The term "employee" in the various workers' compensation acts includes all persons who perform services for hire and includes aliens. It should be pointed out, however, that some acts require that one be a state resident in order to receive workers' compensation benefits. States are not uniform in this regard and in the absence of a provision to the contrary, it is generally said that residency is not a requirement for compensation. It should be noted that certain classes of nonresident alien dependents are often excluded from the receipt of death benefits. See Jurado v. Popejoy Constr. Co. (1993) (constitutional challenge); Alvarez Martinez v. Industrial Commission (1986).

10.　MINORS

Generally, any person may be an "employee" for the purposes of workers' compensation coverage, and one is not excluded from such coverage simply because of minority. Most states have specific provisions in their compensation acts regarding minors. In some states minors are entitled to double compensation, and in others minors may either opt for compensation or sue for damages. A minor's unlawful employment may itself provide a separate tort basis for liability. See Restatement (Second) of Torts § 286 Comment e (1966).

11.　ILLEGAL EMPLOYMENTS

Illegally employed workers can present unique coverage problems. The difficulty usually relates to the question of whether the employment itself is prohibited by statute; for example, prostitution would be a prohibited employment in most jurisdictions, and thus if one is employed to perform acts in violation of a penal statute, coverage would be denied. On the other hand, one who has been illegally employed still enjoys coverage when the employment contract is unlawful because of a provision relating to the legality of such an agreement; for example, laws prohibiting the employment of a minor should not interfere with coverage if a minor is injured in an otherwise lawful employment.

12. INDEPENDENT CONTRACTORS

If one is classified as an independent contractor, rather than the servant or employee of another, one may lose the right to workers' compensation coverage. The independent contractor issue is one of the most frequently litigated questions in the law of workers' compensation. The Restatement (Second) of Agency, § 220 provides the usual definition and tests utilized in this area. The most common factors considered are: the right of control; the method of payment; the providing of materials, tools, or supplies; control over the work site; and the right to discharge the employee.

Independent contractor decisions are often conflicting and irreconcilable. The difficulty in this area stems from attempts by the courts to resolve independent contractor issues in tort cases in which the question is one of vicarious liability. It is questionable whether an inquiry aimed at the avoidance of vicarious liability should be of any relevance to a determination of workers' compensation coverage, given the social and economic policies underlying workers' compensation legislation. See Laurel Daily Leader, Inc. v. James (1955). See also 1 C. Larson § 43.50. Professor Larson argues that a relative nature of work test should be used because it is supported by workers' compensation theory. This test provides that any worker whose efforts are regularly and continually included in the costs of products or services should receive compensation from the manufacturer of such products, or the provider of such services.

13. PROFESSIONAL EMPLOYEES

While often professionals may be viewed as independent contractors, it is certainly possible for them in certain employment circumstances to be employees for purposes of workers' compensation coverage. For example nurses and interns regularly employed by hospitals are generally employees and included within coverage. Additionally, it is possible for an attorney to have an employer and be an "employee" for workers' compensation coverage. See Egan v. New York State Joint Legislative Committee (1956).

C. EMPLOYERS GENERALLY

Workers' compensation acts must be consulted for the definition of "employer." As in the case of "employees" the statutory definition of "employer" is the controlling one to the extent that common law concepts of master and servant are modified. Typically, "employer" means a master or principal who employs another to perform services for hire; who controls or has the right of control of the other; and who usually pays another's wages directly. Situations may arise in which an employee appears to have two employers. For example, an employer's employee may hire another without informing the hiree of the true employer's identity. Since an employer for workers' compensation coverage is usually provided on agency theories, the employee is permitted to elect a covered "employer" for compensation purposes. See Hesse v. J. J. Oys & Co. (1958).

1.   MINIMUM NUMBER OF EMPLOYEES

A minority of workers' compensation acts contain provisions that mandate coverage only in situations in which an employer has a specified number of regular employees. Typical provisions of this nature would, for example, require coverage in the case of three or more employees. Minimum employee requirements are liberally construed in favor of coverage. See Jackson v. Fly (1952).

Furthermore, the usual requirement of workers "regularly" employed does not necessarily mean constant or continuous employment in order to meet the minimum threshold for coverage.

2.   GENERAL AND SPECIAL EMPLOYERS

General and special employer issues usually arise in loaned employee cases. The term "general employer" refers to a worker's original employer, while the term "special employer" refers to the one to whom a worker is loaned. It is possible for one to be the employee of both at the same time, and thus seek compensation against one or both. Special employment relationships require the consent and knowledge of the employee. The basic test for determining one's employer in the loaned employee situation is: who had the right of control and direction over the worker at the relevant time. The pertinent factors, inter alia, include: the power to fire; who paid the wages; and whose business was being furthered. See also Chapter 4, A.4., Loaned Employees, supra.

3. SUBCONTRACTORS AND STATUTORY EMPLOYERS

A majority of states have provisions in their workers' compensation acts which are designed to prevent a general contractor from shielding himself from compensation liability through the use of subcontractors. These "statutory employer" or "contracting under" provisions are intended to provide protection for employees injured or killed while working for uninsured or judgment proof subcontractors. In order to successfully maintain a compensation claim against a statutory employer, the subcontractor's employee must establish that the work that gave rise to the injury was a part of the regular business of the statutory employer. The statutory employer may also be benefited in that tort liability can be precluded. See Black v. Cabot Petroleum Corp. (1989) (exclusive remedy protection involving upstream and downstream contractors); Kelpfer v. Joyce (1961). It must be pointed out, however, that issues of primary versus secondary liability, the status of the statutory employer as guarantor or insurer under some acts, and the subcontractor's failure to carry insurance, may affect third party tort liability on the part of the statutory employer, even if he has paid workers' compensation benefits. See 2 A. Larson, § 72.31. The possibility exists for a statutory employer to obtain reimbursement from a solvent subcontractor. See, e.g., New York-McKinney's Workers' Compensation Law § 56.

4. CHARITABLE ORGANIZATIONS

Employees of charitable or nonprofit organizations may not be covered by workers' compensation in some states. Some acts expressly exclude charitable employers. Charities and nonprofit organizations may be excluded as employers because they involve employments not carried on "for pecuniary gain." In those jurisdictions that require that one be engaged "in the trade or business of the employer" in order to be covered there are conflicting decisions with regard to the coverage of an employee of a charitable organization. The better view allows coverage. See Smith v. Lincoln Memorial University (1957).

5. CONCURRENT EMPLOYERS

An employee may have more than one employer for workers' compensation purposes. These employers may be characterized as either concurrent employers or as joint employers. When one is injured or killed in the service of such employers, several approaches have been taken toward compensation. Liability may be joint, or apportioned, or placed upon only one employer. In apportionment situations employers may be required to provide compensation in proportion to the wages they paid the employee. See Newman v. Bennett (1973).

6. SUCCESSIVE EMPLOYERS

It is not uncommon for an employee to have successive employers, and difficulties can arise in determining which employer is the "employer" for workers' compensation purposes. One method of determining one's responsible employer is to focus simply on the date of injury, and to view the employer at that time as the appropriate one. In those cases in which a disability or injury has resulted from successive employments, the various employers may be required to provide compensation on the basis of their contribution to such disability or injury. Some injuries and certainly death, as in tort cases, can be viewed as single and indivisible, or as incapable of apportionment, with entire liability imposed upon the employers.

In cases of occupational disease and successive employers the following possibilities exist: liability is placed upon the employer in whose service the disease was contracted; liability is borne by the last employer in whose employ the worker was last exposed to the disease's hazards; or liability may be apportioned among several employers. Statutory variations exist with respect to the foregoing possibilities, but given the objectives and policies of workers' compensation, there should be complete compensation for employment related diseases whenever a solvent contributing employer exists.

CHAPTER 5

THE COVERAGE FORMULA–
NECESSITY FOR A "PERSONAL
INJURY BY ACCIDENT
ARISING OUT OF AND
IN THE COURSE OF
EMPLOYMENT"

A. THE COVERAGE INQUIRY

Since the inception of workers' compensation legislation, there have been difficulties in fixing and defining the boundaries of coverage. Problems in this area have largely been the result of a failure to properly identify and inquire into the issue of the scope of the risk. The early cases took a tort law, proximate cause approach toward the risk inquiry. Needless to say, a fault based risk analysis is totally incompatible with the objective and policies of workers' compensation. Subsequent decisions developed various doctrines aimed at defining the scope of the risk, e.g., the "peculiar risk" doctrine, see infra.

One can best understand scope of the risk questions by reference to three broad categories of risks. First, there are definite employment related risks, as the loss of limb by a machinery operator; all would agree that this type of injury is within the scope of the risk of employment and covered by workers' compensation. Second, there are personal risks, such as an injury produced by an epileptic seizure while at work, but unrelated to the employment; this injury might be covered by hospital insurance, but not by workers' compensation because the injury arose from a purely personal condition and was unrelated to a risk of employment. Third, there are neutral risks, such as acts of God, or random acts of violence unrelated to one's employment. These risks are neutral because they bear no relation to one's employment, and they cannot be classified as personal risks. Neutral risks are the cause of a great deal of conflict and confusion.

In a further effort to define the boundaries of coverage, an inquiry is made with regard to whether a sufficient relation exists between one's employment and one's injury. Factors such as time, place and circumstances are considered; however, scope of the risk issues with concomitant confusion also arise in this context. For example, an employee traveling to and from work could be excluded from coverage because at the time of injury the employee was not at work and was off the employer's business premises. While time, place, and circumstances may be relevant, the true question in to and from work situations may be whether the perils of such a journey should be within the scope of the risk created by one's employment, given the policies and purposes of workers' compensation.

An additional inquiry which must be made in an effort to define coverage boundaries is that of factual cause. This refers to the necessity for a factual connection between one's activities at the time of injury and the injury of which one complains; i.e., did the employment in which one was allegedly engaged produce the medical complaint for which one now seeks compensation. For example, did one's employment activity contribute to or cause a heart attack that occurred while one was at work.

In summary, the principal elements directed at coverage in workers' compensation cases are:

1. scope of the risk;

2. sufficient relation to employment, and;

3. factual cause.

The preceding issues arise in the context of the statutory language or coverage formula found in workers' compensation legislation. The coverage formula used in the vast majority of workers' compensation acts requires a "personal injury or death by accident arising out of and in the course of employment." The "arising out of" requirement refers to the scope of the risk issue previously discussed in this section and which will be more fully discussed hereinafter. The "in the course of" requirement refers to the sufficient relation to employment issue (time, place, and circumstances factors) which was discussed above and which will be more fully developed later. Factual causation issues will also be discussed.

The coverage formula requirements of "personal injury by accident" have posed problems in cases involving diseases, mental illnesses, and injuries to artificial limbs. Originally, injuries to artificial limbs were not considered "personal injuries," and disabilities from disease that developed over long time periods were excluded from coverage because no personal inquiry "by accident" had occurred.

It should be noted that while the coverage formula speaks in terms of "personal injury," workers' compensation legislation also provides coverage for death cases. Thus, much of what ordinarily is stated with regard to injuries is also applicable to death situations. Therefore, the analysis of various circumstances producing injuries in the following sections is also applicable when those circumstances have resulted in death.

B. THE "ARISING OUT OF" CONCEPT

One can best understand the "arising out of" concept by comparing it to the scope of the risk question asked and resolved by courts on the basis of policy considerations in tort cases. Sometimes this issue is dealt with in tort cases through the use of proximate cause terminology. It is important to remember that this is a question of law and policy exclusively for the court, and certainly scope of the risk issues should be approached in a similar fashion in workers' compensation cases. In light of the objectives and policies of workers' compensation it is submitted that a much broader approach should be taken toward the scope of the risk than is taken in tort cases.

There appears to be five basic risk doctrines employed by the courts to determine the scope of the risk.

1. THE FIVE BASIC RISK DOCTRINES

a. *Proximate Cause*

Originally judges had difficulty divorcing themselves from tort law with its proximate cause and fault concepts, and some early cases, therefore adopted the fault-related proximate cause test for the "arising out of" concept, which required that one's employment be the proximate cause of one's injury. This approach is much too narrow, and it is incompatible and in conflict with the objectives of any statutory no-fault compensation system.

b. *Peculiar Risk*

An early device which resulted in hardship to employees was the peculiar risk doctrine. This risk concept excluded coverage for injuries caused by risks which, admittedly were within the course of one's employment, but which were commonly shared by others, even though the employee was exposed for a longer period of time by virtue of the nature of the employee's employment. For example, an employee who suffered a sunstroke while delivering coal for his employer was viewed as not having been "peculiarly exposed" to the danger of sunstroke because he was not subjected to a materially greater risk of sunstroke than other outdoor workers. Dougherty's Case,   (1921). The peculiar risk theory is generally rejected in modern compensation cases because it is unrealistic and allows only limited coverage.

c. *Increased Risk*

A modern approach which provides broader coverage than the peculiar risk test is the increased risk doctrine. This approach includes within the scope of the risk those risks to which an employee has been exposed for a longer period of time than the public, even though the risk is commonly shared by all. If one's employment results in a greater exposure to a risk there would be coverage even though the risk is not one that is qualitatively different from that shared by others. For example, one constantly exposed to extreme heat on the job and who suffers from heatstroke should be entitled to compensation under the increased risk theory.

d. *Actual Risk*

A liberal approach toward the scope of the risk issue can be found in the actual risk doctrine. The sole question to be answered is whether the risk realized was in fact a risk of one's employment, regardless of whether the risk is commonly shared by the public. For example, heat prostration would be compensable if the nature of the employment exposed the employee to the risk; the fact that the risk is common to all who are exposed to the sun's rays on a hot day would be immaterial. Hughes v. Trustees of St. Patrick's Cathedral (1927).

e. Positional Risk

The positional risk doctrine is the most liberal of the scope of the risk theories, and it has been adopted in a minority of jurisdictions. The only inquiry under a positional risk theory is whether one's employment was responsible for one's being at the time and place where an injury occurred.

Even the most neutral of risks can be included; for example, an employee at work who was accidentally struck by an arrow fired by a small boy next door, would be covered. Gargiulo v. Gargiulo (1952).

2. A MISCELLANY OF RISKS

a. Acts of God

While acts of God such as windstorms, tornadoes, exposure, lightning, floods, earthquakes, etc., would at first appear to be outside the employment risk, it is generally agreed that if one's employment has enhanced or "increased" the risk of injury from these sources, the injury would be compensable. In addition to an increased risk approach to recovery, it may be possible to recover on the basis of "actual risk" or "positional risk" theories. The "proximate cause" or "peculiar risk" approaches would disallow compensation.

b. Street Risk Doctrine

Frequently employees find themselves on the streets and highways in the course of their employment. Early decisions denied recovery to employees who were injured as a result of the realization of risks associated with the use of streets and highways because these were viewed as common risks or hazards to the general public and not risks peculiar to one's employment. The situation is somewhat different today, and an employee who is subjected to a greater exposure to the risks of the street, despite the fact that such risks are common to the public, may be covered. Coverage in these cases can be provided on the basis of the increased risk approach; also, coverage can be had on the basis of the actual risk or positional risk doctrines.

c. *Imported Dangers Doctrine*

It is not uncommon for employees to be exposed to a risk of harm which they or their fellow employees have imported to the worksite; e.g., matches, explosives, firearms, etc. Traditionally, risks imported by the injured employee were viewed as "personal" and outside of the scope of the risk of employment. A danger imported by one's co-employee, while it may appear to be a neutral risk, could nevertheless give rise to recovery on the basis of increased, actual or positional risk theories. In Ward v. Halliburton Co. (1966), compensation was denied to an employee who was killed when his hunting gun accidentally discharged while he was getting a work uniform from his car; the court indicated that recovery would have been allowed if the gun had belonged to another employee. Additionally, an employee might be able to recover for the realization of a personal risk that the employee has imported, if it could be established that the employment had increased such a risk.

d. *Assault*

Assaults are held to be within the scope of the risk and to arise out of one's employment when the nature of the employment (e.g., policeman or security guard) increases the likelihood of such an occurrence, or if the assault has grown out of a controversy that is work related. Ordinarily assaults are not within the scope of the risk if they have been prompted by malice or personal motives; however, even these assaults may be included if in some manner one's work has contributed to the occurrence. Assaults in some cases, such as those by strangers, lunatics, children, etc., may be viewed as neutral risks outside coverage; however, it may be possible for these to be covered through the use of the positional risk doctrine.

Early cases recognized the aggressor defense which denied compensation to an aggressor in work-related assaults. The aggressor defense has been discredited today because it creates a fault based defense in a no-fault system. Despite the rejection of the aggressor defense, a substantial minority of jurisdictions by statute exclude from coverage those who have been harmed as a result of their "willful intent to injure" others. Generally these statutes require a greater degree of fault and wrongdoing than is required for the aggressor defense.

e. Horseplay

Frequently injuries occur in the workplace as a result of horseplay. There is little difficulty in providing coverage for a non-participant who is a victim of a horseplay injury; such an injury is viewed as being within the scope of the risk of one's employment. Difficult problems are posed, however, when one instigates or actively participates in horseplay and receives an injury. These cases may be disposed of on the basis of whether they occurred "in the course of" employment; however, the better analysis is one that focuses on the scope of the risk inquiry with the increased, actual, or positional risk doctrines determining coverage. In any event, an instigator or willing participant may be able to recover on the basis of the longevity and customary nature of the practice.

f. Heart Cases

One of the most problematic areas in the law of workers' compensation is that of heart cases. Commonly these cases are approached on the basis of whether or not a personal injury "by accident" has occurred. This approach requires that "unusual" strain or exertion precipitate the heart attack. This is an impractical and unsatisfactory test for coverage in heart cases; distinctions between "usual" and "unusual" strains are practically impossible to make, and serve to confuse the issue.

The better approach is one that focuses on the scope of the risk; thus if one's employment has contributed to the heart attack because of exertion or other work-related circumstances, the attack may be found to have arisen out of one's employment; otherwise heart attacks occurring on the job would involve personal risks. Professor Larson advocates the utilization of both a legal test and a medical test in heart cases. The legal test would be met on the basis of work-related exertion, and the medical test would simply require proof of a causal connection between such work-related exertion and the heart attack. This inquiry would be the same as that previously characterized as factual cause and would necessitate expert medical testimony.

As a result of the difficulties in this area, some jurisdictions have special provisions directed at heart and exertion cases.

g.   *Pre-existing Injury or Disease*

It is certainly not uncommon for employees to bring pre-existing medical problems to the workplace. The difficulty posed in this area stems from the fact that pre-existing medical problems constitute personal risks which would fall outside of coverage; however, if one is able to demonstrate that one's employment exacerbated or aggravated a pre-existing medical problem, then recovery may be permitted. The obvious problem facing employees is that of factual cause and medical proof. One must establish through expert medical testimony the fact of aggravation and a causal connection between one's employment and the claimed injury. Some jurisdictions address this problem area through special provisions in their workers' compensation act.

h. Unexplained Accidents

Coverage questions arise in cases of unexplained deaths, unexplained falls, and idiopathic falls. A strict application of the neutral risk or personal risk theories could result in a denial of coverage, even if a fall or death occurred in the course of employment. An application of the positional risk doctrine can result in recovery even if the cause of a fall or death is unknown, because of the employment relation that existed at the time. The positional risk doctrine could also permit recovery in idiopathic fall situations in which the fall was the result of a purely personal condition, if, for example, the fall occurred at work.

In an effort to resolve the problems posed by an unexplained employee death, courts will generally employ a presumption that the death was one that arose out of employment if the death occurred at the appropriate time and in the appropriate work situation. Given the objectives and policies of workers' compensation legislation every effort should be made to resolve unexplained injury and death cases in favor of the employee or his survivors.

C. THE "IN THE COURSE OF" CONCEPT

1. AN INTRODUCTION AND PERSPECTIVE

The statutory formula for workers' compensation coverage generally requires a personal injury by accident arising out of and "in the course of" one's employment. The "in the course of" requirement refers to the necessity for a sufficiently close relationship between one's employment and injury. This inquiry focuses on considerations of time, place, and circumstances, as they relate to one's employment.

Problems in this area usually occur for two reasons. First, the "in the course of" concept may be confused with the vicarious liability requirement of the same terms used in tort cases to establish liability; for example, a master is liable for the torts of a servant committed in the course of employment. The vicarious liability "in the course of" requirement certainly may be of assistance in many workers' compensation cases in establishing the requisite employment connection or relation; however, it should not be determinative in those cases in which it conflicts with the policies and coverage objectives of workers' compensation legislation. For example, if one's employment has produced an injury which occurs or manifests itself while one is not at work and off the employer's premises, there should still be coverage. In other words, one need not be acting within the course and scope of one's employment when an employment related harm produces injury. The only issue is one of causal connection between one's employment and injury. Rogers v. Allis Chalmers Manufacturing Co. (1949); see 1 A. Larson § 29.22. In Technical Tape Corp. v. Industrial Commission (1974), the inhalation of chemical fumes at work produced residual intoxication causing an employee to have an automobile accident after leaving the workplace; compensation was allowed.

The second cause of difficulties in this area stems from confusing the "in the course of" requirement with the scope of the risk inquiry which is made in conjunction with the "arising out of" requirement. In other words, the time, place, and circumstances considerations involved in the "in the course of" question may be permitted to dictate the answer to the scope of the risk issue. The scope of the risk issue should always be viewed as a question directed at the scope of workers' compensation coverage, with the necessity for a liberal and broad approach toward employment risks. The "in the course of" requirement really should do no more than estab- lish the necessary relation to one's employment required for workers' compensation coverage. The more liberal a jurisdiction's approach toward the selection of a risk theory, then the less that will probably be required to meet the "in the course of" test. If a positional risk theory is employed, little would probably be required to establish the neces- sary employment relation. For example, a salesman who suffers harm some distance from the employ- er's place of business, and on the premises of anoth- er, could be covered. See Wiseman v. Industrial Accident Commission (1956).

2. COMMON "IN THE COURSE OF" PROBLEMS

a. *Going to and From Work*

Injuries occurring while employees are traveling to and from work have constituted a large portion of workers' compensation litigation, and there is a lack of uniformity in this area. It should be noted at the outset that the problems posed with regard to coverage stem from a failure to recognize that many of these cases should be addressed on the basis of the "arising out of" requirement with its concomitant scope of the risk inquiry.

Generally, those accidents that take place while one is on the way to or from work are viewed as outside the course of one's employment; however, if one is on the employer's premises (having not yet arrived at work or in the process of leaving work) ordinarily there would be coverage. The key issue thus becomes the boundaries of the employer's premises. Various devices have been employed to resolve coverage issues for those injured off of but near the employer's premises; included are: the parking lot exception; the "so-close" rule; the "proximity" rule; and the "threshold" doctrine. Some jurisdictions have special provisions in their compensation laws to deal with "going to and from work" problems.

An employee may well be found "in the course of" in the following special circumstances, even if the injury has occurred while going to or coming from work. These special circumstances exist if: the employer provides the transportation or travel expenses; the employer compensates the employee for time spent in travel; or the employee is on call and travel constitutes a significant portion of employment duties. In many situations employees are required, as a regular part of their employment, to spend time away from home or office and difficult questions arise here because of the myriad of circumstances in which one might receive an injury; e.g., sleeping, eating, recreation, etc., in conjunction with work-related travel. Again it must be emphasized that the crux of the "in the course of" problem is to be found in a failure to address many of these cases on the basis of the scope of the risk.

b. *Mixed-Purpose Trips*

An area in which the rules of vicarious liability have created confusion with regard to workers' compensation coverage is that of mixed-purpose trips. On occasion an employee may be injured while on a trip that is both for the employee's benefit and for that of the employer; these are sometimes called "dual purpose" cases. Certainly, if the trip is primarily for the benefit of the employer there should be coverage despite the fact that the trip also involves some personal benefit or personal purpose; this is generally called the dominant purpose rule. Marks' Dependents v. Gray (1929).

Just as in cases of vicarious liability, issues of frolic and detour arise. It should be kept in mind that in vicarious liability situations the issue is one of possible employer liability to a third person, whereas in compensation cases the issue is one of coverage for the injured employee. Given the question in workers' compensation cases a more liberal approach is required and less emphasis should be placed upon the vicarious liability meaning of "in the course of." Little should be required in the way of employment connection, and the major inquiry should focus on the scope of the risk. In some jurisdictions a liberalizing trend is evident in this area. For example, coverage was extended to an employee who, prior to going to work, was injured in an accident while driving his child to school in a company truck; this would certainly appear to have been a personal trip, but the presence of the company's name and address on the truck seemingly determined the outcome. Thomas v. Certified Refrigeration, Inc. (1974).

c. *Recreation*

Various approaches have been taken toward compensation coverage when accidents have occurred during recreational or social activities. There may be liability when injuries from these sources have occurred on the employer's premises. Some decisions take a scope of employment approach toward the activity that produced the injury, while others insist upon some kind of benefit to the employer, direct or indirect. Recreational cases may frequently involve "going to and from" work and personal comfort issues (see infra). The more liberal a jurisdiction's risk theory, the greater the likelihood of coverage in recreation cases, and the less that is required for an activity to be "in the course of" employment.

d. Personal Comfort Doctrine

Employees who are injured while engaged in activities aimed at their personal comfort, e.g., drinking, eating, resting, smoking, using toilet facilities, etc., generally enjoy compensation coverage if their activities bear the necessary relationship to their employment. An employee may, however, remove oneself from the course of employment if, in efforts to satisfy personal needs, one abandons one's work or employs means which move the employee outside of the employment relation, thus indicating that a purely personal or neutral risk has been realized. For example, a deliveryman injured while attempting to dislodge a rabbit from a culvert was denied compensation. Ranger Insurance Co. v. Valerio (1977).

e. Emergencies

Employees injured while attempting rescues, or otherwise in emergency situations, are viewed as having acted within the course of their employment if an interest of the employer was furthered by the effort or activity. The good will of the employer alone may constitute a sufficient interest for coverage. As a matter of policy, very little should be required for a finding of "in the course of" when employees receive injuries during rescue attempts. The positional risk theory should be employed to provide coverage when an employee, motivated by common humanity and decency, is injured while attempting to rescue a stranger who bears no relation to the employer's business. See Food Products Corp. v. Industrial Commission of Arizona (1981).

f. Wilful Misconduct and Violation of Laws, Regulations and Safety Rules

The question of wilful misconduct on the part of an employee may arise in two important contexts: (1) it may provide the basis for a statutorily created defense in a minority of jurisdictions or, (2) in the absence of such a statute, it may be relevant to the issue of whether an employee was outside of the course of employment at the time of injury. The wilful misconduct defense is usually a difficult one to establish, because employee fault should not bar recovery under workers' compensation theory. The term "wilful" is strictly construed, and gross negligence will not suffice. The issue of wilful misconduct may also arise in the "in the course of" context in conjunction with questions concerning personal comfort, going to and from work, recreation, etc.

Some jurisdictions provide the employer with a statutory defense when an employee has wilfully violated safety rules, regulations, or statutes. The wilful violation defense is in some ways comparable to the assumption of the risk defense in tort cases. The employer must establish actual knowledge of the rule or statute and an appreciation of the risk connected with non-compliance. Additionally, excuses may exist for non-compliance. The justification and wisdom of the wilful violation defense is open to question in light of the no-fault nature of workers' compensation and the inevitability of employee injuries which are in large part the result of human frailty.

g. *Intoxication*

Employee intoxication is addressed statutorily in a majority of jurisdictions, and it may constitute a separate defense to coverage. The key question in employee intoxication cases is one of causation. The "sole cause" approach taken by some statutes appears to be the one most compatible with the policies of workers' compensation legislation; if there has been some work-related contribution to the injury, there should be coverage.

The coverage question in intoxication cases may also be addressed on the basis of a scope of the risk inquiry, an "in the course of" requirement, or as an issue of whether an injury "by accident" has occurred.

h. *Suicides*

Suicides have traditionally posed problems because they may be viewed as the result of a wilful act on the part of an employee, which severs the causal connection between a job related injury and one's death. The minority view, which parallels the traditional tort view, would only allow recovery in those cases in which one committed suicide in a state of delirium or as a result of an uncontrollable impulse evidencing an inability to make a conscious decision with regard to the taking of one's life. Under the minority approach there would need to be medical testimony of a mental disorder sufficiently serious to deprive one of volition.

A more liberal approach is generally taken in many jurisdictions, and if an unbroken chain of causation can be established between a work related injury and a mental condition that leads to a suicide, then compensation may be permitted. See City of Tampa v. Scott (1981).

Given the difficulties involved in establishing the requisite causal relation between employment related injuries and suicides, a better approach would be one requiring simply a demonstration of some contribution to the suicide by an employment related physical or psychic injury. See Lopucki v. Ford Motor Co. (1981). A broad approach should be taken toward the scope of the risk in suicide cases, and such deaths should be viewed as in the course of one's employment when a work relation can be shown.

D. THE NECESSITY OF "PERSONAL INJURY BY ACCIDENT"

1. THE PROBLEMS

Traditionally most workers' compensation acts have required as a part of their coverage formula a "personal injury by accident" or "accidental injury." Difficulties have arisen in interpreting the meanings of "accident" and "personal injury." Historically, problems have existed in this area because of the failure to take a pragmatic and liberal approach toward these requirements as they relate to the scope of the employment risk.

Furthermore, difficulties in this area were compounded by factual causation issues which were disposed of under the guise of "personal injury by accident," and which more appropriately should have been addressed as a part of the employment risk question, with very little required in the way of the cause in fact.

The personal injury by accident requirement has caused confusion and worked hardships in the following three major areas: occupational diseases; mental illness; and diseases, illnesses or injuries that have developed over a gradual period of time. Additionally controversies sometimes exist as to whether injuries to artificial limbs are excluded from coverage by the "personal injury" or "accidental injury" requirement. See Self v. Riverside Companies, Inc. (1980). A growing number of jurisdictions treat artificial limb injuries by special statutory provisions.

Initially occupational diseases were excluded from workers' compensation coverage because it was generally thought that this was an area for private health insurance. There was thus no provision for disease coverage in early compensation legislation, and the courts refused to find coverage because no "personal injury by accident" had occurred; after all, all diseases were considered to be personal or neutral risks commonly shared by everyone. In more modern times the necessity for occupational disease coverage has been candidly recognized either by broad judicial interpretations of the formula wording, or by special occupational disease provisions in the compensation acts.

Another difficulty with the "personal injury by accident" requirement is that presented by mental illnesses. Certainly today, on the basis of medical science, mental illness is recognized as a legitimate form of injury that may be causally connected to a risk of one's employment. The basic employment-related, mental illness fact patterns that commonly arise are: (1) physical trauma producing a nervous disorder; (2) nervous shock producing a physical disorder; (3) nervous shock producing a nervous condition or neurosis; (4) mental distress produced by prolonged work-related stress and anxiety; and (5) compensation neurosis; i.e., an unconscious desire to prolong compensation or a fear that compensation will not be paid. Little difficulty is presented for coverage by the foregoing first two fact patterns; however, coverage issues exist in the latter three. There is authority for compensation recovery in all five areas, and given the current state of medical science, there should be coverage for all the patterns when a mental illness is proven and the requisite employment connection is established. Given the pace and complexity of the modern industrial state with its rapid technological changes, mental disorders may well be within the scope of the risk of one's employment. See generally, Wade v. Anchorage School Dist. (1987).

Originally the formula coverage requirement of an "accident" was generally said to necessitate an "unusual," or "unforeseen," or "unexpected," or "external" event as the cause of an injury. In addition to an "unexpected event," it was also generally said that an injury had to have been sustained on a definite occasion or at a certain time. This approach created insoluble coverage problems because of the apparent necessity of distinguishing between "unexpected" or "unusual" and "expected" or "usual" risks; e.g., was the strain, exertion or hernia caused by an unusual or usual work related event. Furthermore, the definite occasion requirement in "accident" cases resulted in the exclusion of occupational diseases which had gradually developed over a long period of time.

2.   THE SOLUTION

The enormous coverage problems caused by the "accident" interpretations in many jurisdictions prompted the National Commission on State Workmen's Compensation Laws to recommend the elimination of this coverage requirement. It should be pointed out that the confusion created by the language "personal injury by accident" can be avoided simply by focusing upon scope of the risk, work connection, and factual cause.

E. OCCUPATIONAL DISEASE

1. COVERAGE SCHEMES

General compensation coverage for occupational diseases is currently provided in all jurisdictions, but the coverage methods vary considerably. The exclusive remedy provisions in the various acts, in recent years, have provided an increasingly important area of employer immunity. See Buford v. American Tel. & Tel. Co. (7th Cir.1989). At least five schemes of occupational disease coverage are identifiable: (1) use of a general definition of occupational disease in the workers' compensation act; (2) use of an expanded definition of "injury" or "personal injury" to include occupational disease; (3) use of a scheduled list of occupational diseases coupled with a general disease catch-all definition; (4) use of an unrestricted disease coverage provision; and (5) use of a separate occupational disease act. In addition to the foregoing general occupational disease coverage schemes, it is not uncommon to find specific legislative provisions dealing with loss of hearing, hernias, radiation, and various diseases of the lungs. Finally, the area of coal miner pneumoconiosis or "black lung" has virtually been preempted by federal legislation and programs; see supra Chapter 1, E., 5. and infra Chapter 15.

2. COVERAGE PROBLEMS

a. *Occupational Disease Versus Accident*

As mentioned previously, early workers' compensation acts contained no provision for occupational disease coverage, and most courts interpreted the formula "personal injury by accident" to exclude all diseases from workers' compensation coverage. As might be expected, the grey area between the definition of personal injury and disease became a conceptually difficult one. With the passage of special occupational disease legislation, however, the distinctions between disease and injury by accident definitions became less important. It should be kept in mind that an occupational disease can in fact occur through accidental means; for example, one can contract many diseases as a result of an accidental cut or skin breakage that is work related. See Wilson Foods Corp. v. Porter (1980).

b. *Occupational Disease Versus Common Diseases*

The major problem area today in occupational disease cases is to be found in the identification of those ordinary diseases of life that are said to be common to the public and not distinctively associated with a particular employment. Most jurisdictions attempt to give a detailed definition of the term "occupational disease," and despite the wording chosen, the ultimate issue of coverage is usually decided by the particular jurisdiction's approach to the scope of the employment risk of the disease in question. This is probably the case even though many jurisdictions fail to realize that their decisions are being made on this basis. For example, coverage problems of this nature could easily arise for a delivery man who is regularly exposed to rain, sleet and snow in the winter months, and who claims that his pneumonia is sufficiently work-related to be compensable. Pneumonia may be an ordinary disease of life, common to the public, and certainly not peculiar to his employment; however, deliveries made in winter weather may increase the risk of pneumonia, or make it an actual risk of employment, or place the delivery man in a position to contract the disease.

c. *Occupational Disease and Medical Causation*

In the foregoing example of the delivery man who contracted pneumonia in the winter months, difficulties also arise with regard to medical causation. A medical expert might testify that the employee's exposure because of his working conditions was a minor causative factor in the contraction of the pneumonia, or the expert might testify that the employee was subjected to both employment and non-employment related exposure, either of which could have caused the disease. The key inquiry should be whether the employment exposure caused or substantially contributed to the pneumonia. If the employment relation, as the cause in fact of the disease, is unclear, vague, or uncertain in the medical sense, then there is a likelihood that no coverage will be found. See Florida State Hospital v. Potter (1980).

The medical cause in fact inquiry poses real difficulties because of the frequent merger of the scope of the risk issue with the medical-factual causation question, and the surrounding confusion that this produces. The entire area of occupational disease is confusing and troublesome, and as recognized by the 1972 Report of The National Commission on State Workmen's Compensation Laws, "the determination of the etiology or 'cause' of a disease in a medical sense is often difficult or even impossible."

3.   SPECIAL COVERAGE RESTRICTIONS

It has been fairly common for various states to place unique restrictions on recovery for certain occupational diseases. Those diseases which receive restrictive treatment are generally diseases of the lungs, such as silicosis, asbestosis, black lung, etc. Typical restrictions are those that preclude recovery unless death or disability has occurred within a certain number of years from the date of last injurious exposure or from the date of the last employment in a particular area. Another example of restriction is to be found in the denial of benefits to one who has suffered less than total disability as a result of a particular occupational disease. Sometimes one finds that employees are precluded from compensation unless they can demonstrate their exposure to the hazards of a particular disease for a specified period of time. The policies and practices of each jurisdiction should be examined. In some instances there are even special provisions granting greater compensation than normal for certain lung diseases.

CHAPTER 6

DEATH

A. DEATH BENEFITS GENERALLY

Death benefits are provided by workers' compensation legislation to certain classes of beneficiaries. These benefits include burial expenses, with a statutory limit placed on the expenses, and compensation for the beneficiaries that is calculated on the basis of the appropriate statutory formula of the particular jurisdiction. The right to death benefits is a right created by statute, and it is not dependent upon any rights of the deceased worker. Therefore, a worker's release, compromise, or settlement, or unfavorable compensation decision, would be no bar to the claims of beneficiaries. A beneficiary's claim is legally separate and distinct from the worker's claim for compensation during his lifetime, and the worker generally has no right to control or dispose of the claims of the beneficiaries.

B. DEPENDENCY AND PARTIAL DEPENDENCY

As a general proposition only those beneficiaries who are viewed by the compensation act as "dependents" are entitled to death benefits. The acts vary, but generally compensation statutes require a showing of either actual dependency (complete or partial), and/or membership in a designated class or group before there can be recovery. In many instances those bearing certain relationships to the deceased, e.g., wife or child, enjoy a presumption of dependency and need not demonstrate actual dependency.

It is always important at the outset to determine who can be classified as complete or total dependents as opposed to partial dependents, because the former group is given preference and may recover compensation to the exclusion of the latter group. Anyone claiming death benefits other than one who enjoys a statutory presumption of dependency, must prove actual dependency, and membership in the statutory class entitled to compensation. The statutory classes are defined differently from jurisdiction to jurisdiction. Some acts provide fixed lists of persons, e.g., widow or widower, child, parent, brother, etc. Other acts use classes defined by the terms "next of kin," or "member of the employee's family," or "member of the employee's household." While the term "next of kin" may sometimes mean blood relatives only, a liberal approach should be taken toward the classifications, and for example, an unadopted dependent child living in the deceased's household should be included as a beneficiary. See generally Ryan–Walsh Stevedoring Co., Inc. v. Trainer (5th Cir.1979).

In those cases in which one does not receive the benefit of a presumption of total dependency, either total or partial dependency actually must be proven. Generally, total dependency may be proven despite the fact that a dependent had some other minor sources of support; however, one would not be totally dependent if a substantial source of support was received from other than the deceased. Partial dependency is a question of fact, and can be found to exist even if one's own sources provide substantial support. A majority of jurisdictions take a liberal approach toward the definition of "dependent"; see Tabor v. Industrial Accident Fund (1952).

C. WIDOW

In a majority of jurisdictions a widow is conclusively presumed to be totally dependent upon the deceased for workers' compensation purposes. Widowers should receive equal treatment. See Wengler v. Druggists Mutual Insurance Co. (1980). When no legal presumption exists, proof of dependency would be required. A claimant's marital status at the time of the death of the employee is often a key factor because some jurisdictions fix compensation rights as of the time of death. Other jurisdictions, sometimes with inequitable results, fix relationships and dependency as of the time of the accident or injury producing death. See generally, Dunn v. Industrial Commission (1994). For example, widows have been denied death benefits when they married an employee after the date of an injury that ultimately produced death.

1. LIVING WITH OR APART

In most jurisdictions a surviving spouse enjoys a presumption of dependency only if living with the deceased employee at the time of injury or death. "Living with" does not necessarily mean residing together; for example, economic necessity or considerations of health might dictate a separation. Additionally, a separation may be the result of desertion or other wrongful conduct on the part of the deceased employee's spouse which does not affect the legal obligation to provide support. If a separation has occurred that relieves the deceased employee's spouse of the legal obligation to provide support, the "living with" requirement would not be met, and there would be no presumption of dependency.

2. COMMON–LAW MARRIAGE

The domestic relations laws of a particular jurisdiction control whether a surviving common-law spouse may recover death benefits. For example, a common-law wife may be viewed as a "widow" or "wife" for workers' compensation purposes. See National Union Fire Insurance Co. v. Britton (1960). Even in jurisdictions in which the relationship is considered illicit, one may be entitled to compensation benefits as an actual dependent member of the deceased's "household." Furthermore, in some jurisdictions an illicit relationship is no bar to recovery if it was entered into in a "good faith" belief in legality by the surviving spouse. See Dawson v. Hatfield Wire & Cable Co. (1971). Bigamous marriage situations are often resolved on the basis of the "last marriage rule," which presumes that the last marriage was the legal one for compensation purposes. See Gibson v. Hughes (1961).

D. CHILDREN

Death benefits are generally provided for the "child" or "children" of a deceased employee on the basis of specific statutory language that includes them within the group conclusively presumed to be dependent. Illegitimate children, stepchildren, posthumous children, and other children who were not the subject of a legal obligation for support on the part of the deceased employee, have posed coverage problems. Coverage has sometimes been afforded under the dependent classifications of "member of the family" or "member of the household," and under specific statutory provisions addressing acknowledged illegitimate children. Today the difficulties previously posed by illegitimate children have been largely eliminated by the Supreme Court decision of Weber v. Aetna Casualty & Surety Co. (1972), in which the Louisiana Workers' Compensation Act was declared unconstitutional in so far as unacknowledged illegitimate children were denied coverage. This was held to be violative of the Equal Protection Clause of the Fourteenth Amendment. Proof problems with regard to paternity still remain.

E. FAMILY AND HOUSEHOLD MEMBERS

While the exact statutory language may vary, many workers' compensation acts permit the recovery of death benefits to one who can qualify as a "member of the family" or "member of the household." On the basis of the creation of these classifications it may be possible for stepchildren, stepgrandchildren, stepmothers, illegitimate children, nephews, mothers-in-law, and even unrelated children, etc., who can establish some dependency upon the deceased to receive death benefits. The liberal approach taken toward these groupings is supported by the humane objectives of workers' compensation.

F. PRIORITIES

Death benefit priorities are statutorily established in workers' compensation acts. Family relationships and/or dependency dictate priorities and benefits. For example, it is sometimes provided that a surviving spouse and minor children are to receive an entire award to the exclusion of others claiming dependency. Ordinarily that class which consists of total dependents are entitled to receive death benefits even if this means no recovery for partial dependents. When more than one wholly dependent claimant exists, there may be an equal division of benefits or statutorily fixed proportions may be allocated. It is possible, however, on the basis of some acts, for both total and partial dependents to receive compensation, but this should only occur after full compensation has been had by total dependents. As a caveat, it should be noted that compensation accrued and due a deceased employee must be paid either to the deceased's estate for distribution, or to the dependents under a compensation act, depending upon the jurisdiction.

CHAPTER 7

MEDICAL EXPENSES, DISABILITIES AND BENEFITS

A. INTRODUCTION TO RECOVERIES

The three broad categories of recovery under workers' compensation are: (1) medical and related expenses; (2) disability benefits; and (3) death benefits. Under the first group, medical expenses, rehabilitation costs, nursing costs, drugs, etc., are recoverable. Disability benefits are designed to provide compensation for the loss of earnings or earning power, and they are usually determined on the basis of either medical loss or wage loss theories, or some combination thereof; these benefits are determined by statutory formulas that may result in weekly, monthly, or sometimes lump sum payments. Death benefits are paid to the dependents of a deceased worker and such benefits are based on a statutory formula; additional amounts are specified for funeral or burial expenses. For reference and comparison purposes, the U. S. Chamber of Commerce compiles, on an annual basis, comprehensive charts of the state, federal and Canadian compensation requirements and benefits. U. S. Chamber of Commerce, Analysis of Workers' Compensation Laws.

B. MEDICAL EXPENSES AND REHABILITATION

At one time workers' compensation acts placed limitations on the amounts recoverable for medical expenses. Today most jurisdictions permit the recovery of unlimited medical expenses so long as a worker's condition necessitates continued treatment and care. A liberal approach is taken toward medical expenses, and commonly the costs of doctors, nurses, specialists, hospitalization, medical equipment, prosthetic devices, psychiatric treatment, drugs, medicines, etc. are included. It should be noted that in those cases in which an injured worker's spouse provides home nursing services, there can be recovery for the value of such services under the heading of medical expenses. See Kushay v. Sexton Dairy Co. (1975).

There is a lack of uniformity among workers' compensation statutes with regard to the recovery of physical and vocational rehabilitation costs. Ordinarily, those costs reasonably necessary for medical rehabilitation are recoverable, however, very few statutes provide complete coverage for the costs of vocational rehabilitation and related expenses necessary for a worker's return to full employment.

It should be remembered that in those cases in which medical complications, bad results, and even greater disabilities from medical malpractice occur, these events can be viewed as a part of the employee's original "injury", and all increased medical costs and benefits should be recoverable. See, e.g.,

Mallette v. Mercury Outboard Supply Co., Inc. (1959).

It should also be noted that the avoidable consequences rule has been applied to workers' compensation cases by statutes or case law. Employees who unreasonably refuse to submit to medical aid and treatment may jeopardize their rights to benefits. See Commonwealth, Department of Highways v. Lindon (1964).

C. SELECTION OF PHYSICIAN

The right to choose freely one's physician has been the subject of a great deal of controversy under workers' compensation laws. Some acts permit an employee to select a physician and others require that a selection be made from a panel of physicians chosen by the employer. Other acts require that treating physicians be approved by the medical profession for workers' compensation practice.

The physician selection controversy revolves around the need for physician-patient confidentiality and confidence on the one hand, versus the need to control medical costs and to provide effective medical treatment on the other hand. No matter what the physician selection rule of the particular jurisdiction may be, an injured employee cannot generally seek medical assistance without the employer's prior knowledge and consent, except for emergency situations. Of course, if after notice, an employer fails to provide the necessary medical care, an employee is free to procure medical assistance and submit claim for reimbursement. It should be noted that osteopaths and chiropractors may be selected. See Wetzel v. Goodwin Brothers, GMC Truck (1981).

D. MEDICAL LOSS AND WAGE LOSS

The key to understanding compensable disabilities is to be found in medical loss and wage loss theories; both theoretically compensate an injured worker for loss of earnings or earning power, but they achieve this result by different methods. The medical loss theory focuses upon the physical injury or impairment suffered by a worker. Compensation may be based on "pure" medical losses; for example, workers' compensation acts usually contain "schedules" which provide a predetermined amount of compensation for specific enumerated medical losses; i.e., a schedule might provide a specified amount of compensation for the loss of a hand, regardless of the economic impact of such a loss. In other words, certain enumerated medical losses, are clearly recognized as disabilities and a loss of earnings or earning power is conclusively presumed on the basis of the inclusion of the loss in a medical loss schedule.

The wage loss theory attempts to provide compensation for an injured employee on the basis of the employee's actual earnings that have been lost due to an injury. For example, a "pure" wage loss approach might award compensation to an injured employee on the basis of actual lost wages incurred during the period of incapacity. In many jurisdictions wage loss determinations are made by comparing actual earnings prior to the date of injury with one's "earning capacity" after the injury. This "diminished earning capacity" concept permits an injured worker to recover compensation even if there has been no actual loss of earnings. See, e.g., Karr v. Armstrong Tire & Rubber Co. (1953).

No compensation system today employs pure medical loss or pure wage loss theory, rather, one finds that compensation acts utilize both in varying degrees. For example, a compensation act that contains an injury schedule may also provide compensation for an unscheduled injury that has resulted in a medical impairment. The severity of the impairment and the degree of one's disability (i.e., temporary total, permanent total, temporary partial, and permanent partial) commonly are used to determine the duration and amount of the employee's economic losses.

A tremendous amount of controversy exists with regard to the proper use of medical and wage loss theories in the determination of the appropriate amount of compensation for injured workers. See A. Larson, "The Wage–Loss Principle in Workers' Compensation," 6 Wm. Mitchell L.Rev. 501 (1980). While it is desirable for compensation awards to bear a reasonable relation to one's past wages, and to be based upon a reduction in one's earning capacity, rather than on the basis of arbitrary amounts dictated by the type of medical injury sustained, it must be stressed that no wage loss or medical loss approach actually attempts to provide compensation on the basis of the injury's true economic impact on the particular worker or on the worker's earning power or earning capacity. All legislation in this area represents compromises which have resulted in a no-fault system of reduced but fairly certain compensation for work-related injuries.

E.   THE AVERAGE WAGE AND FORMULAS

The cornerstone of compensation calculations is an employee's average wage, commonly specified as an "average weekly wage" or as some other average wage based upon a unit of time such as months or days. The average weekly wage, average monthly wage or the like represents an average earnings figure, which, when multiplied times a jurisdiction's fixed statutory percentage (ranging from 50 to 66⅔%), produces the employee's basic weekly or monthly benefit. Statutory formulas vary from jurisdiction to jurisdiction, but commonly, compensation benefits are determined on the basis of weeks or months of eligibility. In addition, it is commonly provided that maximums and minimums are to be placed on the amount of the weekly or monthly benefits; further, limitations may be placed upon the number of weeks or months of eligibility.

Frequently, issues arise with regard to the composition of the average weekly wage, and whether, for example, tips, fringe benefits, bonuses, meals, transportation, etc., should be considered. Every effort should be made to make the employee's average weekly wage computation as complete as possible. See Jess Parrish Memorial Hospital v. Ansell (1980); but see Morrison–Knudsen Construction Co. v. Director, OWCP (1983).

Difficulties may also arise because of an employee's temporary, irregular, or erratic work history. The average wage may sometimes be calculated with reference to the wages of a comparably situated employee. Most statutes permit calculations of average wages in a discretionary manner, if a just and fair result for the employee cannot be obtained by the use of the normal statutory formulas.

F.　DISABILITIES

1.　DISABILITIES GENERALLY

Workers' compensation statutes ordinarily provide four classifications of disability. These classifications are determined by the severity or extent of the disability with the disability characterized as either partial or total. Additionally, disabilities are affected by their duration and are characterized as either permanent or temporary. The four common disability classifications are: temporary partial, temporary total, permanent partial, and permanent total. These disability classifications in conjunction with the employee's average wages, and appropriate statutory formulas provide the basis for disability benefit computation.

2. TEMPORARY PARTIAL

A temporary partial disability is present when an employee, who has been injured on the job, is no longer able to perform that job, but for the period of disability is able to engage in some kind of gainful employment. Temporary partial disability compensation is designed to pay an injured worker for lost wages, and thus wage loss theory is generally employed in making awards. Additionally, this classification promotes the prompt return of an injured employee to the workforce. Examples of injuries that commonly produce temporary partial disabilities are sprains, minor fractures, contusions and lacerations.

The critical factor in determining the temporary partial classification may be the impairment of the employee's earning capacity. For example, an employee who has received a minor injury that has resulted in no loss of time at work and who has suffered no actual wage losses, may still be entitled to temporary partial compensation if some impairment to earning capacity can be proven.

3. TEMPORARY TOTAL

The condition of temporary total disability exists when an employee is unable to work at all for a temporary but undetermined amount of time. One may be totally disabled even though not completely helpless or wholly disabled. Examples of injuries that can result in temporary total disability are serious illnesses, heat exhaustion and disabling back injuries. Temporary total disability is designed to provide compensation to an injured worker for the economic losses incurred during a recuperative period.

4. PERMANENT PARTIAL

A permanent partial disability may be found when a permanent and irreparable injury has occurred to an employee, i.e., one that probably will continue for an indefinite period with no present indication of recovery. For example, one who loses a foot on the job will experience a period of temporary total disability during hospitalization and recuperation. At the point in time when maximum medical improvement has been attained, the disability should be classified as permanent partial; a foot has been lost, but the employee is able to perform some gainful work. The purpose of permanent partial disability is to provide compensation for the employee's reduced earning capacity, even though this is often accomplished through the use of a medical loss schedule. It should be noted that the majority view is to the effect that if a scheduled injury produces additional disability to other parts of the body, the employee will be able to recover an amount in excess of that provided in the schedule, for example, loss of a foot could produce traumatic neurosis. See Gonzales v. Gackle Drilling Co. (1962).

5.   PERMANENT TOTAL

The condition of permanent total disability exists when an employment related injury renders an employee permanently and indefinitely unable to perform any gainful work. An employee need not be entirely helpless or completely incapacitated in a medical sense. The so-called "odd-lot" doctrine permits the finding of a permanent total disability for workers who are not completely incapacitated, but are handicapped to such an extent that they cannot become regularly employed in any well-known branch of the labor market; the worker is said to have been left in the position of an "odd lot" in the labor market. Cardiff Corp. v. Hall, [1911]. One may receive a permanent total disability on the basis of a scheduled loss; for example, loss of sight in both eyes can be a scheduled loss that requires compensation as a permanent total disability. It is difficult to generalize about permanent total disabilities, but the following factors are generally relevant to such determinations: age; experience; skills and training; education; nature and extent of injury; employment history and nature of employment at the time of injury.

6.   DISFIGUREMENT

The great majority of jurisdictions address disfigurement by special provision. Compensation for disfigurement is generally provided in much the same way that compensation is provided for scheduled injuries. In the absence of special disfigurement provisions it may be difficult for a worker to establish an impairment to earning capacity because of disfigurement, scars or the like. These special provisions candidly recognize the need for compensation in disfigurement cases, and thus like medical loss schedules, conclusively presume a wage loss that dictates compensation. Occasionally, the issue may arise with regard to whether an employee may receive compensation both on the basis of a disability classification and disfigurement. It may be possible to obtain compensation on the basis of both. For example, compensation has been awarded for permanent partial disability resulting from burns with additional compensation awarded for disfigurement. Kerr–McGee Corp. v. Washington (1970).

G. MULTIPLE AND SUCCESSIVE INJURIES

Difficulties sometimes arise when multiple injuries are received by a worker from the same accident. Often this problem is addressed statutorily in the particular workers' compensation act. In the absence of a specific provision an approach should be taken that provides the injured employee with the greatest possible coverage and compensation for the most serious degree of disability that can be demonstrated. For example, a worker might receive concurrent injuries to two different fingers on the same hand. These injuries could result in the complete loss of use of both fingers, and the compensation paid could simply amount to twice the scheduled amount for the loss of a finger. This amount might be less than the compensation to which the worker would be entitled on the basis of a percentage disability to the hand as a whole. In other words, an employee should not be confined to an injury schedule when multiple injuries have been sustained and the disability is greater than the sum of the scheduled losses. The reverse should also be the case, and when the sum of the scheduled losses provides greater compensation than the percentage of disability, then the greater amount should be awarded. See Emerson Electric Co. v. Powers (1980); Holcombe v. Fireman's Fund Insurance Co. (1960).

Successive injuries may present problems because the cumulative effect of the injuries may produce a greater degree of disability and dictate greater compensation than the amount that would have been paid on the basis of separate scheduled injuries. For example, an employee who has lost one hand may lose the other hand in another work-related accident. The worker has thus suffered a much greater loss than the sum of single hand losses on a schedule. Three possible approaches are taken to the problem. First, the employer can be required to provide compensation for the entire resulting disability. Second, there may be apportionment statutes requiring the employer to provide compensation on the basis of the disability the employee would have experienced without taking into effect the previous disability. It should be noted that if a greater disability is suffered because of some pre-existing illness, disorder, weakness, or disease on the part of the employee, apportionment may not be permitted; as a general rule, an employer takes an employee as he finds him with regard to latent and pre-existing conditions that result in greater disabilities than otherwise would have been suffered. Third, "second injury funds" may exist (discussed infra) and therefore assure that an employee is fully compensated for an entire disability.

H. SECOND INJURY FUNDS

Second injury funds (sometimes called "subsequent injury funds") offer the best solution to the problem of the worker who suffers a greater degree of disability, as the result of a work-related injury, because of some pre-existing disability or condition. The second injury fund is designed to encourage the employment and retention of handicapped workers. There is little incentive for their employment if the last employer faces entire liability for a disability in part due to pre-existing causes. The second injury fund provides an equitable solution to the problem of the handicapped employee by allowing the employer to pay only that amount he would have been required to pay in the absence of the pre-existing difficulty. An issue exists in second injury situations with regard to what will qualify as an "injury" or "disability" for purposes of the utilization of the second injury fund. Traditionally employers take their employees as they find them; however, it is questionable whether the last employer of an injured employee should bear the complete burden of an employee's disability that is in part the result of a previous work related injury or disability. It is also questionable whether the last employer should bear the complete burden of an employee's disability that is in part the result of a previous nonwork-related injury. See Lawson v. Suwanee Fruit & Steamship Co. (1949). It should be noted that second injury fund liability cannot be established when the sequence of injuries is reversed; subsequent nonwork-related accidents make no difference in compensation awards.

A liberal approach should be taken toward the utilization of second injury funds because handicapped workers are often the subject of job discrimination. Furthermore, workers' compensation legislation should strive to provide compensation for the entire extent of a disability suffered as a result of a work-related injury regardless of whether that disability has been contributed to by some purely personal condition or previous work-related injury.

I. DEATH AFTER DISABILITY

When death follows disability several issues may arise. In analyzing the problems in this area it should always be remembered that an employee's right to compensation benefits is separate and distinct from the right of an employee's dependents to death benefits. (See supra Chapter 6, A.) For that reason, death benefits should not be reduced by compensation paid to an injured worker prior to the worker's death unless there is a statutory provision to the contrary; for example, some jurisdictions statutorily reduce the dependency period by the period of disability compensation payments. An additional problem area is that of accrued compensation benefits that have not been paid prior to a worker's death. Generally these accrued amounts are paid to the employee's estate or to the employee's dependents, depending on the jurisdiction. Reference should be had to particular statutes that address this issue.

J.   DEATH COMPENSATION BENEFITS

In the case of complete or total dependents, death compensation benefits are generally computed on the basis of statutorily fixed percentages of a workers' average wage, just as in the case of computing a worker's disability compensation benefits. The majority of compensation acts place maximum limits on death benefits. Statutes vary considerably with regard to the computation of death benefits for those classified as partial dependents. A popular method of computing benefits for partial dependents is to provide compensation on the basis of the amounts of the deceased worker's contributions. It must be stressed that the formulas and methods employed in computing death benefits for all dependents vary considerably, and generalizations are inappropriate regarding exact computations. Usually, the most important legal issues involved in this area are those mentioned in Chapter 6, supra.

CHAPTER 8

ADMINISTRATION

A. INTRODUCTION

A statutory scheme of no-fault compensation can be no better than its administration. Efficient and effective administration is especially necessary in the workers' compensation context, because a majority of claims are uncontested, and the prompt delivery of compensation benefits is of critical importance to a worker and the worker's family.

According to the 1972 Report of the National Commission on State Workmen's Compensation Laws there are six primary obligations of administration:

(1) to take initiatives in administering the act;

(2) to provide for continuing review and seek periodic revision of both the workmen's compensation statute and supporting regulations and procedures, based on research findings, changing needs, and the evidence of experience;

(3) to advise employees of their rights and obligations and to assure workers of their benefits under the law;

(4) to apprise employers, carriers, and others involved of their rights, obligations, and privileges;

(5) to assist voluntary resolutions of disputes, consistent with the law; and

(6) to adjudicate disputes which do not yield to voluntary negotiation.

The National Commission clearly pointed out that the adjudication of disputes should be the least burdensome of the six obligations when the other five obligations are properly executed.

B. COMMISSIONS VERSUS COURTS

Only a few jurisdictions permit the initial judicial adjudication of disputed compensation claims. The great majority of the states have administrative agencies that supervise, administer, and adjudicate workers' compensation matters, subject to subsequent judicial appellate review.

It is generally accepted that the judiciary is ill equipped to administer adequately and effectively compensation matters and accomplish the six primary obligations of administration identified by the National Commission on Workmen's Compensation, supra, Chapter 8, A. Furthermore, the adversary nature of judicial proceedings insures unhealthy conflict between employers and employees and is incompatible with the goals and objectives of workers' compensation. State systems of administration vary, however, the best approach appears to be the one recommended by the National Commission on State Workmen's Compensation Laws. Under its recommendation there would be an executive officer and staff who devote their time solely to administration, with a separate and independent board of compensation appeals. The appellate board would review the decisions of hearing officers in contested compensation cases. An informal procedures unit would handle all claims initially, and those claims that are incapable of voluntary resolution would be forwarded to a hearing officer for a formal determination. Only questions of law from the appellate board would receive judicial review.

C. NOTICES

Almost all workers' compensation acts contain provisions requiring that an employee promptly inform the employer of an injury. Some statutes may require that notice of injury be given within a specified period of time. The purpose of the notice requirement is to facilitate prompt medical treatment and care, and to minimize the extent of an employee's injury. Additionally, notice provides the employer with a timely opportunity to investigate the causes and conditions of injury.

A rigid approach should not be taken, and generally it is not taken toward notice requirements. The employee's failure to comply with the notice requirement should be excused if there is actual knowledge on the part of the employer or one whose knowledge can be imputed to the employer. Certainly, knowledge can be found on the basis of compensation or medical payments to an employee. Additionally, an employee's lack of compliance should be excused if it has not resulted in prejudice to the employer. Many reasonable excuses can exist for non-compliance with formal notice requirements.

D. STATUTES OF LIMITATION

There are generally two types of limitation statutes that govern the timely filing of workers' compensation claims for disability. In one type of statute, the limitation period runs from the date of injury, and in the other type of statute the period commences on the date of the employee's accident. In jurisdictions using date of injury, a liberal approach is usually taken, and the appropriate date may be the time when the injury became apparent or reasonably should have become apparent to the employee. In date of accident jurisdictions, an inflexible and literal approach is sometimes taken toward the time of the accident; this may result in the loss of a worker's claim, because of a personal failure to discover the injury or its work connection prior to the running of the statute. This type of statute of limitations has been the subject of a great deal of criticism. See 3 Larson § 78.42(c).

Generally in death cases, statutes of limitation begin to run at the date of an employee's death; however, some statutes of limitation commence at the time of the accident or injury producing death. A literal approach should not be taken to date of accident or injury statutes in recognition of the fact that dependents' rights do not arise until the date of an employee's death.

The possibility always exists for a finding of a waiver of the limitations period on the part of the employer. A recognition of liability, the payment of compensation or medical benefits, or the failure to raise the defense of the statute of limitations in a timely manner, can result in waiver.

E. WAITING PERIODS

Waiting periods may be found in workers' compensation statutes. These provisions authorize compensation only after the passage of a specific amount of time from the date of an employee's injury. Waiting periods are generally inapplicable to medical benefits and to death benefits. In an effort to discourage malingering and to promote a prompt return to the workforce, many waiting period provisions are directed specifically at temporary total disability claims.

By way of illustration, the Council of State Government's Model Act, Part III, Section 15, proposes a waiting period of three days, with retroactive payment if the total period of disability exceeds fourteen days. This follows the recommendation of the 1972 Report of the National Commission on State Workmen's Compensation Laws. As a general proposition, it should be noted that the longer the waiting or qualifying periods, then the less the costs of workers' compensation programs; however, this results in reduced benefits for workers.

F. HEARINGS, EVIDENCE AND REVIEW

In practically all jurisdictions, disputed workers' compensation cases are handled by an administrative process rather than by the courts. A less formal, more expeditious and more flexible approach is taken than in a normal judicial civil trial. It is always desirable for some part of the administrative machinery to be available for the resolution of contested claims through the use of an informal procedure; however, a formal administrative adjudicative process must be available for those contested claims which cannot otherwise be resolved informally.

The workers' compensation administrative process may vary somewhat from jurisdiction to jurisdiction, and despite occasional commentary to the contrary, the proceedings in contested cases are all marked by a degree of practical formality consistent with the adjudication of substantive rights. One should exercise some caution when one encounters the often repeated phrase that compensation proceedings are to be informal with the ordinary rules of evidence relaxed.

In every jurisdiction, administrative compensation decisions can ultimately be the subject of judicial review. In most jurisdictions, judicial review is limited to questions of law, and administrative findings of fact will not generally be disturbed.

The common law rules of evidence generally do not apply to compensation proceedings, however, they can serve as a guide. Appellate review sometimes occurs because of the admission of hearsay evidence. Wide discretion is permitted in compensation hearings, and the admission of evidence that would be inadmissible in a court of law is allowed. While the admission of hearsay evidence may not constitute error, if an undue amount of weight has been given to such evidence in the administrative decision, then error may have been committed. A jurisdiction's approach to the treatment of hearsay is particularly important to claimants who are prone to present a great deal of hearsay evidence; indeed, in many cases, only hearsay evidence may be available on key issues. In reviewing compensation decisions, four different approaches have been taken toward the use of hearsay evidence. First, hearsay is admissible and may provide the basis for the decision. Second is the residuum and majority rule which permits administrative decisions to be based upon hearsay evidence, but some of the evidence supporting the decision must have been admissible. Third, the admission of the hearsay is not reversible error; however, if the decision would not have been rendered but for the hearsay evidence, the decision must be reversed. Finally, there is some authority declaring hearsay evidence inadmissible and its admission to be reversible error.

Generally the standard of review in appeals of administratively decided compensation cases is whether there is substantial evidence to support the decision. For variations on the above standard of review, see 3 Larson § 80.26(a)-(i).

G. COMPROMISE, SETTLEMENT, AND LUMP SUM COMMUTATION

The policy considerations in workers' compensation cases differ from those found in the adversary and uncertain environment of the tort system with regard to compromises, agreements, and settlements. As a result of these differences most jurisdictions by statute or by judicial decision deny the claimants the right to settle, adjust, or compromise a claim for less than the statutory amount regardless of whether the claim is disputed or undisputed. See Southern v. Department of Labor and Industries (1951). The minority view would permit compromises and settlements for less than the statutory amounts when disputed questions of liability exist; even so, approval of the compromise, agreement, or settlement would ordinarily be required by the appropriate workers' compensation authority.

It may be possible for a claimant to receive compensation benefits in a "lump sum" rather than by way of periodic payments, depending upon the jurisdiction. This method of payment is subject to criticism given the objectives of compensation benefits to replace lost wages and to provide economic benefits over a period of time. Lump summing generally takes the form of a reduction of periodic benefits to present value with the use of a percentage discount. There may be some situations in which the best interests of a claimant can dictate a lump sum approval, as for example, in the cases of a worker who needs the entire amount for legitimate educational, retraining, or rehabilitation costs. Tremendous potential for harm exists, however, when lump summing is indiscriminately permitted because of the likelihood that the entire award will be quickly and unwisely spent. See Malmedal v. Industrial Accident Board (1959). The use of lump sums and the difficulties that surround their use have been exacerbated by the desire of some claimants' attorneys to obtain their entire fees at once rather than over a period of time.

H.　REOPENING, MODIFICATION, TERMINATION, AND REDISTRIBUTION

Statutes vary from jurisdiction to jurisdiction with regard to the details of reopening and modification of compensation awards; however, reopening and modification is usually permitted on the basis of a disabled worker's changed condition. Modification may take the form of increased or decreased benefits, or a cessation of benefits. Time limits for reopening can be found in a majority of jurisdictions. Fraud, mutual mistake of fact, and sometimes "any good cause" can provide grounds for reopening. A minority of jurisdictions permit reopening at any time for changed conditions.

In death benefit cases, the possibility exists for termination or redistribution of benefits based upon certain dependents' changes in status. For example, the remarriage of a widow may result in the termination of benefits; a redistribution could also occur as a result of the death of a minor dependent.

I. INSURANCE

There are three methods of insuring workers' compensation benefits. First of all there is the private insurance system, which provides a majority of the benefits paid in the United States, and which may be utilized in the vast majority of states. Secondly, there is self-insurance, which is also available in a vast majority of states, but which provides a small overall percentage of the benefits paid in the United States. Third, there are state insurance fund systems, which provide almost a fourth of the benefits paid in the United States; six states mandate participation in the state fund, while twelve states permit private insurance competition with their state insurance funds. It is difficult to determine whether any one insurance method is superior to another, and as long as proper controls exist for the adequate protection of compensation claimants, any of the methods accomplish their purposes. Perhaps, lower insurance costs can be achieved through the use of state insurance funds.

It must be stressed that the object of insurance in workers' compensation systems is to provide security for the payment of benefits. If for some reason the insurance carrier or employer is unable to provide insurance or to guarantee benefits, then machinery and resources should be in existence to provide workers and their dependents the benefits to which they are entitled. For example, Michigan has a self-insurer's security fund. See McQueen v. Great Markwestern Packing Co. (1974). Most states do not have direct security systems, but rely upon indirect or administrative supervision of insurance carriers and self-insurers. The Council of State Government's Model Workmen's Compensation and Rehabilitation Law contains special fund provisions which would provide payments in the case of insolvent employers or insurers. See Part IV, Insurance; Section 55, Special Fund.

Workers' Compensation insurance is designed for the benefit and protection of both the employee and the employer. In an effort to maximize the security of the employee and dependent claimants, the defenses which could be used by an insurer against an employer should not be available against claimants. For example, the employer's failure to pay a premium should not provide an effective bar to an otherwise eligible compensation claimant. See Home Life & Accident Co. v. Orchard (1920).

Each state has a workers' compensation insurance regulatory authority which establishes rates based upon experience ratings and loss experiences. Rate making service organizations have a direct impact on this process. While a few states have independent data gathering organizations, the majority of states use the National Council on Compensation Insurance (NCCI) to collect data for rate

making purposes. Its website address is: http://
www.ncci.com.

J. REMOVAL

Under 28 U.S.C.A. § 1445, actions brought under
the FELA and Jones Act in state court generally
cannot be removed to federal court. The same code
section also prohibits removal of actions under
workers' compensation laws of the state in which
the federal district court is sitting. This would include suits for retaliatory discharge for filing a
worker's compensation claim. See Wallace v. Ryan–
Walsh Stevedoring Co. (1989). The federal statute
reflects a Congressional policy of allowing states
local control over their workers' compensation systems without federal court interference in the local
administrative process. It should be noted that 28
U.S.C.A. § 1332(c), the direct action provision, does
not apply to actions initiated in federal court by a
workers' compensation insurer; actions against
such an insurer initiated in federal court are not
allowed. Northbrook National Insurance Co. v.
Brewer (1989).

CHAPTER 9

EXTRATERRITORIAL PROBLEMS AND OVERLAPPING COVERAGES

A. CONFLICT OF LAWS

Conflict of laws and full faith and credit problems often arise in workers' compensation cases because of the inevitable multi-state contacts which are encountered by today's employees. For example, an employee may reside in Texas, sign a contract of employment in Oklahoma, work for a company whose home office is in Arkansas, on a job based in Wyoming, and receive a compensable injury while on company business in Louisiana. Conflicts questions ordinarily are concerned with which state's workers' compensation statute is applicable. As a general rule, the rights provided by the workers' compensation act of one state cannot be enforced in other states. See 4 Larson § 84.20.

The following fact patterns usually give rise to most conflicts problems: (1) the accident is local and the employment contract is foreign; (2) the employment contract is local and the accident is foreign; (3) both the accident and the employment contract are foreign; and (4) the accident is foreign to the state of the employer's principal place of business or legal residence. Most states have specific statutory provisions which address conflict of laws issues. Normally, if a compensable injury has taken place within a state, that fact alone may provide a basis for the utilization of local law.

State statutes addressing out of state injuries commonly provide for the application of the law of the forum on the basis of the contract of employment being entered into within the forum state, or on the basis of employment connections, relations, or contacts with the forum state. Where both the employment contract and state of injury are foreign, a proceeding under the law of an unrelated forum is generally inappropriate. Finally, the domicile or residence of the claimant, and/or the location of the employer's home office or legal residence, can affect the application of a particular state's workers' compensation act. In order to avoid the conflicts difficulties in workers' compensation cases, the Report of the National Commission on State Workmen's Compensation Laws recommended that a worker or dependents have the choice of claiming compensation in the state where the injury or death occurred, or where the employment was principally localized, or where the employee was hired. This recommendation would probably eliminate the problem of the employee who could be without compensation coverage in any state, because of multi-state contacts. The Restatement (Second) of Conflicts § 181 takes a liberal and expansive approach toward the circumstances that may bring the workers' compensation law of the forum into play. It is suggested that resort should be had to this restatement section when statutes of a forum state fail to address a workers' compensation conflict problem. This restatement section is compatible with the objectives and policies of workers' compensation legislation.

B. FULL FAITH AND CREDIT

The full faith and credit clause has posed two major problems for workers' compensation: (1) the extent to which the workers' compensation laws of one state should be recognized and given weight in the decisions of another state; and (2) to what extent should successive compensation awards be permitted from state to state for the same injury or death.

The primary difficulties created in the first situation were the result of Bradford Electric Light Co. v. Clapper (1932), in which the Supreme Court held that New Hampshire was forced to recognize the Vermont workers' compensation statute under the full faith and credit clause. A subsequent series of Supreme Court decisions have virtually abolished the Clapper doctrine, and the full faith and credit clause's requirement of the recognition of foreign law, now presents few problems when the forum state wishes to apply its own workers' compensation act. See Carroll v. Lanza (1955); Kelly v. Guyon General Piping, Inc. (4th Cir.1989) (Virginia would apply North Carolina exclusive remedy provision to bar tort claim arising out of accident in South Carolina).

The full faith and credit clause has been the source of a great deal of controversy because of the difficulties posed when more than one state awards compensation to a claimant for the same injury or death. The Supreme Court resolved a major area of controversy in Thomas v. Washington Gas Light Co. (1980). This case held that one jurisdiction has no legitimate interest in preventing another jurisdiction from awarding supplemental compensation, when that second jurisdiction had the power in the first instance to apply its compensation law and to make an award. The full faith and credit clause is not to be construed in such a way as to bar another state's successive award of workers' compensation, so long as credit is given for the prior state's award. In other words, a worker is entitled to receive the largest single amount of compensation to which one would be entitled under the applicable compensation acts.

C. THE PROBLEM OF OVERLAPPING COVERAGE

The coverage boundaries between state workers' compensation acts and certain federal remedies and programs are unclear. These vague boundaries create difficulties for claimants because of the possibility of federal preemption, and an improper election of remedies which could result in a denial of compensation or in a lesser award than that to which a claimant could be entitled. The federal remedies that pose potential problems in this area are: the

Longshore and Harbor Workers' Compensation Act (LHWCA); personal injury and death actions by seamen or their survivors based upon Jones Act negligence, general maritime law unseaworthiness, and maintenance and cure; and personal injury and death actions based upon the Federal Employers' Liability Act.

In LHWCA situations the "twilight zone" doctrine has been recognized by the Supreme Court. Davis v. Department of Labor & Industries (1942). This doctrine eliminates the risk of an initial mistake on the part of a claimant, by allowing a presumption of coverage under the first act providing a basis for the claim. Additionally, the Supreme Court has indicated that concurrent jurisdiction may exist in borderline cases, particularly in regard to injuries or deaths occurring on land. Sun Ship, Inc. v. Pennsylvania (1980). The possibility of successive and supplementary awards exists in the LHWCA area by analogy to the policies contained in Thomas v. Washington Gas Light Co., supra, even though the constitutional bases would be different. Certainly, no double recovery should be permitted. It should be noted that the LHWCA generally provides more generous benefits than the various state compensation acts.

The coverage problems of seamen involving either the LHWCA or state workers' compensation acts usually depend upon a factual determination of one's status as a seaman. The LHWCA specifically excludes from coverage a master or member of the crew of a vessel. Borderline cases involving state compensation acts may also receive "twilight zone" doctrine treatment. See Maryland Casualty Co. v. Toups (5th Cir.1949). But see Anderson v. Alaska Packers Association (1981). Successive awards are sometimes allowed on the basis of concurrent jurisdiction theories when federal seamen's remedies are pursued after an acceptance of state workers' compensation benefits. See Manuel Caceres v. San Juan Barge Co. (1st Cir.1975).

The Federal Employers' Liability Act (FELA) provides a negligence remedy for all interstate railway workers whose jobs affect interstate commerce, including employees engaged in auxiliary activities related to interstate railroads. Motor carrier, airline, and other interstate transportation workers are not covered by the FELA. If an employee is covered by the FELA, then it is said to be the exclusive remedy because of federal preemption in the field of interstate commerce, and thus state compensation acts have no application. The LHWCA provides the exclusive remedy for covered workers and bars actions under the FELA. See Chesapeake & Ohio Railway Co. v. Schwalb (1989).

As an additional note on overlapping coverages, it should be remembered that the payment of workers' compensation benefits may have a direct impact upon one's social security benefits, because the Social Security Act provides for the reduction of benefits to the extent that they are duplicated by state or federal workers' compensation payments. See 42 U.S.C.A. § 424a; 20 C.F.R. § 404.408; Sciarotta v. Bowen (3d Cir.1988). In 14 states, however, there are statutory provisions that reduce worker's compensation benefits when a worker is entitled to social security. The FELA is not considered a workers' compensation law or plan for the purposes of 42 U.S.C.A. § 424a.

In addition, approximately one-half of the states treat workers' compensation payments as disqualifying income for unemployment compensation purposes. There is a lack of uniformity on this issue. See Page v. General Electric Co. (1978).

It should also be noted that tensions can arise in the context of the Americans with Disabilities Act (ADA) and workers' compensation. For example, settlement of permanent partial disability claims usually involve carefully crafted releases. Other issues include the effects of ADA violations on state claims for compensation. See Caldwell v. Aarlin/Holcombe Armature (1997). In 1996, the EEOC published a guide entitled, Workers' Compensation and the Americans with Disabilities Act (Pub. No. 915.002).

Finally, an issue of claim preclusion can arise when a workers' compensation or social security disability claimant alleges total disability but seeks to maintain an ADA action. See Dush v. Appleton Electric Co. (8th Cir.1997); Swanks v. Washington Metro. Transit Authority (D.C.Cir.1997).

CHAPTER 10

THIRD PARTY ACTIONS

A. EXCLUSIVE NATURE OF COMPENSATION ACT

Workers' compensation legislation provides employees and their dependents with their exclusive remedy against the employer and insurance carrier for all injuries and deaths which arise out of and in the course of employment. The exclusivity provisions of workers' compensation acts have generally withstood constitutional attacks for the most part in recent times, and their continued vitality remains the keystone of compensation legislation. Constitutional questions concerning exclusivity may, however, be of importance in certain areas. See Chapter 3, B., supra. See also Fleischman v. Flowers (1971). Generally, the immunities provided to the employer and others are difficult to avoid. Kimball v. Millet (1988).

The exclusive nature of the workers' compensation remedy can sometimes result in a denial of compensation in cases in which damage has clearly occurred. For example, injuries to sexual organs, the senses, the psyche and sometimes disfigurement, and non-disabling pain and suffering may go uncompensated, if the injuries producing these results fall within the workers' compensation formula, because most workers' compensation acts fail to provide compensation for these results.

It should always be remembered that an employer may be sued in tort despite the exclusivity provision, on the basis of intentional tort theories and in situations giving rise to nonphysical torts. Lopez v. S.B. Thomas, Inc. (2d Cir.1987) (emotional distress under 42 U.S.C.A. § 1981). See Chapter 3, B., supra.

B. WHO ARE THIRD PARTIES

The exclusivity provision of workers' compensation legislation applies only to employers and others who may be so treated, such as insurance carriers and co-employees. Generally the rights of employees and survivors to pursue common law and statutory remedies against a "third party" whose conduct has caused or contributed to an injury or death, remain intact. Frequently issues arise with regard to who are "third parties" subject to separate actions for damages. One of the most troublesome groups, is that of co-employees. A majority of jurisdictions, either on the basis of statute or judicial decision, have extended the employer's immunity to co-employees. A minority of jurisdictions view co-employees as "third persons" outside of the immunity enjoyed by the employer.

It is difficult to generalize about who are third parties, however, third parties have from time to time been found among the following: physicians, product manufacturers, co-employees (including possibly corporate officers, directors, or stockholders), supervisory employees, compensation carriers and their safety inspectors, unions and their safety inspectors, governmental entities, owners and occupiers of land, etc. See chapter 3, supra.

C. THIRD PARTY ACTIONS AGAINST THE EMPLOYER

Questions of contribution and indemnity may arise when third parties attempt to recover over against the employers of injured or killed employees. Most jurisdictions deny a third party the right to contribution from an employer whose negligence has played a part in an employee's harm, because of the general common law rule that there can only be contribution from one who is liable to the plaintiff. The exclusivity provision of workers' compensation legislation relieves the employer of tort liability for injuries or deaths falling within the coverage formula; thus, generally employers cannot be the subjects of contribution actions. Third party indemnity actions present a problem for all workers' compensation jurisdictions. Prof. Larson describes this issue as an evenly-balanced controversy in workers' compensation law. Larson, "Third Party Action Over Against Workers' Compensation Employer," 1982 Duke L.J. 483, 484. Despite the exclusivity provisions in workers' compensation acts, and despite the necessity of inquiries directed at fault in noncontractual indemnity situations, the possibility of employer liability certainly exists under substantive indemnity law. See Lockheed Aircraft Corp. v. United States (1983). Additionally, in appropriate cases, indemnity may be obtained from an employer on the basis of an express or implied agreement, or on the basis of a separate and independent duty owed by the employer to the third person. See Carneiro v. Alfred B. King Co. (1975).

D. DEFENSES OF THIRD PARTIES

Normally third parties who are defendants in actions brought by employees, employers, or insurance carriers, may employ any defenses which could be utilized against the employee. Thus, regardless of whether or not the action is one for damages on the part of the employee, or a subrogation action brought by an employer or insurer, the employee's negligence or the statute of limitations may be used as defenses. Since the action, even in subrogation cases, is that of the employee, the contributory fault of an employer, may not generally be raised as a defense. Mermigis v. Servicemaster Industries, Inc. (1989) (jury not allowed to consider employer negligence in order to reduce award). See Baker v. Traders & General Insurance Co. (10th Cir.1952).

E. SUBROGATION

It is difficult to generalize about subrogation rights and procedures, but almost all jurisdictions have subrogation statutes that affect workers' compensation cases. The common-law background of subrogation arose out of duties that are no longer popular. See Seavey, "Liability to Master for Negligent Harm to Servant," 1956 Wash. U.L.Q. 309. There appears to be a common-law basis for subrogation in some compensation cases. See Federal Marine Terminals, Inc. v. Burnside Shipping Co. (1969). A variety of statutory approaches may be found. Some statutes grant employees priority in actions against third parties, and if the employee fails to take advantage of the priority, then the subrogee may maintain the action. Other statutes provide the employer or carrier with priority to proceed against third parties. Still other statutes grant no priority and allow both to proceed against third parties independently or jointly. A few jurisdictions deny subrogation rights altogether, while others bestow all rights upon the subrogee.

The central policy issue to be found in the subrogation area centers on the conflict between the desire for full and adequate compensation, and the potential problem of double recovery if subrogation is not allowed. Additional policy issues involve the following: the possibility of workers' compensation payments inuring to the benefit of a wrongdoer; the desire to impose liability on a third party at fault; and the need for a third party to indemnify those who have been required to pay workers' compensation benefits. See 6 Larson, § 74.00.

F. UNINSURED MOTORIST INSURANCE AND NO-FAULT INSURANCE

Special problems have been created by the off-set provisions contained in uninsured motorist and no-fault insurance policies when claims also involve workers' compensation benefits. No uniform solution to these problems has been found, and each state's insurance statutes and public policy must be examined.

Where there is uninsured motorist insurance, some courts have held the off-set provisions invalid or void as being contrary to public policy because the insurance provision reduces effective coverage below that required by statute. Often legislation is enacted to alter this result. See generally, Mountain States Mutual Cas. Co. v. Vigil (Ct.App.1996); see also National Union Fire Ins. Co. v. Figaratto (1996). Other courts have held that insurance contracts are valid which allow insurers to reduce uninsured motorist liability by the amount of workers' compensation paid. Ullman v. Wolverine Ins. Co. (1970). In those states which allow the off-set for workers' compensation, there are divided authorities on the issue of whether reduction should be made from an insured's total damages or from the amount of insurer liability under the insurance policy; see, e.g., Waggaman v. Northwestern Security Ins. Co., (1971); American Ins. Co. v. Tutt (1974); Michigan Mutual Liability Co. v. Mesner (1966).

No-fault insurance creates a similar off-set problem when a workers' compensation claim is involved. See, e.g., Neel v. State (Utah 1995). It can be argued that the exclusive remedy provision in the workers' compensation act precludes any recovery of no-fault benefits regardless of statutes that would require workers' compensation benefits to be off-set. On the other hand, the exclusive remedy provision does not bar receipt of no-fault benefits and due process and equal protection are not violated. Mathis v. Interstate Motor Freight System (1980). In jurisdictions where reduction or off-set is allowed, no-fault coverage should be recoverable only to the extent that damages exceed workers' compensation benefits received by an injured worker. See 6 Larson, § 71.24(e).

CHAPTER 11

FUTURE OF WORKERS' COMPENSATION

A. THE NATIONAL COMMISSION ON STATE WORKMEN'S COMPENSATION LAWS

The Occupational Safety and Health Act of 1970, (29 U.S.C.A. § 651 et seq.) Section 27, established a National Commission on State Workmen's Compensation Laws and authorized "an effective study and objective evaluation of state workmen's compensation laws in order to determine if such laws provide an adequate, prompt, and equitable system of compensation for injury or death arising out of or in the course of employment." Section 27(a)(2). The National Commission submitted its report to the President and Congress on July 31, 1972, in which it made 84 recommendations for minimum state standards. The report indicated that 19 of its proposed state standards were "essential," and that the states should comply with these by July 1, 1975, or else congressional action should be taken in the form of a national minimum standards law. The National Commission found five major objectives for modern workers' compensation programs:

(1) Broad coverage of employees and work-related injuries and diseases;

(2) Substantial protection against interruption of income;

(3) Provision of sufficient medical care and rehabilitation services;

(4) Encouragement of safety; and

(5) An effective system for delivery of benefits and services.

Some of the National Commission's recommended "essential" elements of workers' compensation laws were:

(1) Compulsory coverage;

(2) No Occupational or Numerical Exemptions to coverage;

(3) Full coverage of work-related diseases;

(4) Full medical and physical rehabilitation services without arbitrary limits;

(5) Employee's choice of jurisdiction for filing interstate claims;

(6) Adequate weekly cash benefits for temporary total, permanent total, and death cases; and

(7) No arbitrary limits on duration or sum of benefits.

To date the 19 "essential" recommendations of the National Commission have not been adopted by any state, but many states have used the recommendations as a basis for the improvement of their particular workers' compensation acts. In 1976, an Inter–Agency Workers' Compensation Task Force reported in its findings that there was a need to reform state workers' compensation programs. The recommendations of both the National Commission and the Task Force have been used as a basis for a proposed National Workers' Compensation Standards Act.

The Council of State Governments took the 84 recommendations and incorporated them into a Model Act (as revised). This effort brought about some modifications in state workers' compensation laws.

The International Association of Industrial Accident Boards (IAIABC) studies workers' compensation issues and makes recommendations for legislative changes. Its website address is: http://www.iaiabc.org.

B. NATIONAL WORKERS' COM-PENSATION STANDARDS ACT PROPOSALS

Neither the National Commission nor the Inter–Agency Task Force (later merged with the Division of State Workers' Compensation Standards within the Department of Labor's Office of Workers' Compensation Programs) recommended the replacement of state workers' compensation laws with an overall federal program, but both emphasized the overall need to reform state programs. As a result of these studies, several bills have been introduced in Congress from time to time to set federal "minimum standards" for all state workers' compensation systems with one overall federal program. For example, Senate Bill 420 was introduced in the 96th Congress in an effort to create the "National Workers' Compensation Standards Act of 1979". There has never been sufficient political support for these proposals in Congress.

C. ALLOCATION OF FUTURE ECONOMIC AND SOCIAL BURDENS FOR INDUSTRIAL ACCIDENTS AND DISEASES

Despite the many justifiable criticisms of state workers' compensation laws, these acts will probably continue to serve as the chief vehicles for compensating workers for employment related injuries and deaths. The Report of the National Commission on State Workmen's Compensation laws indicates that workers' compensation is preferable to tort actions because of the fact that: (1) in many cases both employee and employer fault and causation produce industrial accidents; (2) the tort process is expensive, lengthy, and uncertain in nature with an assurance of no compensation to some victims; and (3) the tort system contains an inherent deterrence to rehabilitation.

The National Commission also indicated that presently it would be impracticable and unbeneficial to attempt to disassemble the present workers' compensation system and place its various branches under other social programs. The report further noted that it is unlikely that acceptable medical program alternatives to workers' compensation with regard to medical care will be established in the foreseeable future. Furthermore, the report observed that no other delivery system is more effective than workers' compensation. In summary, the conclusion of the National Commission was to the effect that workers' compensation systems, with recommended changes, should continue. See Report of the National Commission on State Workmen's Compensation Laws, pp. 119–121 (1972).

It is certainly likely that in the future there will be federal and state social programs which, to some extent, may overlap with workers' compensation. Every effort should be made to avoid a duplication of benefits and to insure the coordination of complementary systems. See 4 Larson §§ 96, 97.

It is possible that tort reform in the future will look to the workers' compensation model for guidance, particularly in the areas of medical malpractice and catastrophic injuries.

There is definitely a trend toward managed health care in workers' compensation programs throughout the states. See Hashimoto, The Future Role of Managed Care and Capitation in Workers' Compensation, 22 Am. J.L. & Med. 233 (1996). The insurance industry has debated genetic testing as a part of various insurance plans, including workers' compensation, but to date the political environment has not been receptive to these ideas.

In 1998, Executive Order No. 13078 created a National Task Force on Employment of Adults with Disabilities which will include studies and recommendations concerning workers' compensation laws.

PART 3

EMPLOYEE PROTECTION LEGISLATION

CHAPTER 12

UNEMPLOYMENT COMPENSATION

A. BACKGROUND

In 1935, an unemployment insurance system was established in order to provide economic security for workers during periods of temporary unemployment. The original system was created by Title IX of the Social Security Act of 1935. In 1939, the tax provisions of Title IX became the Federal Unemployment Tax Act, under the Internal Revenue Code. Today the Social Security Act, the Federal Unemployment Tax Act, and numerous amendments to these acts provide the statutory basis for federal unemployment compensation programs in the United States. Constitutional challenges to the system have met with little success. Chas. C. Steward Machine Co. v. Davis (1937); Carmichael v. Southern Coal and Coke Co. (1937); W.H.H. Chamberlin v. Andrews (1936). Recent constitutional challenges have generally been unsuccessful. See

McKay v. Horn (1981). This is not to say that the unemployment insurance system is free from all constitutional problems. For example, payment or nonpayment of compensation during labor disputes creates a federal preemption question under the Supremacy Clause; see Nash v. Florida Industrial Commission (1967). First Amendment rights can also pose problems. Frazee v. Illinois Dept. of Employment Security (1989).

The principal federal statutes comprising the basis of the unemployment insurance system today are: the Federal Unemployment Tax Act (I.R.C. §§ 3301–3311); the Social Security Act, Titles III, IX, and XII; 5 U.S.C.A. §§ 8501–8508, 8521–8525; the Wagner–Peyser Act; the Social Security Amendments of 1960; the Manpower Development and Training Act of 1962; the Federal State Extended Unemployment Compensation Act of 1970; the Employment Security Amendments of 1970; the Disaster Relief Act of 1970; the Emergency Unemployment Compensation Act of 1971; the Disaster Relief Act of 1974; the Trade Act of 1974; the Emergency Unemployment Compensation Act of 1974; the Emergency Jobs and Unemployment Assistance Act of 1974, as amended; the Emergency Compensation and Special Unemployment Assistance Act of 1975; the Unemployment Compensation Act Amendments of 1976; the Emergency Unemployment Compensation Act of 1977; the Omnibus Reconciliation Act of 1980; the Omnibus Budget Reconciliation Act of 1981; the Tax Equity and Fiscal Responsibility Act of 1982; the Social Security Amendments of 1983;

the Omnibus Budget Reconciliation Acts of 1987 and 1990; the Emergency Unemployment Compensation Act of 1991; the Unemployment Compensation Amendments of 1993; the Personal Responsibility and Work Opportunity Reconciliation Act of 1996; the Balanced Budget Act of 1997; and the Taxpayer Relief Act of 1997. In addition to the foregoing, each state, the District of Columbia, Puerto Rico, and the Virgin Islands have separate unemployment compensation laws.

The unemployment insurance system relies on cooperative federal-state programs. Federal laws provide general guidelines, standards, and requirements, with administration left to the states under their particular unemployment legislation. The unemployment compensation system is generally funded by unemployment insurance taxes or "contributions" imposed upon employers. The federal taxes are generally applied to the costs of administration, while the state taxes provide trust funds for the payment of benefits. Federal taxes are paid into a Federal Unemployment Trust Fund from which administrative costs and the federal share of extended benefits are paid. The Fund is also used to establish a Federal Unemployment Account from which the states can borrow if their state trust funds become depleted. Unemployment taxes should not be confused with the separate Social Security taxes imposed by the federal government, or with the separate disability benefits taxes imposed by some states. It should be noted that unemployment benefits are taxable as ordinary income.

The U.S. Department of Labor maintains a useful website at: http://www.dol.gov.

B. FEDERAL UNEMPLOYMENT INSURANCE PROGRAMS

1. REGULAR STATE PROGRAMS

a. Overview

The principal vehicle for providing weekly unemployment benefits is referred to as the regular state program. Subject to federal guidelines, the states determine: (1) qualifying requirements; (2) amounts of benefits; (3) duration; and (4) grounds for disqualification.

While state unemployment compensation laws can vary, ordinarily qualification requires a demonstration of: employment by an employer subject to the unemployment tax of a particular jurisdiction, and employment during a "base period" (a recent 12 month period); and generally one must have been employed in more than one quarter.

Payments usually take the form of weekly benefits. The weekly amount is calculated on the basis of a particular jurisdiction's formula. Commonly an employee's average weekly wage provides the basis for the weekly benefit amount, and this average amount is determined by dividing one's high quarter wages by the 13 weeks in a quarter; one-half of the result is the weekly benefit amount paid to the worker. There may be a waiting period prior to the initial payment of benefits. In some jurisdictions this may be referred to as the "waiting week;" however, not all jurisdictions impose an unemployment period of one week prior to the payment of compensation. Normally, claimants have a "benefit year" of a designated 52 weeks within which to receive or "draw out" all compensation entitlements.

The duration of unemployment compensation benefits varies with the particular jurisdiction; however, the vast majority of jurisdictions determine duration on the basis of the length of employment or the amount earned (variable duration approach). The longer the length or the greater the amount, the more weeks of benefits one can receive. A minority of jurisdictions consider an employee's work history to be irrelevant, and all claimants who qualify for benefits are treated in the same manner; i.e., each uniformly receives the same number of weeks of benefits on the theory that benefits should be tied to that period of time necessary to secure new employment (uniform duration approach).

Workers are denied compensation benefits if certain grounds for disqualification exist. Unemployment compensation policy dictates payment only to those employees who have lost their jobs through no fault on their part. In all jurisdictions an employee is disqualified from benefits if the worker: (1) voluntarily quits employment without good cause; or (2) is discharged for employment related misconduct. Additionally, disqualification can occur at any time if a claimant or benefit recipient refuses to accept suitable employment without good cause. Finally, in order for benefits to continue, a claimant must: (1) register for employment with the jurisdiction's Employment Service; (2) be able to work; (3) be available for work; and (4) seek work on one's own.

b. Procedures and Appeals

Representatives of the state employment agencies, who may be called deputies or claims examiners, make initial findings of fact (usually on the basis of interviews) which lead to a grant or a denial of unemployment compensation benefits. The appellate rights of a dissatisfied claimant are generally guaranteed by Title III of the Social Security Act, Section 303(a), which requires administration by the states in a manner "reasonably calculated to insure full payment of unemployment benefits when due," and which requires an "opportunity for a fair hearing before an impartial tribunal for all individuals whose claims for unemployment are denied." See Graves v. Meystrik (1977). It should be noted that employers have appellate rights as well, and they frequently exercise these rights because an employer's unemployment experience rating affects the amounts that an employer is required to contribute. Appellate procedures vary from state to state, but all jurisdictions allow access to the state judicial system for appellate review, once administrative remedies have been exhausted (usually after a hearing before an appeals tribunal whose decision may or may not be then reviewed by a board or some other state administrative body). A state administrative practice of permitting the automatic suspension of benefit payments upon the filing of an appeal by an employer was enjoined by the Supreme Court. California Department of Human Resources Development v. Java (1971). See Jenkins v. Bowling (7th Cir.1982).

c. *Extended and Supplemental Benefits*

In recent times, certain amendments have provided extended, supplemental or special unemployment benefits, thus increasing unemployment compensation for many unemployed persons in the United States. The Federal–State Extended Benefits Program pays "exhaustees" (individuals who have exhausted their regular program entitlements) further unemployment compensation, with the costs shared equally by the federal and state governments. The Omnibus Budget Reconciliation Act of 1981, repealed the national "on" and "off" triggering indicators which automatically regulated the extended benefits program. The Federal Supplemental Compensation Act of 1982 made additional unemployment benefits available in states experiencing periods of "higher unemployment;" these benefits are funded out of general federal revenues. The Social Security Amendments of 1983 extended the Federal Supplemental Compensation program. More recent federal acts have made similar adjustments.

2.   FEDERAL EMPLOYEES
AND EX–SERVICEMEN

In 1956, unemployment compensation coverage was extended to federal employees. The state law of the jurisdiction in which a claimant worked as a federal employee usually determines an employee's eligibility. This eligibility may also be determined by the law of the state in which a claimant subsequently worked in privately covered employment, or by the law of the state in which a claimant resides at the time of the filing of the claim. The amount of benefits is determined by state law. The conditions and eligibility requirements for compensation are also governed by state law, but findings of fact provided by the employing federal agency with regard to federal employment, wages, and the reasons for separation (which have been made under U.S. Department of Labor procedures) are binding upon the states.

In 1958, unemployment compensation coverage was extended to ex-servicemen. The state law of the jurisdiction in which a claimant first files an unemployment compensation claim which establishes a benefit year after the claimant's most recent separation from active duty, determines eligibility. A U.S. Department of Labor schedule prescribes applicable wages for benefit purposes. These are based upon a claimant's pay grade at the time of one's latest discharge or release from federal service. If a claimant is eligible for certain Veterans Administration benefits (subsistence or educational), the claimant is not entitled to unemployment compensation during these periods of eligibility.

3.   DISASTER UNEMPLOYMENT ASSISTANCE

Those employees who suffer unemployment as a result of major disasters are entitled to unemployment benefit assistance. This program is now generally known as the Disaster Relief and Emergency Assistance (DREA) program. The President makes disaster area declarations. The states generally administer the payment of benefits, and these are strictly derived from federal revenues. Individual benefits are payable for the period of unemployment caused by the disaster, or until suitable reemployment is obtained, but in no event longer than the prescribed disaster assistance period.

4.   TRADE ADJUSTMENT ASSISTANCE

Direct assistance is provided to employees who find themselves unemployed because of foreign competition. These benefits are provided only to those employees whose terminations are the result of foreign imports. These imports must be a substantial cause of actual or threatened termination. Assistance is paid out of federal revenues and is generally administered by the states. This assistance takes the form of weekly benefits, training allowances, relocation allowances, and job search allowances.

C. STATE FINANCED PROGRAMS

1. EXTENDED AND ADDITIONAL BENEFITS

A few states have enacted supplemental unemployment programs. These programs are financed completely by the particular jurisdiction, and they are usually aimed at providing extended benefits during high unemployment periods. California, Connecticut, and Puerto Rico have state extended benefit programs. Hawaii has enacted an Additional Unemployment Compensation Benefits Law that provides benefits for unemployment resulting from disasters.

2. UNEMPLOYMENT COMPENSATION DISABILITY BENEFITS

Six jurisdictions in the United States have enacted special disability benefit programs to assist workers who are ineligible for either unemployment compensation or workers' compensation. Workers' compensation generally excludes disabilities arising out of nonwork-related diseases or injuries; benefits are not payable through unemployment insurance programs to disabled workers because the ability to work is a condition of eligibility. California, Hawaii, New Jersey, New York, Rhode Island, and Puerto Rico have special unemployment disability benefit programs that fill the gap between workers' compensation and unemployment compensation laws. A branch of the particular jurisdiction's labor agency administers the program. Contribution by employers to state funds, private insurance, or self-insurance finance the programs. Some states make distinctions between the employed and the unemployed in their benefit formulas, while other jurisdictions do not.

CHAPTER 13

FAIR LABOR STANDARDS ACT

A. INTRODUCTION

The federal attempt to regulate the wages and hours of employees began in 1892 with the passage of the Eight–Hour Law. Later, the Supreme Court in Hammer v. Dagenhart (1918), held that Congress could not properly exercise its power under the Commerce Clause to prohibit the shipment of goods produced by child labor in interstate commerce. The Fair Labor Standards Act of 1938, 29 U.S.C.A. § 201 et seq. (hereinafter referred to as "FLSA") was enacted to regulate wages and hours (set minimum wage and overtime requirements) and child labor. The FLSA was upheld as constitutional in United States v. Darby (1941), in which the Hammer v. Dagenhart case, supra, was overruled. Over the years Congress has amended the FLSA and added major and minor acts to the federal wage-hour laws. The Equal Pay Act of 1963 was an important amendment to the FLSA; it generally prohibits sex-based wage discrimination by requiring equal pay for equal work regardless of sex. The Congressional extension of wage and hour coverage to public schools and hospitals was upheld as constitutional in Maryland v. Wirtz (1968), but this decision was overruled in National League of Cities v. Usery (1976). In this latter case, the Supreme Court held that the attempted Congressional regulation of wages and hours of employees of state and local governments constituted an unconstitutional infringement on state sovereignty. Constitutional issues again reached the Supreme Court in Garcia v. San Antonio Metro. Transit Authority (1985), in which a divided court upheld the application of the FLSA to state and local governments, overruling National League of Cities v. Usery. Congress passed the Fair Labor Standards Amendments of 1985 in order to lessen the impact of Garcia by authorizing the use of compensatory time in the place of overtime for state and local government employees.

The FLSA may be applied to a nonprofit religious organization that derives income largely from commercial business, despite constitutional challenges based upon the First Amendment. Tony and Susan Alamo Foundation v. Secretary of Labor (1985).

The Fair Labor Standards Amendments of 1989 created a "training wage" for eligible employees under 19 years of age at rates less than the minimum wage. The Small Business Job Protection Act of 1996 increased the minimum wage, and it replaced the "training wage" with an "opportunity wage."

Today the FLSA, as amended, provides compensation standards and regulation in four basic areas: (1) minimum wages; (2) overtime compensation; (3) sex-based wage discrimination (equal pay for equal work); and (4) child labor. The FLSA, as amended, is liberally construed by the courts, and, with certain exceptions, it applies generally to interstate commerce and industry. Other federal acts apply compensation standards to federally financed public works contracts (Davis–Bacon Act), government service contracts (Service Contract Act), and government supply contracts (Walsh–Healey Public Contracts Act). Some states have enacted higher compensation standards than those existing under federal law. These higher state standards are not superseded or preempted, and the federal standards cannot be used to excuse noncompliance with the higher state ones. If employees are covered by both federal and state compensation standards, then the stricter federal or state standards are applicable.

B. STANDARDS AND REQUIREMENTS

1. MINIMUM WAGE

Congress changes the minimum wage rate from time to time, and as of September 1, 1997, the FLSA established the minimum hourly rate for all covered employees at $5.15. This means, for example, that employees who are paid on a monthly basis and who are working 40 hour weeks, must be paid at least $892.67 per month; employees who are paid semi-monthly must be paid $446.33; employees who are paid weekly must be paid $206.00 per week. The foregoing are monthly, semi-monthly, and weekly average standards; the FLSA does not require an employer to pay these amounts each period, but the average standards must be met (based upon 8 hour work days; 40 hour work weeks; and 2,080 work hours in a year).

It must always be remembered that the work-week is the longest unit of time over which wages can be averaged in order to determine whether the minimum wage has been paid. This does not mean that all employees must be paid solely on an hourly rate basis; they can be paid on a salary, commission, or piecework basis that is monthly, semi-monthly, or weekly, but the minimum hourly rate must be received by them. If employees are paid solely on an hourly rate basis, then the minimum hourly rate must be met.

Problems sometime arise because certain deductions may be legally made from an employee's wages. Wages must be paid in cash or "facilities furnished," and thus the reasonable costs of board, lodging or other facilities can be used in meeting minimum wage requirements. Payment in scrip, tokens, coupons, etc., is prohibited. Gifts, talent fees, discretionary bonuses, and certain other payments are excluded from wage calculations. The application of the minimum wage to particular employees requires detailed research, because of the complexity and exceptions contained in the FLSA and related wage and hour laws.

2.   OVERTIME COMPENSATION

The federal wage and hour laws do not limit the number of hours that an employee can work in a workweek, but the employee must be paid time and one-half the employee's regular rate of pay for each hour worked over 40 in a workweek. It should be noted that an employee's regular rate of pay can be higher than the minimum hourly rate set by law for these purposes. The workweek is the longest period over which earnings may be averaged in arriving at an employee's regular hourly rate of pay. For example, if an employee works 45 hours in one week and 35 in the next week, the employee must be paid overtime for five hours in the first week, despite the fact that the employee's hourly average over two weeks is 40 hours per week. Time lost on the job must be made up in the same workweek, or else overtime must be paid for all hours subsequently worked over 40 in any other workweek. Overtime exceptions and exemptions exist that must be researched in particular cases.

Many disputes arise because employers and employees fail to agree on what activities are to be considered "working time." For example, time spent on call may or may not be considered as working time. The Portal-to-Portal Act of 1947, excludes preliminary and postliminary activities from working time not otherwise compensable by contract, custom, or practice. Premium pay can also create overtime calculation difficulties. This is pay received in excess of basic straight-time wages, and it can take the form of holiday pay, contracted overtime, gifts, bonuses, sick pay, etc. If premium pay is considered to be part of an employee's regular earnings, then FLSA overtime is increased, otherwise premium pay may be offset against the statutory overtime pay.

3. SEX–BASED WAGE DISCRIMINATION

The Equal Pay Act of 1963 amended the minimum wage provisions of the FLSA, and prohibited wage discrimination based upon sex. The provisions require equal pay for equal work for men and women doing equal work on jobs requiring equal skill, effort and responsibility and that are performed under similar working conditions. Minimum, overtime, and premium wages for men and women must be equal if the work is equal, and the wages of one sex cannot be lowered in order to comply with the law. Exceptions are allowed for: (1) seniority systems; (2) merit systems; (3) systems measuring earnings by quantity or quality of production; and (4) factors other than sex. The act prohibits sex-based wage discrimination only in "any establishment" operated by an employer. The act does not cover discriminatory rates as between an employer's two or more legitimate "establishments." It should be noted that wage differences authorized by the Equal Pay Act are valid pay practices for the purposes of the Civil Rights Act of 1964, Title VII; however, it is possible for sex-based discrimination involving pay practices, beyond the reach of the Equal Pay Act, to be remedied under Title VII. In order for equal pay coverage to exist, an employee generally must be covered by the FLSA minimum wage provisions. It should also be pointed out that amendments in 1972, placed executive, administrative, and professional employees within equal pay coverage. See Ch.20, B., infra.

4. CHILD LABOR

The FLSA prohibits "oppressive child labor" in commerce or in the production of goods for commerce. There is a "hot goods" ban that prohibits the interstate shipment of goods from establishments that have employed oppressive child labor. Enterprise coverage is used to prohibit the use of oppressive child labor, regardless of whether the work of children has an interstate impact or is purely local in nature. The FLSA defines "oppressive child labor" through the use of age restrictions. Essentially, minors under 14 cannot be employed, except in agriculture; minors 14 to 16 can work limited hours outside of their school hours in a limited class of jobs; and minors 16 to 18 cannot be employed in certain hazardous occupations. Employers generally obtain age or permit certificates for each minor in accordance with Department of Labor regulations and state guidelines.

C. COVERAGES

Compensation standards have been imposed by Congress through the exercise of its powers to regulate interstate commerce and through it powers to control federal government contracts and federally financed projects. All geographical areas under the jurisdiction of the United States, including possessions and leased bases in foreign countries, are subject to the FLSA. Two forms of coverage are provided by the FLSA: (1) "enterprise" coverage; and (2) "individual employee" coverage. Enterprise coverage generally exists if an employer has two or more workers engaged in interstate commerce, or in the production of goods for interstate commerce, while meeting a requirement of business volume. If enterprise coverage exists, then all employees of the enterprise are covered. Individual employee coverage can exist even if an employer's business does not qualify for enterprise coverage. An individual employee can be covered if the employee is engaged in commerce or in the production of goods for commerce, or is employed in a closely related process or occupation directly essential to the production of goods. The FLSA contains a number of exemptions based upon the type of industry or the type of employee. Once FLSA coverage is found to exist, the minimum wage, overtime, equal pay and child labor provisions are applicable, unless a specific exemption governs.

In those situations in which government contract laws impose compensation standards, the particular transaction and the appropriate federal act must be considered. For example, the Walsh–Healey Act imposes employee compensation standards through the terms and conditions of federal government supply contracts.

D.   ENFORCEMENT AND REMEDIES

The administration and enforcement of federal compensation standards primarily rests with the

U.S. Department of Labor, Employment Standards Administration. The Wage and Hour Division performs inspections and investigations, makes compliance determinations, and issues rules and regulations. The Equal Employment Opportunity Commission is now charged with the enforcement of the equal pay provisions.

The Secretary of Labor is authorized to file suit on behalf of employees to collect wages and overtime, plus liquidated damages in an equal amount. The Secretary is also empowered to file suits enjoining or restraining employer violations; the Secretary can also seek civil contempt citations against employers for continued violations of decrees. It should be noted that a "clearly erroneous" standard of review is to be used by courts of appeal in reviewing the application of an exemption to the FLSA. Icicle Seafoods, Inc. v. Worthington (1986). The U.S. Department of Justice can prosecute wilful violators in criminal proceedings. Employees are authorized to file suit for reinstatement, back wages, liquidated damages in an equal amount, reasonable attorney's fees, and costs. A three year statute of limitations exists for wilful violations, while a two year statute exists for other violations. McLaughlin v. Richland Shoe Co. (1988) (definition of "willful" in connection with 3 year statute of limitations). It should be noted that employees generally do not have the right to release employers for less than the full amounts owing or to waive their rights to compensation. See D.A. Schulte, Inc. v.

Gangi (1946); Brooklyn Savings Bank v. O'Neil (1945).

CHAPTER 14

OCCUPATIONAL SAFETY
AND HEALTH ACT

A. BACKGROUND AND SCOPE

In 1970, Congress enacted the Occupational Safety and Health Act, 29 U.S.C.A. § 651 et seq., for the purpose of assuring as far as possible that safe and healthful working conditions exist for all workers in the United States. The basic act has withstood constitutional challenge; Atlas Roofing Co. v. OSHRC (1977); but some procedural difficulties have been encountered. See Marshall v. Barlow's, Inc. (1978). The act extends geographically to all areas under U.S. jurisdiction, including territories, possessions, and the outer continental shelves. The act provides coverage and applies to all employers engaged in a business that affects interstate commerce, and the act's jurisdictional scope has been broadly construed. See Usery v. Lacy (1980). State and local governments are excluded from coverage. Federal employees are not covered, but special safety and health programs are required by Executive Order 12196. See 29 C.F.R. Part 1960.

Essentially, the act imposes a twofold obligation upon all employers: (1) there is a "general duty" clause requiring employers to furnish a workplace free from recognized hazards that are likely to cause serious injury or death to workers, and (2) there are safety and health standards that employers must meet. Employers are required by the act to keep records of accidents, illnesses, deaths, and particular hazards. The posting of OSHA information and citations for violations are also required under the act. Finally, employers are required to make reports to OSHA.

Of importance to both employers and employees is OSHA's Hazard Communication Program. 29 C.F.R. § 1926.59. The purpose of this program is to give employers and employees vital information about chemical hazards through product container labeling and dissemination of "material safety data sheets." Some states have enacted "right to know" legislation that may be preempted by OSHA unless the particular state is operating under an approved plan.

Several federal agencies administer and enforce the act. Safety and health standards are usually recommended on the basis of research by the National Institute for Occupational Safety and Health, and they fall under the responsibility of the Secretary of Health and Human Services. The Occupational Safety and Health Administration (OSHA) of the U.S. Department of Labor promulgates and enforces standards. An independent agency, the Occupational Safety and Health Review Commission adjudicates contested cases through the use of administrative law judges. Judicial review of commission decisions rests with the federal circuit courts of appeal.

The act provides that the states may assume responsibility for workplace safety and health by adopting a plan of standards and enforcement that is at least as effective as the federal one. See generally, Gade v. National Solid Wastes Management Ass'n. (1992). All state plans must receive approval from the Occupational Safety and Health Administration. Upon approval, the states are entitled to enforce their own laws. A minority of states have adopted these plans.

It should be kept in mind that no private rights of action are created against employers for violation of standards under the act. See Russell v. Bartley (1974). Citations and standards, however, can have a significant impact on private damage actions. The safety and health standards can be evidence of an employer's standard of care in tort actions. See Donovan v. General Motors (1985) (standard of care issue); Schroeder v. C.F. Braun & Co. (1974). See also, Hines v. Brandon Steel Decks, Inc. (1989) (use of OSHA reports as evidence in civil trial).

B. STANDARDS AND VARIANCES

There are three types of safety and health standards, and two types of variances that come into play under the act. First of all, there are interim or "start-up" standards based upon existing federal and national consensus standards. The existing or already established federal standards originate from the Service Contract Act, the Longshore and Harbor Workers' Compensation Act, the Construction Safety Act, and the Walsh–Healey Act. The consensus standards originate from national standards organizations such as the American National Standards Institute, the National Fire Protection Association, and the American Society for Testing and Materials. Consensus standards also originate from federal procedures permitting consideration of opposing views or from designated standards of the Secretary of Labor after consultation with particular federal agencies.

A second type of standard is called a permanent standard. Permanent standards are designed to replace or supplement the interim ones, and they generally come into being after advisory committee recommendation, publication in the Federal Register, receipt of comment by interested parties, and public hearing. The Secretary of Labor then makes a permanent standard determination.

The third type of safety and health standard is called a temporary emergency standard, which the Secretary of Labor establishes when the Secretary determines that new safety and health findings demonstrate that employees are exposed to grave dangers.

All of the three foregoing types of safety and health standards are subject to judicial review by the U.S. Circuit Courts of Appeal upon petition by any person affected by the standard, within 60 days of a standard being set. The development and promulgation of safety and health standards can be the subject of serious judicial scrutiny. See Industrial Union Department, AFL–CIO v. American Petroleum Institute (1980).

An employer may obtain either a permanent or a temporary variance from the safety and health standards in certain circumstances. A permanent variance is obtained after application and a showing that an employer's working conditions, practices, methods, etc. are as safe and healthful as those provided by the standards. Applications are filed with the Assistant Secretary of Labor for Occupational Safety and Health. Temporary variances may be obtained from the Secretary of Labor if an employer can demonstrate either that necessary equipment or personnel are not immediately available or that the construction or alteration of required facilities or controls cannot be completed by a standard's effective date. Economic hardship is not a consideration in these determinations, and temporary variances are only good for a limited time period.

C. ENFORCEMENT AND PROCEDURES

The enforcement of the act usually involves OSHA inspections, and citations of employers for: (1) breach of the general duty obligation; (2) breach of specific safety and health standards; or (3) failure to keep records, make reports, or post notices required by the act.

Upon the presentation of appropriate credentials, OSHA inspectors are authorized to enter without delay and at reasonable times an employer's premises. These investigations are to occur at reasonable times, within reasonable limits, and be conducted in a reasonable manner. OSHA inspectors are entitled to private interviews with employers, owners, agents, employees or operators. If an OSHA inspector is denied entry, a search warrant may be obtained from a U.S. District Court by the Solicitor of Labor. The probable cause requirements are less stringent than those in criminal cases. See Marshall v. Barlow's, Inc., supra. Ex parte warrants are obtainable under OSHA regulations. It should be noted that it is unlawful to discriminate against employees or to discharge them for OSHA inspection requests, testimony in OSHA inspection requests, testimony in OSHA proceedings, or for the exercise of any rights under the act.

When a violation is discovered, a written citation, proposed penalty, and correction date are furnished to the employer. Citations may be contested, and in such cases, administrative law judges are assigned by the Occupational Safety and Health Review Commission, to conduct hearings. The commission may or may not grant review of an administrative law judge's decision; commission review is not a matter of right. If commission review is not undertaken, then the judge's decision becomes the final order of the commission 30 days after receipt. In any event once a decision is final, it may be appealed by any aggrieved party to the appropriate U.S. Circuit Court of Appeals within 60 days.

Civil and criminal penalties exist for various violations. Penalties are usually accessed in a monetary on a per day per violation basis, and criminal fines, along with imprisonment, are allowed. In cases involving civil penalties, it is important, as a matter of practice, to distinguish between serious and nonserious violations. Serious violations require that a penalty be proposed. In nonserious violation cases, penalties are rarely proposed. It should be noted that employers can be cited by OSHA and still be subject to prosecution without violating the ban on double jeopardy. See Herman v. S.A. Healy (1997); Hudson v. United States (1997).

The Secretary of Labor is further empowered by the act to obtain temporary restraining orders shutting down business operations that create imminent dangers of death or serious injury. This procedure is available when imminent dangers cannot be eliminated through regular OSHA enforcement procedures.

CHAPTER 15

FEDERAL BLACK LUNG BENEFITS LEGISLATION

A. BACKGROUND AND SCOPE

The Federal Coal Mine Health and Safety Act of 1969, 30 U.S.C.A. § 801 et seq., was enacted in an effort to provide standards for safety and health for coal mines in the United States. It also provided compensation benefits for coal miners and their dependents, or survivors, when a miner's disability or death was the result of pneumoconiosis, otherwise known as "black lung," a chronic dust disease of the lungs, which is more fully defined in the act. This act has been the subject of several important amendments: the Black Lung Benefits Act of 1972; the Black Lung Benefits Reform Act of 1977; the Black Lung Benefits Review Act of 1977; the Black Lung Benefits Revenue Act of 1981; the Black Lung Benefits Amendments of 1981 and the Consolidated Omnibus Budget Reconciliation Act of 1985. The constitutionality of federal black lung legislation was upheld in Turner Elkhorn Mining Co. v. Usery (1976). See Pauley v. Bethenergy Mines, Inc. (1991)(upholding rebuttal regulations).

The original federal black lung legislation attempted to place the responsibility for compensation and medical expenses on responsible mine operators whose identities could be determined, but the federal government assumed these obligations when no responsible mine operator could be determined. Various devices have been employed by the federal government to insure the payment of black lung benefits. Reforms in 1977, created a Black Lung Disability Trust Fund which is administered jointly by the Secretaries of Labor, Treasury, and Health and Human Services. This fund is financed primarily by excise taxes on mined coal. The Black Lung Disability Trust Fund has suffered from a chronic lack of funding, and this resulted in amendments in 1981 aimed at preserving the fund through increased excise taxes and through benefit limitations. From 1974 through 1996, over $10.7 billion in black lung payments were made to claimants.

Originally, claims were processed by the Social Security Administration; however, the Department of Labor has assumed this responsibility. This was logical, in light of the fact that the Department of Labor is the responsible agency for mining health and safety. Claims filed up to July 1, 1973, continued to be under the Social Security Administration's jurisdiction, but claims filed after July 1, 1973, are administered by the Department of Labor. The Black Lung Benefits Reform Act of 1977, broadened entitlement and provided review for some previously denied claims, either by the Social Security Administration or the Department of Labor. Current claims procedures are set forth in detail in 20 C.F.R. § 410.101 et seq. and in 20 C.F.R. § 718.1 et seq. See 20 C.F.R. Parts 722, 725, 726 & 727.

B. ELIGIBILITY AND BENEFITS

Monthly cash benefits are payable under the federal black lung program to past and present coal miners who are totally disabled as a result of pneumoconiosis; a miner's compensation increases if there are dependents. Additionally, in miner death cases, widows, children, surviving divorced wives, parents, brothers and sisters may receive benefits. If a widow was entitled to benefits at the time of her death, her children may receive benefits.

The basic benefit for a disabled coal miner is equal to 37½ percent of the monthly pay of a federal employee in the Grade of GS–2, step 1, who is totally disabled. A surviving widow is paid the same benefit. Any single surviving child would receive the same benefit that a surviving widow would have received. Single surviving children are entitled to a full widow's benefit, if a widow dies while receiving benefits. Miner's benefits and the benefits of dependents are increased based upon the number of dependents. Benefits are reduced by state workers' compensation, unemployment compensation, state disability insurance, or excess earnings under the Social Security Act.

In order to be eligible for benefits under the federal black lung program, a coverage formula must be met. See Mullins Coal Co. v. Director

(1987). The formula requires: (1) a "miner," who is (2) "totally disabled due to pneumoconiosis." In order to qualify as a "miner," a person must have worked as an employee in a coal mine whether underground or above ground, performing functions in extracting the coal or preparing the coal so extracted. The definition of "miner" has undergone several statutory changes since the original act, and in 1977, it was expanded to provide coverage for self-employed miners, and certain others in the coal mine construction and transportation industries. See Baker v. United States Steel Corp. (1989) (liberal construction given to the term "miner"). Once "miner" status is established, a claimant must prove total disability due to pneumoconiosis. In proving total disability due to pneumoconiosis, claimants traditionally enjoyed the assistance of certain rebuttable and irrebuttable presumptions. The 1981 amendments effectively eliminated some presumptions, however, two important ones remain: (1) a miner with pneumoconiosis who was exposed for 10 or more years is rebuttably presumed to have pneumoconiosis that arose out of employment; and (2) a miner with complicated pneumoconiosis receives an irrebuttable presumption of the necessary total disability, or in death cases, that death was due to the pneumoconiosis; or additionally in death cases that total disability from pneumoconiosis existed at the time of death. See generally, Pittston Coal Group v. Sebben (1988).

The 1981 amendments also addressed the issue of proof and provided that after the effective date of the 1981 amendments, the Secretary of Labor need not accept a radiologist's interpretation of chest x-rays, and could consider second interpretations. Furthermore, the Secretary need not accept as binding the affidavits of interested persons who are eligible for benefits in death cases.

C. PROCEDURES

Claims for black lung benefits may be filed at certain offices of the Department of Labor, Social Security district offices, or Foreign Service offices of the United States by mail or presentation. The Department of Labor's Office of Workers' Compensation supervises the claims procedures, and once a claim has been forwarded to them, a deputy commissioner conducts an initial investigation which is designed to determine a claimant's eligibility for benefits, and if a responsible operator exists.

Deputy commissioner decisions in contested cases are assigned to Administrative Law Judges for formal hearings in accordance with the Administrative Procedure Act. See Pyro Mining Co. v. Slaton (1989). Appeals from these hearings are lodged with the Benefits Review Board, which may enter a final decision or remand the case either to the Administrative Law Judge or to the deputy commissioner. Final decisions of the Benefits Review Board may be appealed to the U.S. Circuit Court of Appeals in the circuit where the miner was last employed.

D. MINING SAFETY AND HEALTH

The Federal Mine Safety Act of 1997, 30 U.S.C.A. § 801 et seq., protects persons working on mine properties. The Mine Safety and Health Administration (MSHA) administers the Act. Responsibility is placed upon employers for miners' safety and health. Regular inspections are required for both underground and surface mines. Miners' training requirements have been established, and dangerous mines can be closed. The Act prescribes penalties for health and safety violations, and specific health and safety regulations cover mining hazards.

CHAPTER 16

SOCIAL SECURITY

A. INTRODUCTION

The federal Social Security system began in 1935 in an effort to provide limited retirement or death benefits for workers in commerce and industry. Since 1935, the system has greatly expanded, and benefits have increased dramatically.

Historically significant changes occurred as follows: in 1954, coverage became almost universal; in 1956, disability insurance benefits were added; in 1958, disability eligibility was liberalized, and benefits were added for dependents of disability insurance recipients; in 1961, early but reduced retirement was permitted for men at age 62; in 1965, medicare benefits were added; in 1972, automatic cost-of-living-adjustments (COLA) were added to the benefit system; in 1977, substantial increases in tax rates were enacted to cover projected long term deficits; and in 1981, short term deficits were financed by interfund borrowing.

Amendments in 1983 resulted in the taxation of certain social security benefits for the first time; called for the normal retirement age to be gradually changed from 65 to 67; established mandatory coverage for employees of nonprofit organizations;

resulted in some federal workers being covered by social security rather than by civil service; established deferred compensation plan taxation for social security purposes; prohibited states from' terminating coverage of state and local government employees; altered cost-of-living-adjustment computation methods; and eliminated several gender-based distinctions previously made by the social security laws. The Disability Reform Act of 1984 changed the standard of review for terminating disability benefits and, among other changes, provided for the evaluation of pain. Technical amendments were passed in 1986 and 1987. Catastrophic health care coverage and financing was enacted under the Medicare Catastrophic Coverage Act of 1988, however, Congress voted to repeal this Act in 1989. The Omnibus Budget Reconciliation Act of 1990, the Omnibus Budget Reconciliation Act of 1993, the Social Security Domestic Employment Reform Act of 1994, the Social Security Independence and Program Improvements Act of 1994, and the Contract with America Advancement Act of 1996, have added other changes in policies.

Today, the Social Security system contains the following benefit programs: (1) Retirement and survivors benefits (Old–Age and Survivors Insurance–OASI); (2) Disability benefits (Disability Insurance–DI); (3) Medicare benefits (Hospitalization Insurance–HI; a separate Medicare Medical Insurance (MMI) program requires enrollment and premium payments); and (4) Supplemental Security Income benefits (SSI). With the exception of state and local governments, and certain non-profit organizations, coverage is generally mandatory; election of coverage is permitted, however, for these groups.

For the most part, Social Security benefits are financed by taxes or "contributions" collected from employers, employees, and self-employed persons who work in employments covered by Social Security. The Federal Insurance Contributions Act (FICA) which falls within the Internal Revenue Code, governs taxation and collection. The maximum yearly social security tax paid by employees based on wages for OASDI is $4,240.80. As of 1994, all wages became subject to the hospital insurance (HI) tax without limitation on the amount of yearly wages. The combined OASDI and HI 1998 FICA withholding rate was 7.65% (6.20% OASDI and 1.45% HI)on wages. These collected taxes pay for retirement, survivors, disability, and hospital insurance benefits. In the case of certain persons, however, hospital insurance benefits are paid from the general revenues of the United States, and it should also be noted that supplementary medical insurance benefits are generally financed through the collection of monthly premiums. The general revenues of the United States pay for supplemental security income benefits.

Three basic trust funds hold Social Security contributions: (1) the Old–Age and Survivors Insurance Trust Fund; (2) the Disability Insurance Trust Fund; and (3) the Hospital Insurance Trust Fund (this fund also receives general revenues in order to pay benefits to uninsured persons 65 and older).

The Supplementary Medical Insurance Trust Fund receives premium collections and general revenues that have been appropriated for the fund. A Board of Trustees, consisting of the Secretaries of Health and Human Services, Treasury, and Labor, hold these funds, and amounts not currently needed are invested in federal securities that bear interest.

The Department of Health and Human Services, through its Social Security Administration, basically administers the retirement, survivors, disability, hospital and medical insurance, and supplemental security income programs. Other public assistance and welfare services programs are financed separately, and they are generally administered by the states in cooperation with the federal government; these include: aid to needy families with children; medical assistance, maternal and child-health services; crippled children services; child support and welfare services; food stamps; and energy assistance.

The Department of Health and Human Services maintains websites at: http://www.hhs.gov and http://www.ssa.gov.

B. RETIREMENT AND SURVIVORS INSURANCE (OASI)

1. ELIGIBILITY FOR OASI

Eligibility for retirement and survivors benefits depends upon the "insured status" of an employee. Generally, an employee's insured status is established by the number of "quarters of coverage" that have been earned in work covered by Social Security. A worker and family can become "fully insured" with as little as 31 quarters (eight years) of work. The requisite age and quarters of coverage can vary. 20 C.F.R. § 404.115 (chart of age and quarters). If a worker is "currently insured," benefits can be paid to survivors upon the worker's death; six quarters of coverage in the 13 quarters preceding death gives rise to this "currently insured status." OASI benefits are conditioned upon the attainment of retirement age or death. Full OASI benefits are payable at age 65; reduced benefits are available at 62. The 1983 amendments will gradually increase the retirement age to 67. Other OASI benefits have age eligibility variations. OASI benefits are in the form of monthly benefit payments.

2. OASI BENEFIT CALCULATIONS

The past earnings of covered workers generally determine the benefit levels which are to be paid to retired employees, disabled workers, dependents and survivors. Four basic concepts govern benefit calculations: (1) computation years; (2) index earnings; (3) average indexed monthly earnings (AIME); and (4) primary insurance amount (PIA). The "computation years" is essentially the number of years worked in employment covered by Social Security. The "index earnings" represents the earnings of each year which have been converted to reflect increases in wage levels over the years; this indexing creates an earnings record. The "average indexed monthly earnings" (AIME) is the result of having divided the total indexed earnings by the number of months in the "computation years." Finally, a "primary insurance amount" (PIA) or basic benefit level is obtained by applying a percentage formula to the AIME; the 1997 percentage formula is: 90% of the first $455.00 or less of AIME, plus 32% of any AIME over $455.00 to $2,741.00, plus 15% of any AIME over $2,741.00. All benefit levels are subject to periodic cost-of-living-adjustments (COLA).

3. OASI BENEFITS

The figure which provides the basis for almost all benefit amounts is the primary insurance amount (PIA). Lump sum death benefits are fixed; special benefits are sometimes paid without reference to the PIA. The OASI types of benefits payable and the percentage of the primary insurance amount (PIA) receivable in for retirees, disabled workers, dependents and survivors are generally as follows:

(1) *Full retirement*—100% of PIA (eligible at age 65); reduced benefits available at 62.

(2) *Widowed spouses*—100% of PIA (eligible at age 65); reduced benefits available at 60.

(3) *Spouses*—50% of the PIA (eligible at age 65 or younger if caring for a disabled child, or child under 16); reduced benefits available at 62.

(4) *Divorced spouses*—50% of PIA (eligible on the same basis as spouses, supra, but 10 years of marriage also required).

(5) *Children*—50% of PIA (eligible until age 18 if a child of a retired or deceased insured employee; eligible while attending full-time elementary or secondary school).

(6) *Surviving children*—75% of PIA (eligible on the same basis as children, supra).

(7) *Parents*—82½% of PIA if one parent entitled; 75% of PIA if more than one parent entitled.

(8) *Maximum family benefits*—175% of PIA.

(9) *Lump sum death benefit*—$255 payment to survivors (not a percent of PIA).

(10) *Transitionally insured benefits*—Not a percent of PIA (eligible if over 65 with insufficient quarters of coverage).

(11) *Special age 72*—Not a percent of PIA (eligible if over 72 with insufficient quarters of coverage to permit retiree benefits; must not receive public assistance).

(12) *Special minimum*—Not a percent of PIA (eligible are workers with low average earnings).

(13) *Currently insured*—OASDI benefits (eligible if survivor of worker not fully insured so long as deceased employee worked at least 6 of the 13 quarters in covered employment preceding death).

It should be noted that there can be reduction in all benefits based upon a beneficiary's annual earnings. See 20 C.F.R. Subpart E. This reduction can vary, but generally all benefits are charged on the basis of $1.00 of excess earnings for each $1.00 of monthly benefits. In 1996, Congress enacted changes that will gradually increase the annual exempt amount for beneficiaries ages 65 to 69. Self employment at age 70 and thereafter is exempt.

C. DISABILITY INSURANCE (DI)

1. ELIGIBILITY

In general, the test for disability benefit eligibility employs the same "insured status" concept used by OASI, supra. Disability eligibility requires that an employee be both: (1) "fully insured" under OASI; and (2) "disability insured." The disability insured requirement is met if a worker has 20 quarters of coverage in the 40 quarters immediately preceding disability. A waiting period of 5 months exists before these benefits can be paid. At age 65, disability benefits cease, and regular full retirement benefits are paid. In making eligibility determinations, "disability" is generally defined as the inability to engage in gainful activity by reason of any medically determinable physical or mental impairment that can be expected to last at least 12 continuous months or to result in death. Social Security disability benefits are generally offset by any other disability benefits.

2. DI BENEFITS

Generally, there are five fundamental types of disability insurance benefits:

(1) *Disabled worker*—100% of PIA (eligible 5 months after disability if fully insured under OASI and disability insured).

(2) *Disabled surviving spouse*—100% of PIA (eligible at age 60; benefits available at age 50, if disabled).

(3) *Disabled surviving divorced spouse*—50% of PIA (eligible at age 60; benefits available at age 50 if disabled).

(4) *Disabled child*—50% of PIA (eligible at age 18).

(5) *Disabled surviving child*—75% of PIA (eligible at age 18).

It must be pointed out that the Disability Insurance Trust Fund only pays benefits to disabled workers and their dependents. The benefits payable to "disabled surviving spouses" and "disabled surviving children" are paid from the Old–Age and Survivors Insurance Trust Fund. The 1980 amendments provided for the review and assessment of eligibility every three years with the exception of cases of permanent disability. This policy generated a great deal of controversy and litigation, and resulted in the Disability Reform Act of 1984.

3. DI EVALUATION

There is a stepped sequential approach to disability determinations. 20 C.F.R. § 404.1520 (20 C.F.R. § 416.920 for supplemental security income disability determinations). The claimant must initially demonstrate physical and/or mental impairments that are severe and meet the duration requirements. There is a five-step evaluation that asks and answers certain key questions. Favorable disability determinations for claimants can be made at steps three and five. (1) Is the claimant working in a substantial gainful activity; if so, then no disability will be found regardless of medical condition or age, education and work experience. (2) Does the claimant have a severe impairment; if there is no impairment or combination of impairments that significantly limit physical or mental ability, then no disability will be found. If a severe impairment(s) does exist, then the following question is necessary. (3) Does the claimant's impairment or impairments meet or equal the "listings," contained in 20 C.F.R. Part 404, Subpart P, Appendix 1, containing specific medical criteria; if so, then a finding of disability will be made without considering age, education and work experience. (4) If a claimant does not meet the "listings," then inquiry is made whether the claimant's impairment(s) prevents the claimant from performing past relevant work. A review of residual functional capacity and the physical and mental demands of past work are evaluated at this point. If the claimant is found able to perform past relevant work, then a finding of no disability will be made. (5) If the claimant cannot perform past relevant work because of severe impairment(s), then the burden shifts to the agency to prove the claimant capable of performing other gainful employment. The question of residual functional capacity to perform other work is therefore evaluated, considering the age, education and past work experience of the claimant. At this point, vocational-expert testimony or Medical–Vocational Guidelines contained in 20 C.F.R. Part 404, Subpart P, Appendix 2 (commonly known as the "Grids") may be used to aid in the ultimate determination of disability. See Bowen v. Yuckert (1987) ("severity regulation" upheld); Heckler v. Campbell (1983) (medical-vocational guidelines are valid).

It should be noted that a constitutional tort challenge to the continuing disability review program was made in Schweiker v. Chilicky (1988), but the Court rejected the cause of action by a narrow margin.

It should also be noted that claims under the Americans with Disabilities Act (ADA) are not automatically barred by the receipt of social security disability benefits. See Tranker v. Figgie International (1998).

D. MEDICARE–HOSPITAL INSURANCE (HI) AND SUPPLEMENTARY MEDICAL INSURANCE (SMI)

Certain disabled and aged persons are entitled to the benefits of a national health insurance program called Medicare. Most persons over 65 are eligible automatically; if not eligible, coverage can be purchased for an annual premium. There are two basic medicare programs: (1) Part A, Hospital Insurance (HI), which is fundamentally financed through special payroll taxes similar to FICA taxes, and which are held in the Hospital Insurance Trust Fund; and (2) Part B, Medicare Medical Insurance (MMI), which is fundamentally financed through individual medical premiums and general revenues of the United States, and which are held in the Supplementary Medical Insurance Trust Fund. Both Part A and Part B benefit programs contain cost-sharing measures, usually in the form of coinsurance and deductibles. The Health Care Financing Administration (HCFA) administers both programs. Part A (HI) payments are generally tied to "benefit periods." If a patient has not been hospitalized for 60 consecutive days, a benefit period is available; there are no limits on the number of benefit periods that patients can have during their lifetime, except for inpatient psychiatric hospital services. Each benefit period under Part A pays for: (1) inpatient hospital care (subject to 90 days of coverage and other limitations); (2) extended care services up to 100 days during each benefit period; (3) home health services; and (4) in lieu of certain other benefits, hospice care, subject to limitation periods. Part B (MMI) was designed as a voluntary program that essentially pays 80% of reasonable charges for doctors, osteopaths, chiropractors, psychiatrists, independent therapists, and most medical, outpatient, and laboratory services that Part A does not cover. The elderly and disabled pay only portions of program premiums and the difference is paid by the federal government from general revenues.

E. SUPPLEMENTAL SECURITY INCOME (SSI)

The Supplemental Security Income (SSI) program provides financial assistance to U.S. citizens and lawfully admitted aliens who meet income and resource criteria. They must be aged, blind, or disabled. The SSI program provides a "floor of income" for these persons, and it is financed by general tax revenues. SSI benefits are paid monthly to persons who are: (1) age 65 or older; or (2) blind; or (3) disabled. Generally, these persons must be U.S. citizens or lawful residents of the 50 states, the District of Columbia or the Northern Mariana Islands. "Federal Benefit Rates" (FBR) help determine the eligibility of individuals and couples. These rates are increased periodically and the FBR is employed on a per month basis in order to compare the income and resource criteria in an effort to determine eligibility. The periodic redetermination of eligibility is required for all recipients. The receipt of Social Security insurance benefits does not necessarily disqualify persons from receiving SSI benefits, but Social Security insurance benefits are included in the income determinations that must be made before SSI benefits can be paid.

F. PROCEDURE

The claims procedure for most Social Security benefits under retirement, survivors, disability, medicare insurance programs and under the supplemental security income program, is initiated on special forms provided by the Social Security Administration. These claim forms are usually filed with a local Social Security office which makes an initial determination of eligibility. If there is a dispute, the claimant or the claimant's representative must request a reconsideration of the initial decision. A claimant who is dissatisfied with a reconsideration decision is entitled to a hearing before an administrative law judge. The administrative law judge's decision becomes final unless Appeals Council review is requested within 60 days of receipt by the claimant, or unless the Appeals Council decides to review the decision on its own motion. An expedited appeals process may be requested in certain instances. Denials of review or decisions of the Appeals Council can be appealed within 60 days to the U.S. District Courts. Attorney's fees are permitted for the representation of claimants. Furthermore in some cases the claimant may be entitled to an additional award of attorney's fees under the Equal Access to Justice Act ("EAJA"), 28 U.S.C.A. § 2412(b).

CHAPTER 17

FEDERAL AND STATE ANTI-DISCRIMINATION LAWS IN GENERAL

A. FEDERAL LAWS

Federal and state laws provide workers with significant safeguards against discrimination in the workplace. The First, Fifth, Thirteenth, and Fourteenth Amendments to the U.S. Constitution, together with the Commerce Clause, form the foundation for most federal anti-discrimination measures affecting employment. Three of the Reconstruction Civil Rights Acts passed in the aftermath of the Civil War—42 U.S.C.A. §§ 1981, 1983, and 1985(3)—are still useful, to differing degrees, in challenging particular kinds of discrimination by state, local, or private employers.

Title VII of the Civil Rights Act of 1964 is the most broadly based and influential federal statute prohibiting discrimination in employment. Its prohibitions on discrimination based on race, color, sex, religion or national origin extend to all "terms, conditions or privileges" of employment. Section 703(a)(1), 42 U.S.C.A. § 2000e–2(a)(1). The federal courts have construed this language quite broadly to embrace any benefit actually conferred or burden

187

actually imposed in the workplace, whether or not provided for by contract. See, e.g., Hishon v. King & Spalding (1984) (right to be considered for law firm partnership). The concept embraces such intangible aspects of employment as workplace assignments, environment, and even mentoring opportunities as well as more tangible problems like refusals to hire or promote, unequal pay or discriminatory discharge. Decisions interpreting Title VII have frequently served as interpretive models for the Age Discrimination in Employment Act of 1967 ("ADEA") and other statutes, including the Reconstruction Civil Rights Acts. See Western Air Lines, Inc. v. Criswell (1985) (ADEA).

Title VII was amended by the Civil Rights Act of 1991. The principal stated purposes of the Act were to "provide appropriate remedies for intentional discrimination and unlawful harassment in the workplace"; to "confirm statutory authority and provide statutory guidelines for the adjudication of disparate impact suits under Title VII...."; and to "respond to recent decisions of the Supreme Court by expanding the scope of relevant civil rights statutes....". Civil Rights Act of 1991, Pub.L. 102–166, §§ 3(1), (3), and (4), 105 Stat. 1071.

In addition to Title VII and the Reconstruction Civil Rights Acts, the federal laws, rules, regulations, and remedies affecting employment discrimination include: the Equal Pay Act of 1963 ("EPA"); ADEA; the Civil Rights Act of 1964; Title IX, Education Amendments of 1972, banning sex discrimination in federally funded education programs; the

Civil Rights Attorney's Fees Awards Act of 1976; the Rehabilitation Act of 1973 ("RHA") and Americans with Disabilities Act of 1990 ("ADA"), prohibiting disability discrimination; the Immigration Reform and Control Act of 1986, or "IRCA"; the Civil Rights Act of 1968, Title I; the Intergovernmental Personnel Act of 1970; the Vietnam Era Veterans Readjustment Act of 1974; the Age Discrimination Act of 1975; the Foreign Boycott Laws (Export Administration Act of 1969, as amended); the Labor Management Relations Act; Executive Order 11246 (Government Contractors and Subcontractors); and Executive Order 11141 (Age Discrimination). Summaries of the more important federal anti-discrimination laws are provided in Chapters 18, 19 and 20. For a fuller treatment of these protections, see Lewis, Civil Rights and Employment Discrimination Law (West 1997)(hornbook) and Lewis, Litigating Civil Rights and Employment Discrimination Laws (West 1996 with 1997–98 Supplement)(practitioners' handbook with forms).

Title VII's broad sweep distinguishes it from statutes, like the EPA, that prohibit employment discrimination solely with respect to one term or condition of employment, like compensation. Further, the Title VII prohibitions on race, color, sex, religious and national origin discrimination set it apart from single-focus employment-related statutes that ban only sex discrimination (EPA and Title IX); age discrimination (ADEA); race, ancestry and possibly national origin discrimination (42 U.S.C.A. § 1981); or disability discrimination (the RHA or ADA).

B. STATE LAWS

Most of the states have enacted anti-discrimination statutes that supplement the remedies available under federal law by extending protection to persons not federally protected or, in some cases, adding grounds of prohibited discrimination or supplementary remedies. For the most part, state laws prohibiting employment discrimination are called "Fair Employment Practices" laws. But Michigan has a Civil Rights Act; California has a Fair Employment and Housing Act; New Mexico has a Human Rights Act; and New York's employment discrimination prohibitions are part of its Executive Law. The federal laws, standards, and programs do not generally preempt these state efforts unless a state law purports to permit conduct that would be federally prohibited or would in practice undermine the enforcement of a federal law.

The state legislation usually forbids discrimination based upon race, religion, color, ancestry, national origin, sex, age, or marital status. Still, there is considerable variation in prohibited grounds. Alabama, for example, has no fair employment laws regulating private employment, while California has enacted laws specifically covering race, age, sex, national origin, religious, arrest record, and blindness discrimination. California also regulates equal pay, pregnancy benefits, and employee records, as well as the employment uses of lie detector tests and voice stress analyzers. A growing minority of states prohibit discrimination on the basis of sexual

orientation, a ground Congress has declined to protect but recurrently reconsiders.

CHAPTER 18

TITLE VII OF THE 1964 CIVIL RIGHTS ACT, AS AMENDED THROUGH 1991

A. SCOPE AND COVERAGE

1. PROTECTION FOR INDIVIDUALS

Title VII's principal provisions defining unlawful employment practices, contained in § 703, extend protection to any "individual," whether or not an employee. There is also a separate definition of employee: "any individual employed by an employer." Relying on § 703's protection of "any individual," courts have had no difficulty according standing to former employees as well as applicants. Further, they have sometimes even recognized claims on behalf of persons who fall outside any common-law understanding of the employee-employer relationship, provided the circumstances satisfy an "economic realities" test that protects those in a position to suffer the kind of discrimination Title VII was designed to prevent. Occasionally, however, a court will rely on the "employee" definition to deny protection to persons who do not satisfy the common law's test for employee status, the "totality of the working relationship." See, e.g., Daniels v. Browner (9th Cir.1995).

By contrast, the § 704 protection against retaliation for opposing unlawful employment practices or participating in proceedings to protest them extends to "employees or applicants for employment." The Supreme Court has resolved a circuit conflict by construing this language to provide protection to former employees who complain of otherwise actionable retaliation—bad references, for example—that occurred after the employment relation was severed. Robinson v. Shell Oil Company (1997).

2. EMPLOYERS GOVERNED BY TITLE VII/ADEA

Title VII applies to employers, employment agencies, apprenticeship programs and labor organizations whose activities affect interstate commerce. There are very few categorical exclusions from the definition of "employer" in either Title VII or ADEA. They include private membership clubs exempt from taxation under the Internal Revenue Code and Indian tribes. See generally Section 701(b), 42 U.S.C.A. § 2000e–5(g) (Title VII) and 29 U.S.C.A. § 626(b), incorporating 29 U.S.C.A. § 216(b) (ADEA).

By far the most significant exclusion is numerical: an employer is covered by Title VII only if it has 15 or more employees, and by ADEA only if it has 20 or more employees, for each working day in 20 or more calendar weeks in the current or prior calendar year. Persons holding an employment relationship with the employer during a calendar week (usually manifested by presence on the payroll) are counted regardless of how many of them actually worked or received compensation on any particular working day in that week. Walters v. Metropolitan Educational Enterprises, Inc. (1997).

Courts have wrestled with: whether to pierce the corporate veil so as to subject a parent corporation to potential liability for the conduct of a subsidiary, Cook v. Arrowsmith Shelburne, Inc. (2d Cir.1995); whether to consider all of an employer's employees when the alleged unlawful employment practice is confined to a discrete operating location, Owens v. Rush (10th Cir.1980); whether to impose liability on a successor employer after a sale of the business or bankruptcy, see, e.g., Rojas v. TK Communications, Inc. (5th Cir.1996); EEOC v. G–K–G, Inc. (7th Cir. 1994); whether a government-appointed receiver is a Title VII "employer" of employees of a failed financial institution, see Nowlin v. Resolution Trust Corp. (5th Cir.1994); whether a contractor is liable for a subcontractor's unlawful employment practice, Fitzgerald v. Mountain States Tel. & Tel. Co. (10th Cir.1995); and whether an employment agency or union meets the statutory "employer" definition even when it has fewer than 15 employees, see Kern v. City of Rochester (2d Cir.1996).

Unions may be liable as labor organizations representing employees in collective bargaining without regard to the number of employees represented, but are liable in their capacity as "employer" only if they satisfy the "employer" definition, including the requirement of at least 15 employees. Yerdon v.

Henry (2d Cir.1996). These and other coverage questions, like the status of nonprofit organizations as employers and the liability of companies for the employment practices of subcontractors, are discussed in detail in several standard works. See generally, Player, Employment Discrimination Law (West 1990).

States, their political subdivisions, and agencies of each are also employers under Title VII and ADEA. Title VII § 701(b) and (a), 42 U.S.C.A. § 2000e(b), (a); ADEA § 11(b)(2), 29 U.S.C.A. § 630(b)(2). The constitutionality of applying Title VII to state defendants, and their amenability to suit in federal court is settled. Title VII's grounding in § 5 of the Fourteenth Amendment empowered Congress to override the Eleventh Amendment barrier to state liability in federal court. Fitzpatrick v. Bitzer (1976). The federal government and its agencies are not defined "employers," Title VII § 701(b), 42 U.S.C.A. § 2000e(b), and ADEA § 11(b)(2), 29 U.S.C.A. § 630(b)(2). But special provisions in each statute mandate that personnel actions affecting most federal employees be made free from discrimination based on any of the grounds those statutes address. Title VII § 717, 42 U.S.C.A. § 2000e–16 and ADEA § 15, 29 U.S.C.A. § 633a. The statute applies only to civilian members of military departments. Randall v. United States (4th Cir.1996).

Both Title VII and ADEA define a covered "employer" to include any "agent" of an employer. 42 U.S.C.A. § 2000e(b) (Title VII); 29 U.S.C.A.

§ 630(b) (ADEA). At a minimum, this definition makes the employer as an entity automatically liable for most unlawful employment practices committed by its employees, through respondeat superior—the major exception being conduct by either supervisory or subordinate employees that creates a hostile work environment. But the circuits that have confronted the issue have usually concluded that a supervisor cannot be subjected to individual liability even though he is an "agent" for the purpose of imputing liability to the employing entity. See Haynes v. Williams (10th Cir.1996). The same court may read the term "agent" broadly for purposes of imposing liability on the employer, E.E.O.C. v. Watergate at Landmark Condominium (4th Cir.1994), yet exclude from its reach the personal liability of an employer officer. Birkbeck v. Marvel Lighting Corp. (4th Cir.1994).

3. AMERICAN CORPORATIONS' EMPLOYEES WORKING ABROAD; "FOREIGN" EMPLOYERS' PERSONNEL IN U.S. AND OVERSEAS; AND NATIONAL ORIGIN, ALIENAGE AND ANCESTRY DISCRIMINATION UNDER TITLE VII, IRCA, AND 42 U.S.C.A. § 1981

Neither Title VII nor ADEA prohibits discrimination on *any* ground against an *alien* (someone who has not yet attained full American citizenship) who works *outside* the United States for either an American or non-U.S. company. Title VII Section 702, 42 U.S.C.A. § 2000e–1, and ADEA § 11(f), 29 U.S.C.A.

§ 630(f). Statutory protection is now available to most U.S. citizens working abroad for American or American-controlled companies, and to most American-based employees, whether citizens or not, working for foreign enterprises.

The ADEA which was amended in 1984 to apply to the overseas work of American corporations and American-controlled foreign corporations, ADEA § 4(h), 29 U.S.C.A. § 623(h). Title VII until recently had no language specifically extending its application to work performed for the thousands of U.S. firms operating tens of thousands of foreign subsidiaries abroad. The Civil Rights Act of 1991 added that protection by defining most covered employees to include U.S. citizens "with respect to employment in a foreign country." Section 701(f), 42 U.S.C.A. § 2000e(f). The 1991 amendments to Title VII may not extend to the overseas work of federal employees (covered for their domestic work under § 717), given the presumption against extraterritorial application of federal statutes announced in EEOC v. Arabian American Oil Co. (1991).

The protection for U.S. citizens working abroad is now coextensive with that earlier provided by the ADEA. Title VII jurisdiction reaches not only U.S. corporations but also those foreign corporations "controlled" by American employers. This follows indirectly from § 702(c)(2), 42 U.S.C.A. § 2000e–1(c)(2), which provides that the "title shall not apply with respect to the foreign operations of an employer that is a foreign person not controlled by an American employer." Section 702(c)(3) identifies four factors critical to the determination of "control" of the foreign enterprise by the American company: interrelationship of operations, common management, centralized control of labor relations, and common ownership or financial control.

The statute appears to provide dual defendants by presuming that unlawful employment practices of the controlled foreign affiliate are engaged in by the controlling (American) employer as well. Section 702(c)(1), 42 U.S.C.A. § 2000e–1(c)(1). But it exempts from coverage practices that would cause any employer to violate the national law of the foreign workplace. Section 702(b), 42 U.S.C.A. § 2000e–1(b). The foreign "law" that would be violated if ADEA were respected may include a collective bargaining agreement with a foreign labor union. Mahoney v. RFE/RL, Inc. (D.C.Cir.1995). This exemption, however, is not triggered simply because the type of discrimination in question is permitted by foreign law; rather, foreign law must affirmatively prohibit the particular employer conduct that compliance with Title VII would mandate absent the exemption.

Although U.S. citizens working abroad meet the amended § 701 definition of "employee," and firms chartered in other nations are not excluded from the definition of "employer," truly foreign corporations—those not "controlled" by a U.S. business—are not subject to Title VII with respect to work outside the United States. Congress in 1991 specifically provided that the basic prohibitions of the Title do not apply "with respect to the foreign

operations of an employer that is a foreign person."
Sections 702(c)(2), 42 U.S.C.A. § 2000e–1(c)(2).

The more than half a million employees of non-U.S. corporations who work *within* the U.S. are generally protected by the federal employment discrimination laws. The foreign parent's employees may usually be aggregated with the number of U.S.-based employees to meet the requisite minimum employee threshold. The foreign employer may be shielded by one of the treaties, discussed below, that authorize discrimination in the selection of executives on the basis of *citizenship*. Or that employer may be able to prove that it is essential to the operation of its business that the incumbent of a particular position have the kind of acquaintance with the customs, mores, or conditions of another nation that only someone born or living there would possess; then the employer could insist on filling that position with a resident of the foreign nation under the narrow but still extant "bona fide occupational qualification" defense of Section 703(e) of Title VII.

While Title VII is generally available to the American-based employees of a foreign employer, it may not afford protection against two common forms of discrimination those employees may encounter. Although Title VII prohibits national origin discrimination, it does not reach discrimination based on alienage (i.e. noncitizenship), which is prohibited by the Immigration Reform and Control Act of 1986 ("IRCA") or on ancestry (i.e., ethnic or physiognomic characteristic transcending national borders, e.g., against Arabs or Jews), which is prohibited by § 1981. Title VII therefore will not avail a plaintiff whose employer, whether U.S or foreign, excludes applicants solely because they lack U.S. citizenship or belong to a distinct ancestral subgroup. IRCA also provides limited protection against national origin discrimination not afforded by Title VII: the covered Title VII "employer" must have 15 or more employees in 20 or more calendar weeks in the current or preceding year, while IRCA § 102's prohibition of national origin discrimination against any individual, 8 U.S.C.A. § 1324b(a)(1)(A) (1986), applies to employers with as few as four employees. 8 U.S.C.A. § 1324b(a)(2)(A).

Since 1988, limited protection against discrimination in hiring because of alienage, i.e. citizenship status, is separately provided to lawfully admitted aliens, and a few others, by IRCA. Section 102, 8 U.S.C.A. § 1324a (1988 & Supp. IV 1992). But unlike the IRCA protection against national origin, which, like Title VII's, extends to "any individual," the IRCA protection against alienage discrimination helps only a narrowly defined "protected individual" who is well on the way to achieving full U.S. citizenship or has been granted refugee or asylum status. Sections 102(a)(1)(B) and 103, 8 U.S.C.A. § 1324b(a)(3) (1986). IRCA also imposes fines and imprisonment on employers who knowingly hire or employ undocumented persons or fail to check their authorization to work—in other words, it requires employers to discriminate against those aliens. Section 101, 8 U.S.C.A. § 1324a. It does not provide

penalties against the undocumented workers themselves for accepting U.S. employment. Only the
fraudulent presentation of employment verification
documents is criminalized. 8 U.S.C.A. § 1324c
(Supp. IV 1992).

The fact that an alien is not lawfully admitted
within the meaning of IRCA does not deprive him of
capacity to sue and receive remedies under Title
VII, although only for the kinds of discrimination
prohibited by the latter statute. See Egbuna v.
Time–Life Libraries, Inc. (4th Cir.1996). This follows not only from the fact that Title VII defines
"employees" broadly as "individuals" employed by
an employer but also from a negative implication of
its alien exemption clause. That clause precludes
application of the statute to the employment of
aliens outside the United States. The Supreme
Court relied on that implication in finding aliens
protected by Title VII against discrimination based
on national origin. Espinoza v. Farah Manufacturing Co. (1973). But as a practical matter aliens will
often be ineligible for important Title VII remedies.
If reinstatement would require the employer to
violate IRCA, the mixed-motive or after-acquired
evidence doctrines, discussed below, would probably
preclude a reinstatement order. A worker's undocumented status may also adversely affect her eligibility for or the amount of back or front pay, since she
may be "unavailable" for work after termination—
either literally (e.g., out of the country) or legally,
because of IRCA.

Discrimination against aliens in general is not, absent adverse impact, treated as discrimination on the basis of any particular national origin, and is therefore not condemned by Title VII. Discrimination against U.S. citizens, in favor of citizens of a particular nation, does amount to prohibited *national origin* discrimination. MacNamara v. Korean Air Lines (3d Cir.1988).

Title VII protection from this "anti-American" discrimination based on national origin is limited, however, by treaty exemptions designed to give foreign companies operating in the United States a free hand in selecting their own citizens for executive positions. The U.S.–Japanese Treaty of Friendship, Commerce and Navigation, for example, authorizes "companies of either party," such as a Japanese-chartered employer, "to engage, within the territories of the other Party ... executive personnel ... of their choice." A U.S.-chartered American subsidiary of a foreign corporation will ordinarily not be deemed a company of the signatory entitled to this exemption. Sumitomo Shoji America, Inc. v. Avagliano (1982). But where a foreign parent dictates the American subsidiary's discriminatory discharges of executives, the subsidiary may assert the parent's treaty rights. Papaila v. Uniden America Corp. (5th Cir.1995). These treaties have in other respects been construed narrowly, though, so as to permit only discrimination based on citizenship and not, for example, based on race, sex or age. *MacNamara.* Nevertheless, they have been read to permit citizenship discrimination even when it has a statistical adverse impact on the basis of national origin. This happens, for example, where the executives preferred by the treaty hail from a homogeneous ethnic population, so that all or virtually all those preferred by virtue of their citizenship also share the same national origin. Thus while companies of signatory countries are, despite these treaties, subject to liability, respecting their executive hiring and firing, for *intentional* discrimination based on national origin (but not citizenship), they cannot be liable for a citizenship-preference practice that merely has a disproportionate adverse impact on a particular national origin. *MacNamara.* Courts have reached this result in order to avoid indirect nullification of the guest company's treaty right to discriminate in favor of its own country's citizens.

4. PURELY OR PARTLY RELIGIOUS EMPLOYERS: COVERAGE, EX-EMPTIONS, DEFENSES

Religious organizations are also viewed as Title VII "employers," and as such may be subject to a specially defined duty not to discriminate on that ground. But they are specifically permitted to make certain employment decisions on the basis of religion. A welter of related and somewhat overlapping statutory and constitutional provisions afford different kinds of covered employers exemptions from or exceptions to liability for religious discrimination. In addition, the special prohibition on religious discrimination—subsuming the ordinary imperative not to discriminate and a duty to make "reasonable accommodation" to an employee's religious beliefs and practices—is subject to the general affirmative defense that permits an employer to discriminate under circumstances where the exclusion is a "bona fide occupational qualification." The two prohibitions on religious discrimination are discussed below. The exemptions, exceptions and BFOQ defense for religious and other employers will be treated here.

a. Overview: Discrimination Because of Religion

The § 702 exemption, strictly limited to pervasively religious institutions like churches, missions and seminaries (EEOC v. Kamehameha Schools/Bishop Estate (9th Cir.1993)), declares Title VII inapplicable with respect to the employment "of individuals of a particular religion" in any of its activities, for any position. Corporation of Presiding Bishop v. Amos (1987).

Section 703(e)(2) excludes from the definition of "unlawful employment practice" the hiring of employees of a particular religion by educational institutions insufficiently religious to qualify for the § 702 exemption but that are (a) substantially owned, supported, controlled or managed by a particular religion or (b) direct their curriculum "toward the propagation of" a particular religion.

If the ground alleged is sex, race, national origin, or age—where, that is, the foregoing statutory exemptions will not avail the employer—it may invoke a Free Exercise or Establishment Clause (excessive government entanglement) override of Title VII or ADEA regulation. These may succeed where the position (e.g., minister) or duties (e.g., teacher of theology) in question lies close to the religious core of the institution, or perhaps where the reason for discharge relates to malperformance of subsidiary religious duties.

b. *Prima Facie Prohibitions*

If no statutory or constitutional exemption applies, one turns to the prima facie case. Section 703(a)(1), amplified by the 701(j) definition of "religion", raises two questions:

(1) Has the employer drawn a distinction because of "religion"? And has it disparately treated the plaintiff "because of" religion, or rather imposed a neutral practice, not specifically targeted to religion, that has adverse impact on plaintiff's particular religion? If the latter, the practice may be defended as justified by job relatedness and business necessity.

(2) Even if an employer has made no hostile discrimination, has it breached the separate 701(j) duty to accommodate:

(a) "Reasonable accommodation" need not fully meet the needs of an employee's religious belief or practice, or be costless to the employee, and the employer need not accept the particular accommodation proposed by employee; and

(b) A reasonable accommodation works "undue hardship" and is thus not legally mandated if it requires an employer to incur more than de minimis cost.

So diluted, § 701(j) does not violate the Establishment Clause.

c. BFOQ Defense

In a refusal to hire case, if statutory exemptions and constitutional overrides fail, and plaintiff establishes a prima facie case of disparate treatment because of religion, an employer still has the BFOQ defense of § 703(e)(1). As restrictively construed by International Union, UAW v. Johnson Controls (1991), an employer must show that its religious exclusion relates to the "essence" of its business and that all or substantially all persons of the excluded faiths could not fulfill the requirements of the job in question. *Kamehameha.*

5. "PURELY" RELIGIOUS ORGANIZATIONS

In general, the more thoroughly "religious" the employer, the more widely it is insulated from liability with respect to terms and conditions of employment and even wholly sectarian activities.

First, any pervasively "religious" employer—the paradigm is a church, mission, seminary—is exempt by virtue of § 702(a) from liability for religious discrimination. This section exempts a "religious corporation, association, educational institution, or society" from Title VII "with respect to the employment of individuals of a particular religion to perform work connected with the carrying on" of any of the institution's "activities." But unless discrimination because of race, gender or national origin is a religious tenet of the defendant, the exemption will not excuse discrimination on those grounds. See Martin v. United Way of Erie County (3d Cir. 1987).

For the most part, only churches or institutions owned or partly owned by them have qualified for the § 702 exemption. See EEOC v. Kamehameha Schools/Bishop Estate (9th Cir.1993). The determination whether an organization, including an educational institution, is eligible for its sweeping protection hinges on whether "the corporation's purpose and character are primarily religious." That question, in turn, is answered on a case-by-case basis, with the court weighing "[a]ll significant religious and secular characteristics."

The § 702 exemption extends to any of the religious employer's activities, secular or sectarian, and applies regardless of the particular term and condition of employment involved. A 1972 amendment to § 702 deleted the word "religious" that had appeared before "activities" in the original 1964 legislation. The exemption has therefore since been understood to shield a covered institution from liability for religious discrimination even with respect to its secular activities, provided those are non-profitmaking. See generally EEOC v. Fremont Christian School (9th Cir.1986).

6. RELIGIOUSLY AFFILIATED EDUCATIONAL INSTITUTIONS

Because relatively few organizations are sufficiently religious to qualify for the broad exemption from Title VII afforded by § 702, Congress added a limited exception from liability designed to benefit religiously affiliated schools.

Under § 703(e)(2) of Title VII, an *educational* institution not qualifying as sufficiently religious to be exempt under § 702(a) but which is substantially supported or directed by a particular religion, or has a religiously oriented curriculum, may "hire and employ" persons of the particular religion with which it is affiliated. Section 702(a), it will be remembered, provides that Title VII "shall not apply" to the "purely" religious institutions it protects. By contrast, § 703(e)(2) more modestly states that it is not an "unlawful employment practice" for an "educational institution or institution of learning to hire and employ employees of a particular religion" if that employer is "in whole or in substantial part, owned, supported, controlled, or managed by a particular religion" (hereinafter, the "structure clause") or maintains a curriculum "directed toward the propagation of a particular religion" (the "curriculum clause").

It is only somewhat easier for a religiously affiliated educational institution to qualify for the more limited § 703(e)(2) hiring immunity than for a religious organization or school to qualify for the broader exemption under § 702. One court, for example, declined to decide whether the defendant university qualified for the § 703(e)(2) exemption even though it had a long history as a Jesuit institution, until 1970 had only Jesuit trustees, still required that more than one-third of the trustees and the President be Jesuit, and whose students were predominantly Catholic. Pime v. Loyola University (7th Cir.1986). And to qualify under the curriculum clause it is not enough that a school require religious education courses, schedule prayers and services, and employ Protestant teachers for principally secular subjects. *Kamehameha.*

Courts have consistently held that the § 703(e)(2) exception, like the § 702 exemption for a religious organization, does not shield the defendant from Title VII liability when the institution discriminates against an employee or applicant (say one who seeks a secular job like science teacher or custodian of a seminary or university) on some basis *other* than religion—sex, race, national origin, or retaliation. *EEOC v. Fremont Christian School.*

ADEA has no express exemption for religious or religiously affiliated institutions. But because ADEA's substantive prohibitions are derived *in haec verba* from Title VII, courts have crafted an immunity from age discrimination liability of the same scope, and with the same limitations, for religious organizations that meet the § 702 (or, apparently, § 703(e)(2)) requirements. See DeMarco v. Holy Cross High School (2d Cir.1993).

7. ALL EMPLOYERS, RELIGIOUS OR NOT: THE "BFOQ" AFFIRMATIVE DEFENSE

Under § 703(e)(1), *any* employer, even one wholly sectarian, may "hire and employ" (a labor organization may "admit or employ" in apprenticeship or retraining programs) on the basis of religion where religion is a "bona fide occupational qualification ['BFOQ'] reasonably necessary to the normal operation" of the enterprise.

Like § 703(e)(2), § 703(e)(1) defends only against hiring discrimination; it does not excuse discrimination concerning subsequent terms and conditions of employment like compensation, promotion, discipline, harassment or discharge. See *EEOC v. Fremont Christian School.*

Moreover, the Supreme Court's decision in Johnson Controls confirms the narrowness of the BFOQ exception to gender, national origin and religious discrimination. The bare language of § 703(e)(1) would appear satisfied if an employer can show that a refusal to hire based on religion, sex, or national origin is reasonably necessary to the normal operation of the defendant's overall "enterprise." Yet the Court has concluded that to prevent the exception from virtually eliminating an applicant's protection, the employer must show that its discriminatory rule bears a "high correlation" to the plaintiff's ability to perform the job in question *and* relates to the "essence" or "central mission" of the employer's business. Relying on *Johnson Controls,* an appellate

court has recently denied the BFOQ defense to a
school that insisted on hiring Protestant teachers to
maintain a Protestant "presence" assertedly important to its general educational goals. *EEOC v.
Kamehameha Schools/Bishop Estate.*

8. CONSTITUTIONAL PROBLEMS SUR-
ROUNDING REGULATION
OF RELIGIOUS
DISCRIMINATION

Subjecting a religiously based institution to Title
VII regulation for discrimination on grounds other
than religion has survived most challenges based on
the Free Exercise Clause. The critical inquiry under
that clause concerns the impact of statutory regulation on the institution's exercise of its sincerely
held religious beliefs. Because of the statutory exemptions, the statutory regulation will not extend
to employment practices motivated or compelled by
the religious beliefs of the employer or its affiliated
church. Accordingly, although defense of an employment discrimination charge may have substantial
adverse impact on a church or other religious institution, the administrative proceeding or action
should have little or no impact on the religious
practices or beliefs of its adherents. Any such incidental impact has been held outweighed by the
government's "compelling" interest in ending employment discrimination. See, e.g., *EEOC v. Fremont Christian School.*

Where, however, the challenged employment practice relates to a staff member who occupies the functional status of clergy within the employer's denominational structure or belief system, courts have construed Title VII and the ADEA not to reach the practice, thereby protecting the free exercise rights of the religious organization or its members. See EEOC v. Catholic Univ. of Am. (D.C.Cir. 1996).

Judicial regulation under Title VII or ADEA that is permissible despite §§ 702 or 703(e)(2) may nevertheless violate the Establishment Clause when it fosters "an excessive government entanglement with religion." Cf. Lemon v. Kurtzman (1971). In N.L.R.B. v. Catholic Bishop of Chicago (1979), where lay faculty sought to unionize under the protection of federal law, the Supreme Court construed the National Labor Relations Act as not affording jurisdiction over religiously associated organizations absent an affirmative, clearly expressed contrary intention of Congress. Yet it later intimated that the First Amendment does leave room for some degree of state intrusion into religious schools' employment practices. Ohio Civil Rights Comm'n v. Dayton Christian Schools, Inc. (1986). And *Catholic Bishop* has been distinguished in employment discrimination cases on the ground that regulation of the labor relations of parochial schools by the National Labor Relations Board under the National Labor Relations Act is far more comprehensive than employer scrutiny by EEOC or in actions under Title VII or ADEA.

B.   TITLE VII: THE BASIC SUB-
STANTIVE PROHIBITIONS

Section 703(a)(1) declares it an "unlawful employment practice" for a covered employer

> to fail or refuse to hire or to discharge any individual, or otherwise to discriminate against any individual with respect to his compensation, terms, conditions or privileges of employment, because of such individual's race, color, religion, sex, or national origin.

Title VII permits manifestly unfair employment practices that are not substantially based on one of its prohibited grounds. At the same time it prohibits otherwise sound management rules or practices that are applied discriminatorily against a member of a protected group. See Johnson v. Arkansas State Police (8th Cir.1993).

Section 703(a)(1) has generated considerable case law defining "disparate treatment" discrimination. The Supreme Court has treated as prohibited gender discrimination certain forms of employer speech and action characterized by sex stereotyping. But the employer must actually have relied on the stereotype as a factor in the challenged employment decision before that decision constitutes an unlawful employment practice under Title VII. Price Waterhouse v. Hopkins (1989). For example, an interviewer's questions about child-bearing and child-rearing plans, asked only of women, did not violate Title VII where the plaintiff could not show that her rejection was attributable to the interviewer's beliefs. Bruno v. Crown Point, Ind. (7th Cir.1991). In this respect Title VII contrasts with some state and local anti-discrimination laws, as well as the Americans With Disabilities Act, which treat questions related to the applicant's protected status as per se violations. In general, the plaintiff must show a nexus between a supervisor's occasional or sporadic slurs related to an employee's protected characteristic and a subsequent adverse employment action. Discrimination "is not preference or aversion; it is acting on the preference or aversion." EEOC v. Consolidated Service Systems (7th Cir. 1993).

Section 703(a)(2) forbids limiting the employment "opportunities" of an applicant or incumbent employee on any of the same grounds. The Supreme Court relied on this section to devise an alternative mode of establishing unlawful discrimination where disparate treatment cannot be proved. Griggs v. Duke Power Co. (1971). That principle, now codified in Title VII by the 1991 Civil Rights Act, allows the plaintiff to show that a "neutral" employment practice that caused plaintiff to be denied a benefit or suffer a burden has a disproportionate adverse impact on plaintiff's group; liability will then be established unless the employer can justify the practice as related to the job for which it is used and necessary to its overall business.

1. THE MEANING OF DISCRIMINATION BECAUSE OF "RACE," "COLOR," "NATIONAL ORIGIN," "RELIGION," AND "SEX"

a. Race

In McDonald v. Santa Fe Trail Transportation Co. (1976), the Court held that the Title VII prohibition on race discrimination is enforceable by whites as well as blacks. But some circuits have required in such single-plaintiff reverse discrimination cases evidence of "background circumstances" tending to prove that the defendant is the unusual employer who discriminates against the majority. See, e.g., Hill v. Burrell Communications Group, Inc. (7th Cir.1995). In a failure to promote situation, the white or male plaintiff can meet this burden by proving that the plaintiff's qualifications were superior to those of the successful minority applicant. Harding v. Gray (D.C.Cir.1993). This is a showing the plaintiff in the ordinary Title VII case need not make. Patterson v. McLean Credit Union (1989). The distinct but little used Title VII prohibition on discrimination because of "color" has supported claims by lighter- or darker-skinned persons based on discrimination by an employer agent of the same race who has skin of a different hue.

b. National Origin, Including Accent Discrimination and Language Rules

Discrimination because of national origin presents special proof difficulties because seldom do defendants refer explicitly to the particular country of origin of the plaintiff or his ancestors. Ethnic slurs more commonly stain an individual's ancestry than her particular national origin. Evidence that the plaintiff's compatriots are as well as or better represented in an employer's workforce than others can defeat a claim that a U.S. citizenship requirement is in fact a smokescreen for intentional national origin discrimination. See Espinoza v. Farah Mfg. Co. (1973). And because citizenship as such is not a forbidden ground of discrimination under Title VII, a rule requiring citizenship as a precondition to hire violates that statute only if in operation it has disproportionate adverse impact on persons of an identifiable national origin. See Gomez v. Allegheny Health Services (3d Cir.1995).

Employer practices or rules based on language characteristics may violate Title VII if applied in ways that are designed to injure, or that have disproportionate adverse impact on, persons of a particular national origin. The leading case relied on an EEOC Guideline to conclude that proof of discrimination based on foreign accent establishes a prima facie case of discrimination based on national origin. Different treatment because of accent is lawful only when the accent "interferes materially with job performance." Fragante v. City and County of Honolulu (9th Cir.1989).

"English-only" rules, too, may be analyzed as neutral employer practices subject to Title VII scrutiny because of their potential adverse effect on non-English and bilingual speakers of particular national origins. EEOC's pertinent guideline declares a presumption that a "speak-English-only" rule, applied at all times in the workplace, discriminates on the basis of national origin. Even if the rule is limited to certain times, the guideline says it must be "justified by business necessity." And as amended by the Civil Rights Act of 1991, Title VII requires employers to demonstrate that any neutral practice having adverse impact be "job related for the position in question and consistent with business necessity." 42 U.S.C.A. § 2000e–2(k)(1)(A) (Supp. 1992) (emphasis added). But circuit court opinions, rejecting EEOC's presumption, have concluded that employees fluent in both English and Spanish were not adversely impacted by even sweeping English-only rules because they could readily comply with the employer's directive and thus avoid tangible employment detriment. Garcia v. Spun Steak Co. (9th Cir.1993). That approach would not pertain to, say, monolingual Spanish speakers, who could not so readily comply with the employer rule. But some of the decisions upholding English-only rules also rested on the alternative ground that even if the employer's rule were discriminatory in effect, it could be defended as a business necessity, for example by facilitating worker safety. That defense would not sustain a rule restricting non-English conversations in an office or conversations during off-duty time.

c. *Discrimination Based on Gender*

Even when gender is an explicit factor in an employer's decision or rule, it is often not the sole factor. For example, consider an employer that refused to hire women, but not men, with pre-school-aged children. As a result it did not exclude all women but excluded only certain women. The Supreme Court found express discrimination, holding that the policy impermissibly created "one hiring policy for women and another for men." It was no defense that the policy discriminated not because of sex alone but because of "sex-plus," the plus factor there being the early stages of motherhood. Phillips v. Martin Marietta Corp. (1971). This logic also makes it unlawful gender discrimination to reject married women, but not married men for initial hire or promotion. See Sprogis v. United Air Lines, Inc. (7th Cir.1971).

Employers have contended that pension plan provisions requiring greater contributions by female employees for benefits equal to those of male employees, or awarding women lesser retirement benefits despite their equal contributions, are geared to the neutral factor of greater average female longevity rather than to gender. The Supreme Court, however, found gender an inadequate proxy for greater female longevity, noting that a significant part of the differential might be explainable by other factors, such as the heavier incidence of smoking among men. In any event, again stressing Title VII's focus on the individual, the Court expressed concern that even an accurate generalization about greater female longevity obscures the fact that many women will live less long than many men, and each such woman is entitled to benefits calculated without regard to gender-based averages. Accordingly, the Court has invalidated plans that require women to make greater contributions or that award them lesser benefits. See, respectively, Los Angeles Department of Water & Power v. Manhart (1978); Arizona Governing Committee v. Norris (1983). These decisions have indirectly forced many insurers to offer employers plans featuring gender-neutral annuity assumptions.

Lower courts have long held, with substantial unanimity, that discrimination because of the plaintiff's sexual orientation or behaviors does not amount to "gender" discrimination prohibited by Title VII. See Garcia v. Elf Atochem North America (5th Cir.1994) (alternative holding); Dillon v. Frank (6th Cir.1992). An anti-homosexual practice "neutral" on its face (because not limited to homosexuals of one gender) and neutrally applied in fact may nevertheless be said to discriminate on the basis of gender because it will often result in disproportionately greater exclusion of male homosexuals, who in many workplaces are more numerous or more readily identifiable. But the impetus for the discrimination is likely anti-homosexual rather than anti-male animus. The circuit opinions accordingly conclude that recognizing the impact theory would amount to an evasion of an assumed Congressional purpose not to forbid discrimination based on sexual orientation. By contrast, disparate enforcement of an anti-homosexual policy in favor of or against members of a particular gender would violate the statute. Despite the absence of national protection, approximately one-third of all Americans live in states or local jurisdictions that provide protection against employment discrimination on the basis of sexual orientation. States in this group include California, Connecticut, Massachusetts, New Jersey, and Minnesota. Over 150 cities and counties have passed similar statutes. See Lewis, Litigating Civil Rights and Employment Discrimination Cases, § 5.22, n.7.5 (West, 1998 Supp.).

Rules prohibiting the employment of spouses in the same office, department or plant of one company have also been viewed as neutral on their face. But they are actionable either if they are disparately enforced against members of a particular gender or if they disproportionately adversely impact wives, and hence women, or husbands, and hence men. See Yuhas v. Libbey–Owens–Ford (7th Cir.1977). See also Sarsha v. Sears, Roebuck & Co. (7th Cir.1993).

Grooming and dress code regulations that on their face limit only one gender—men must have short hair, for example—have nevertheless been analyzed as neutral, rather than expressly discriminatory practices. The leading opinion offered a variety of reasons in support of this conclusion, none of which withstands hard scrutiny. For example, the court wrote that men could readily comply with a short-hair rule because it related to a "mutable" characteristic, and the statute was concerned only with assuring that employment opportunities not be denied on the basis of "immutable" characteristics like race or sex. Willingham v. Macon Telegraph Publishing Co. (5th Cir.1975)(en banc). Other circuits agree that the "primary thrust" of Title VII is to ban employer reliance on sex stereotypes that pose "distinct employment disadvantages for one sex." See, respectively, Craft v. Metromedia, Inc. (8th Cir.1985), and Knott v. Missouri Pacific Railroad (8th Cir.1975). Plaintiffs have also been compelled to litigate no-beard rules within the framework of disproportionate adverse impact rather than disparate treatment. See, e.g., Bradley v. Pizzaco of Nebraska, Inc. (8th Cir.1993).

This tolerant approach to attire and grooming rules may in practice disadvantage more women than men. Even when the employer's rule specifically imposes more demanding clothing and coiffure requirements on one gender than the other, the tendency has been for the courts to assert that the employer has one omnibus grooming regime that naturally must be applied differently to women than to men to account for gender differences. In a variation on this theme, courts will observe that the employer has some grooming standard for each gender and will treat that standard as the common, neutral employer practice. The fact that the employer imposes different, or more stringent, or differentially applied dress or grooming requirements on its employees of different genders is usually just ignored or minimized. Craft v. Metromedia, Inc.; Carroll v. Talman Federal Savings & Loan Association (7th Cir.1979). Employers are consequently far more easily able to justify such rules, as a matter of business necessity and job relatedness, than they would be if the rules were classified as discriminat-

ing facially on the basis of gender. The customary
judicial rejection of women's gender discrimination
complaints about harsher grooming or clothing requirements represents an exception to the Supreme
Court's general recognition that employer practices
driven by sex stereotyping unlawfully discriminate
because of gender. *Price Waterhouse v. Hopkins.*

d. Sexual Harassment

(1) SCOPE AND UNIFORM REQUIREMENTS

Conduct of supervisors, other employer agents, or
co-workers that denigrates or demeans women,
their abilities or status is uniformly considered unlawful gender-based harassment. Early decisions
doubted whether offering benefits for submission to
sexual demands, or imposing detriments for resisting them, constituted discrimination "because of
sex." In part this is because the selection of a
"target" for sexual gratification would usually not
be based on the victim's gender alone; there would
usually be a "plus" factor in the harassing employee's calculus, for example the target's relative at-
tractiveness or vulnerability. But the Supreme
Court has assumed that the target's gender need
not be the sole motivating factor in the superior's
advance in order for the subsequent reprisal to be
actionable. It is sufficient if gender is a "but-for"
cause of the advance. Meritor Savings Bank, FSB v.
Vinson (1986). This of course would be the case in
the most commonly litigated sexual harassment sce-

nario, a heterosexual's advance toward a person of the opposite gender.

Nevertheless, the requirement that the discrimination be based on and directed against a particular gender has continuing significance in the law governing harassment. It undercuts Title VII claims alleging harassment based on the victim's homosexual status or orientation, unless the discrimination is limited to homosexuals of one gender, e.g., lesbians, or there is evidence that homosexuality by an employee of a different gender would be tolerated. It apparently also exempts from Title VII scrutiny sexual advances or reprisals made by a bisexual supervisor, who by definition would usually not select a target because of the target's particular gender. Rabidue v. Osceola Refining Co. (6th Cir. 1986); Vinson v. Taylor (D.C.Cir.1985). Yet claims have been upheld based on nonsexually oriented "equal opportunity harassment" of both men and women, where the evidence supports the conclusion that the harasser would not have sought to demean either victim except for their respective genders. See Steiner v. Showboat Operating Co. (9th Cir. 1994). On the other hand, where a male supervisor's harassing conduct is in fact directed only against women, it is no defense that men might find the supervisor's conduct equally offensive. Hutchison v. Amateur Electronic Supply, Inc. (7th Cir. 1994).

"Same-sex harassment" is actionable when a male harasses another male (or a female another female) not because of the harassee's sexual orientation but "because" of the harassee's gender. The "crucial inquiry is whether the harasser treats ... members ... of one sex differently from members of the other sex." EEOC Compliance Manual, § 615.2(b)(3). A unanimous Supreme Court has recently endorsed this reasoning. Oncale v. Sundowner Offshore Services, Inc. (1998). The victim's gender must be a "but-for" factor in the harassment. For example, conduct motivated by a harasser's homosexual interest in the harassee (rather than by the harassee's own sexual orientation) seems to fall on the actionable side of the line, because such conduct would not occur unless the victim were of a particular gender. By contrast, same-sex harassment inspired by a victim's prudishness, shyness or relative vulnerability to sexually tinged taunting may not be actionable if the particular harasser would for the same reasons harass members of the other gender, too. The issue must be determined case by case, without use of any *presumption* that harassment of a person of the same gender is or is not "because of" that gender. *Oncale.*

The "because of sex" requirement will also usually defeat the typical claim of sexual favoritism, in which a plaintiff denied a job or benefit alleges that another employee was hired or promoted because he or she participated in a consensual romantic relationship with a supervisory or managerial agent of the employer. See Becerra v. Dalton (4th Cir.1996); EEOC Policy Guide on Employer Liability For Sexual Favoritism Under Title VII, 405 FEP Man. (Jan. 12, 1990). In that situation both women and men are disadvantaged for a reason other than, or in addition to, their gender, viz., they were not the object of the agent's sexual interest. Alternatively, the plaintiff's terms and conditions of employment may not be viewed as harmed by a supervisor's romantic relationship with a co-worker. Candelore v. Clark County Sanitation Dist. (9th Cir.1992).

Courts have also been cautious before deciding that sexual harassment constitutes unlawful gender discrimination, because in some cases the alleged harasser's proposition or advance may have been invited or received as welcome. Any sexual harassment plaintiff must therefore show that she or he subjectively perceived a proposition or advance as "unwelcome." Of course this requires first a showing that there was in fact an advance. On this question Congress balanced the scales against the defendant by approving the admission of evidence of past similar conduct by the alleged harasser. For trials commencing after December 1, 1994, Federal Rule of Evidence 415 provides that "evidence of that party's commission of another offense or offenses of sexual assault ... is admissible and may be considered as provided in Rule 413 ... of these rules." Such evidence "may be considered for its bearing on any matter to which it is relevant." Rule 413(a). See Rule 413(c).

If there was an advance, its welcomeness vel non is determined by a subjective test. In *Meritor,* the Supreme Court recognized the potential relevance of a plaintiff's sexually provocative speech or dress to the question of unwelcomeness. And sufficient evidence of the plaintiff's off-hours conduct and attitudes has until recently sufficed to refute her assertion that workplace harassment was unwelcome. Thus employers could sometimes overcome a showing that an actionable level of interference was unwelcome with evidence about the plaintiff's past sexual conduct, "fantasies," or failure to object to sexual advances. The decisions did caution against equating participation in off-duty sex-related activities with acquiescence to sexual advances on the job. For example, evidence that the plaintiff had posed nude for a magazine did not negate her evidence that she did not welcome the employer's sexual advances in the workplace. Burns v. McGregor Electronic Industries (8th Cir.1993); Swentek v. USAIR, Inc. (4th Cir.1987). Indeed even a plaintiff's "vulgar and unladylike" language and behavior on the job did not negate her showing that she did not welcome the crude sexual epithets, sexually insulting messages, and offensive demonstrative conduct directed at her by her male co-workers, where she plainly resented their conduct and complained of it repeatedly to her supervisor. Carr v. Allison Gas Turbine Division (7th Cir.1994).

Federal Rule of Evidence 412 may rule out all but the most important probative evidence of the plaintiff's prior sexual behavior. FRE 412 provides that in a civil action, "evidence offered to prove the sexual behavior or sexual predisposition of any alleged victim is admissible if . . . its probative value *substantially* outweighs the danger of harm to any victim and of unfair prejudice to any party." Fed. R.

Evid. 412(b)(2) (emphasis added). This section also provides that evidence of the alleged victim's "reputation is admissible only if it has been placed in controversy by the alleged victim." That precondition, at least, would seem to be met whenever a plaintiff alleges sexual harassment, since unwelcomeness is an essential element of that claim. But the FRE 412 amendment tilts the scales against admissibility in three respects, as compared to standard probative value-prejudicial impact balancing under FRE 403. First, it reverses the presumptive weighting, by requiring the proponent to justify admissibility rather than requiring the opponent to justify exclusion. Second, the prerequisites for admissibility are more stringent, because the value of the proffered evidence must "substantially" outweigh the specified dangers. Third, harm to the victim must be explicitly placed on the exclusion side of the balance, in addition to party prejudice. Nevertheless, the potential inadmissibility of any such evidence would not necessarily prevent the employer from pursuing these topics in discovery.

(2) "QUID PRO QUO" OR "TANGIBLE TERMS" HARASSMENT

Title VII is violated when submission to an employer's sexual demands is expressly made the "quid pro quo" of gaining a job, promotion, continued employment, pay increase, work assignment or other economic job benefit, or of avoiding demotion, diminished compensation, a disadvantageous transfer, or formal discipline or discharge. *Meritor*; Burlington Industries v. Ellerth (1998); Faragher v. City of Boca Raton (1998). EEOC's Guidelines assert that quid pro quo harassment also occurs when submission to unwelcome sexual advances or conduct is "implicitly" made a term or condition of the target's employment and made the basis for an employment decision. 29 C.F.R. §§ 106.11(a)(1) to (2) (1993).

Relying on the Guidelines, a circuit opinion has held that "quid pro quo sexual harassment occurs whenever an individual explicitly or implicitly conditions a job, a job benefit, or the absence of a job detriment, upon an employee's acceptance of sexual conduct." Nichols v. Frank (9th Cir.1994). The court adopted a per se rule that "a supervisor's intertwining of a request for the performance of sexual favors with a discussion of actual or potential job benefits or detriments in a single conversation constitutes quid pro quo harassment." On this theory, there is quid pro quo discrimination even if, by submitting to the superior's sexual demands, the employee suffers no tangible economic loss. Karibian v. Columbia University (2d Cir.1994). More recently, however, where a harassing superior officer of the employer did not carry out threats to adversely alter the plaintiff's tangible terms of employment despite her refusal to submit, the Supreme Court treated the discrimination as an instance of a hostile work environment, limiting the "quid pro quo" classification to situations in which the threat is consummated. *Burlington Industries*.

This suggests that the Court would analyze "submission" scenarios like the one in *Karibian* as non-quid pro quo, unless perhaps the employer agent does adversely alter the target's terms of employment despite her submission.

In sum, the "quid pro quo" or "tangible terms" sexual harassment plaintiff must prove that (1) he or she encountered verbal, visual or physical propositions or advances of a sexual nature; (2) the harassment was based on her or his gender, and not, for example, sexual orientation; (3) she or he experienced the propositions or advances as *subjectively* unwelcome; and (4) the harassment was perpetrated by a supervisor, manager or other high-ranking agent of the employer who (5) had the authority to and did in fact give the plaintiff a tangible employment benefit for submitting, or imposed a tangible detriment for resisting, the proposition or advance. Remedies available for such harassment would include back pay representing the economic loss of a denied job or promotion; injunctive relief directing the award of the position; emotional distress; for a willful or reckless violation, punitive damages, with the sum of compensatory and punitive damages capped at $50,000 to $300,-000 depending on the number of persons employed by the defendant; and attorney's fees and costs.

(3) EMPLOYER LIABILITY FOR QUID PRO QUO (TANGIBLE TERMS) DISCRIMINATION

Because only supervisors or managers can alter such tangible terms of employment, and they are clothed by the employer with at least apparent authority to do so, a finding of quid pro quo harassment results, as with most other violations of Title VII, in automatic or "strict" liability of the employer. *Nichols v. Frank* (citing cases); Pierce v. Commonwealth Life Ins. Co. (6th Cir.1994); 29 CFR § 1604.11(c); EEOC Policy Guidance on Current Issues of Sexual Harassment, 8 FEP (BNA) 405:6681, 6694 (1990). Dictum in companion cases decided by the Supreme Court in June 1998 confirms that the employer is not only vicariously but strictly or "automatically" liable without more for quid pro quo harassment by a supervisor or other employer agent who has the means to and does in fact alter the plaintiff's tangible terms and conditions of employment. Strict liability means that if the plaintiff demonstrates that her obtaining a tangible job benefit or avoiding a tangible job detriment turned on her compliance or noncompliance with an unwelcome sexual advance, and the employer agent carried out such a promise or threat, the employer will have no affirmative defense. *Burlington; Faragher.* In a "tangible terms" case, the Court reasons, "there is assurance the injury could not have been inflicted absent the agency relation" between the supervisor and a defendant employer. *Burlington.*

(4) "Hostile Environment" Discrimination

Suppose the victim is subjected to worsened working conditions or other "environmental" harassment that affects only intangible aspects of the job? Until Title VII was amended by the Civil Rights Act of 1991, a plaintiff who could prove only an abusive or hostile work environment, without tangible detriment to her employment status, could recover no monetary relief. There was thus little incentive to sue under Title VII for environmental sexual harassment, unaccompanied by termination, demotion, or other adverse action resulting in a reduction or loss of pay or benefits. But Section 102 of the Civil Rights Act of 1991 authorized compensatory and, if appropriate, punitive damages, for all intentional forms of unlawful discrimination, including harassment. (Punitives are not available against government employers). These damages are capped in amounts that vary with the number of employees employed by the defendant.

In *Meritor* and *Oncale* the Supreme Court reaffirmed its traditional broad interpretation of covered "terms and conditions of employment," holding that harassment is actionable, even if it does not affect a tangible term of employment, provided it is sufficiently severe or pervasive to create a hostile or abusive working environment. The "hostile environment" label defines all actionable sexual harassment claims other than "quid pro quo." Thus it includes situations in which the harasser is (a) a co-worker or subordinate without authority to reward or punish with tangible job benefits or detriments; (b) a supervisor whose conduct consists of unwanted verbal or physical sexually oriented advances (or of speech or conduct demeaning to the abilities or status of women), unaccompanied by a tangible job detriment, as in *Faragher*; or (c) a supervisor who threatens but does not fulfill a threat respecting the target's tangible terms of employment, as in *Burlington*. The Court explains that labeling a harasser's conduct as "hostile environment" rather than "quid pro quo" means that the plaintiff will have to show more aggravated or persistent conduct to prove sex discrimination violating Title VII, but the label does not by itself control whether the employer is liable for that conduct.

The "hostile environment" sexual harassment plaintiff must prove that (1) she or he encountered verbal, visual or physical propositions, advances, insults or invasions of person; (2) those propositions or insults were based on her or his gender, as distinct from, for example, her or his sexual orientation; (3) he or she experienced the alleged harasser's conduct as *subjectively* unwelcome; (4) the harassment was of sufficient nature and magnitude (e.g., on one hand, a one-time flagrant physical assault or intimate touching, or, on the other, ongoing, relatively frequent or continual physical or verbal propositions, advances, or insults) to have created an *objectively* intimidating, hostile, offensive, or abusive work environment of a kind that would have unreasonably interfered with the work performance, working conditions, or general well being of a reasonable person in her position; and (5) the harassment was perpetrated by a supervisor, manager or high-ranking agent of the employer, or it was committed by co-workers, subordinates or customers in circumstances that should fasten liability on the employer under general principles of agency law. See *Meritor, Burlington, Faragher.*

The plaintiff's most formidable obstacle here is usually establishing the objectively hostile or abusive work environment element. Whether conduct reaches a level of unreasonable interference with the employee's ability to work, or creates a sufficiently intimidating work environment, "should be evaluated from the objective standpoint of a 'reasonable person.'" EEOC Policy Guidance on Current Issues of Sexual Harassment. Thus a "normal" level of workplace obscenity, isolated sexual suggestiveness or propositions, and even some single instances of unwelcome touching may not amount to unreasonable interference. See McKenzie v. Illinois Dept. of Transportation (7th Cir.1996); DeAngelis v. El Paso Mun. Police Officers Ass'n (5th Cir.1995). The circuit courts are still sorting out whether the "person" from whose standpoint reasonableness should be assessed is the genderless prototype of torts litigation or a reasonable victim, who usually, in this context, would be a woman. Contrast *Rabidue v. Osceola Refining Co.* (reasonable person) with Ellison v. Brady (9th Cir.1991) and Yates v. Avco Corp. (6th Cir.1987)(reasonable woman). The EEOC blurs this division in its Policy Guidance, advocating a "reasonable person" standard but adding that in applying that standard the factfinder "should consider the victim's perspective and not stereotyped notions of acceptable behavior."

The Supreme Court has upheld a "hostile environment" claim when workplace intimidation, ridicule and insult are "sufficiently severe or pervasive to alter the conditions of the victim's environment *and* create an abusive working environment." Harris v. Forklift Systems, Inc. (1993). The plaintiff suffered a series of gender-related insults and unwanted sexual innuendos. Because in totality this conduct may have been sufficient to create an abusive work environment from the standpoint of a hypothetical reasonable person, the Court held that the plaintiff was not required to show that it seriously affected her psychological well-being. The Court located the required level of injury somewhere "between making actionable any conduct that is merely offensive and requiring the conduct to cause a tangible psychological injury." Psychological harm is just another, nonessential factor relevant to the issue of abusiveness.

Justice O'Connor's opinion for the *Harris* majority emphasizes that when the defendant's conduct consists entirely of epithets or sexual innuendo, those must be sufficiently severe or pervasive "to create an objectively hostile or abusive work environment," one that a "reasonable person would find hostile or abusive." In addition, the victim must "subjectively perceive the environment to be abusive." The opinion does little more than identify a number of unweighted, nonexhaustive factors relevant to the objective question of an "abusive" or "hostile" environment: the nature of the discriminatory conduct, i.e., whether it is merely offensive or also physically threatening or humiliating; the conduct's frequency and severity; and whether it unreasonably interfered with the plaintiff's work performance. None of these is identified as indispensable or even preeminent, and this leads the EEOC to conclude that none is. "Enforcement Guidance on Harris."

Justice Ginsburg, concurring, opined that the inquiry should "center, dominantly, on whether the discriminatory conduct has interfered with the plaintiff's work performance." For her this would mean that the plaintiff need show only that the defendant's conduct made it more difficult for her to do her job, and not that the plaintiff's productivity actually declined. A recent court of appeals decision appears to hold just that: a supervisor's sexual innuendo and banter was actionable because it was unwelcome and made it more difficult for plaintiff to do her job, even though it was not of sufficient severity to prevent her from timely meeting her work obligations. But the *Harris* majority did not hold that a showing that the plaintiff's job has been made more difficult suffices. On the other hand, interference with the plaintiff's work performance is not essential to the required demonstration of hostility or abusiveness. It is enough if the offensive conduct is shown, through the totality of the circumstances, to create an abusive work environment, or even just that it adversely affected plaintiff's daily working conditions. See respectively King v. Hillen (Fed.Cir.1994) and Carr v. Allison Gas Turbine Division (7th Cir.1994).

Because no bright line separates merely vulgar banter (usually lawful) from a consistently hostile or severely abusive environment (usually unlawful), some circuits confide the pervasiveness and severity questions to a jury, so long as the district judge is satisfied that the harasser's comments or conducts were "because of sex." See Schwapp v. Town of Avon (2d Cir.1997). Others, however, consider actionable harassment a question of law and accordingly reserve decision on the sufficiency of severity and pervasiveness for the district courts or for themselves. See Konstantopoulos v. Westvaco Corp. (3d Cir.1997).

The environmental brand of sexual harassment, then, "is often a cumulative process rather than a one time event. In its early stages, it may not . . . cross the threshold that separates the nonactionable from the actionable . . . , or may not cause sufficient distress . . . , or may not have gone on long enough to charge the employer with knowledge and a negligent failure to take effective remedial measures." To avoid encouraging premature litigation, therefore, courts will give plaintiffs complaining of environmental sexual harassment the benefit of the "continuing violation" theory, which permits suit on conduct that occurred before the applicable limitations period where that conduct could only have been recognized, within that period, as actionable in light of subsequently occurring events. Galloway v. General Motors Service Parts Operations (7th Cir. 1996).

(5) EMPLOYER LIABILITY FOR PROHIBITED HOSTILE ENVIRONMENT HARASSMENT BY SUPERVISORS AND CO-WORKERS

The plaintiff will ordinarily receive no remedy for sexually harassing conduct of the "hostile environment type" unless the employer as an entity is liable for that conduct. This is because most of the federal appellate circuits addressing the question have held that supervisors, managers and high officials of a covered "employer" cannot be held individually liable, even though the statute defines a covered "employer" to include "any agent of" that employer. See cases collected at Lewis, Litigating Civil Rights and Employment Discrimination Cases (West 1996 as supplemented), § 5.3n.15. So the requirements of employer liability for environmental harassment are critical.

While recognizing that a supervisor's sexually harassing conduct is probably a "frolic and detour" outside the scope of his authority, the Supreme Court has nevertheless held that an employer "is subject to vicarious liability to a victimized employee for an actionable hostile environment created by a supervisor with immediate (or successively higher) authority over the employee." *Burlington* and *Faragher.* As observed above, where the supervisor's harassment culminates in a tangible employment detriment to the victim—where it is "quid pro quo"—employer liability is not only vicarious but strict. But where the supervisor does not impose a tangible employment detriment for nonsubmission to a sexual demand, the employer may avoid liability if by a preponderance of the evidence it carries *both* elements of the following affirmative defense: "(a) that the employer exercised reasonable care to prevent and correct promptly any sexually harassing behavior, and (b) that the plaintiff employee unreasonably failed to take advantage of any corrective opportunities provided by the employer or to avoid harm otherwise." *Burlington; Faragher.*

This test will likely expand employer liability for unlawful hostile environment harassment by supervisors or other high officials. If the compound prongs of the affirmative defense are applied literally, an employer would avoid liability for otherwise actionable supervisory harassment only when it exercised reasonable care to "prevent" and "correct" unlawful environmental harassment *and* when the plaintiff unreasonably failed to use available employer-provided remedies. To show prong (b)—that the plaintiff "unreasonably" failed to utilize corrective opportunities—the employer will probably have to prove that it had in place a policy that specifically condemned sexual harassment, assured victims a means of bypassing the alleged harasser to register a complaint, was widely disseminated among employees, and was adequately enforced in a climate that did not discourage complaints. But because alleged victims will usually take advantage of such policies and procedures, the defense would frequently founder on this second prong.

If that literal reading prevails, the new affirmative defense would seem to deprive employers of the complete defense that circuit courts and EEOC have recognized when an employer takes prompt and appropriate corrective action after an alleged victim *has* complained of a supervisor's hostile environment harassment. See Todd v. Ortho Biotech, Inc. (8th Cir.1998). When the victim complains, or when her failure to complain is not unreasonable, an employer could be liable for a supervisor's unlawful hostile environment discrimination even if it *has* taken prompt appropriate remedial action.

It may be doubted, however, whether the Court's two-pronged defense will be applied so literally. A literal application reduces an employer's incentives to adopt and maintain a fair internal complaints policy by empowering a complainant unilaterally to defeat the defense simply by using the procedure. It would also render employers almost as susceptible to liability for supervisory hostile environment as for tangible discrimination. These consequences run counter to the Court's stated goal in *Faragher* and *Burlington* of encouraging internal resolution of environmental harassment grievances. They also blur the Court's distinction between liability for supervisory tangible harassment, which is strict as well as vicarious, and liability for supervisory environmental harassment, which is also vicarious but potentially defensible.

In the presumably rare situation where a potential plaintiff does unreasonably fail to utilize a fair internal grievance mechanism, how is the employer supposed to learn about alleged harassment in order to carry the distinct burden under prong (a) to "correct promptly any sexually harassing behavior"? Perhaps in such cases the Court will conclude that the plaintiff has deprived the employer of the knowledge it needs to "correct"; it might hold accordingly that the employer has met prong (a) simply by having exercised reasonable care to "prevent." See Farley v. American Cast Iron Pipe Co. (11th Cir.1997). That approach would effectively change the underlined "and" in the Court's two-pronged defense to an "or."

While the literal reading would commonly prevent even explicit, fair and fairly enforced internal grievance procedures from avoiding liability altogether, employers still have an incentive to adopt them. Such procedures will encourage internal complaints, thereby enhancing the employer's ability to take prompt corrective action that will limit its exposure for emotional distress, punitive damages if appropriate, and attorney's fees. And a complete avoidance of liability for supervisory environmental harassment is still possible, even when the plaintiff invokes a complaints procedure and a court applies the literal reading of the compound affirmative defense, for the plaintiff must still carry her prima facie burden of showing a sufficiently severe or hostile environment. The Court hinted in *Faragher* that it intended to continue to insist on palpable harm to the plaintiff's work environment, observing that the *Harris* standards for judging actionable interference "are sufficiently demanding to ensure that Title VII does not become a 'general civility code.' "

In dictum in *Faragher* the Court confirmed the "negligence" standard widely used by the circuit courts and EEOC to determine employer liability for actionable environmental harassment by a plaintiff's co-worker (or subordinate, customer or supplier). Because a co-worker, subordinate or customer cannot independently adversely alter the plaintiff's tangible terms of employment, the underlying violation would be of the "hostile environment" rather than "quid pro quo" variety. It is at least as clear with co-worker as with supervisory environmental harassment that the harasser is not acting on behalf of the employer or carrying out its business. In those cases, therefore, the circuit courts, with the Supreme Court's apparent approval, are unanimous that the employer will be liable only if it actually knew or should have known of the co-worker's (or subordinate's or customer's or supplier's) unlawful harassment and failed to take prompt and effective corrective action. In co-worker or subordinate cases, then, it is clear that the employer can assure non-liability by its own unilateral action.

The EEOC uses the same "subjective" and "objective" standards developed in sexual harassment cases to assess claims of unlawful harassment based on race, religion or national origin. Enforcement Guidance on Harris v. Forklift Systems, Inc., March 8, 1994. The majority's recognition in *Faragher* that the elements of actionable sexual harassment derive from earlier race and national origin decisions may also result in use of the *Faragher/Burlington* standards to determine employer liability for racial or national origin harassment.

Employers have asserted rights to indemnity or contribution with respect to supervisory conduct that has resulted in employer liability. But the Supreme Court has held that no such right is provided by Title VII itself. Northwest Airlines, Inc. v. Transport Workers Union (1981). Claims by supervisors disciplined for violating their employer's anti-sexual harassment policy have not fared well either, most courts reasoning that the employer must enjoy reasonable latitude to conduct a vigorous internal examination without risking additional charges. Thus even a hostile, unprofessional and abusive employer investigation of sexual harassment charges ultimately determined to be unfounded could not support a separate sexual harassment claim by the exonerated suspect. McDonnell v. Cisneros (7th Cir.1996). Similarly, defamation suits based on the same conduct have seldom been successful.

(6) First Amendment Implications of Imposing Liability for Environmentally Harassing Speech

It seems even more likely after *Harris* that speech alone may sometimes violate Title VII; sexually offensive, demeaning or obscene speech or pictorial displays may adversely alter the conditions of the plaintiff's employment. Although federal regulation of such expression, in the form of Title VII procedures and judicial sanctions, may implicate the First Amendment, few courts have decided whether the regulation unconstitutionally abridges worker or employer speech. The potential First Amendment problem is aggravated both by the uncertain line that separates sexual banter from statutory violation and by the reality that employers have an incentive to over regulate the speech of their employees by taking the "prompt and effective corrective action" that may limit their liability.

e.   *The Special Statutory Concept of "Religion"*

Section 703(a)(1) forbids an employer from discriminating because of "religion"; and § 701(j), added in 1972, in turn defines "religion" to include "all aspects of religious observance and practice as well as belief, unless an employer demonstrates that he is unable to reasonably accommodate to an employee's ... religious observance or practice without undue hardship...."

Circuit courts have assumed that employer rules favoring "Protestants," without specifying a denomination, and "Jesuits" (members of one Catholic order) do draw distinctions on the prohibited ground of "religion." *Kamehameha* and *Pime,* respectively. One circuit, finding that a Catholic plaintiff was denied an academic appointment not because of her gender but because her views did not conform to Catholic doctrine, rejected her claim, even though "religion" includes "all aspects of religious ... belief." Maguire v. Marquette University (7th Cir.1987).

More typically, the plaintiff complains of a particular employer practice that burdens the practice of his religion. The prima facie case consists of evidence that an employer practice conflicts with the employee's exercise of a sincerely held religious belief, that the employee has put the employer on notice of the conflict, and the employer has nevertheless imposed an employment detriment. See Ansonia Board of Education v. Philbrook (1986). But two Supreme Court decisions have greatly eased the resulting employer obligation to reasonably accommodate the religious practice.

In *Ansonia,* the Court suggested that if an employer's schedule conflicts with the plaintiff's religious need to refrain from secular employment on holy days, the employer could ordinarily satisfy its accommodation obligation by offering the employee additional unpaid leave. In particular, the employer was not required to accept the plaintiff's proffered fuller accommodation if the employer's own accommodation is "reasonable." The Court wrote that the employer would violate Title VII only if it overtly discriminated against a religiously-necessitated employee absence under circumstances where it would provide paid leave for a non-religious reason. The Court therefore requires the employer to do little more than refrain from the ordinary kinds of discrimination, disparate treatment or neutral-practice/disproportionate adverse impact.

Second, the Court has held that a proposed reasonable accommodation causes the employer "undue hardship," and is therefore not required, when-

ever it results "in more than a *de minimis* cost."
Trans World Airlines, Inc. v. Hardison (1977). But
the hardship must be "real," not merely speculative. Brown v. Polk Co., Iowa (8th Cir.1995). An
accommodation that requires the employer to hire
an additional worker in order to permit the plaintiff
to observe his religion every Saturday works undue
hardship. Cooper v. Oak Rubber Co. (6th Cir.1994).
So do accommodations that permit a religious observer to skip assignments that would have to be
picked up by others, or that allow the observer to
work less than others, even if he reimburses the
employer for the resulting additional costs. Lee v.
ABF Freight System, Inc. (10th Cir.1994). Nor will
a court likely require the employer to accommodate
in a way that requires it to violate a collective
bargaining agreement. See *TWA v. Hardison.* And
when an employee's religious vow commanded her
to wear an anti-abortion button that contained a
graphic photograph, an employer was held to have
adequately accommodated by permitting her to
wear the button with the photograph covered. Wilson v. U.S. West Communications (8th Cir.1995).
But see EEOC v. United Parcel Service (7th Cir.
1996) (directing trial court to consider whether
permitting employee to wear beard in accordance
with dictates of his religion, notwithstanding employer's ban for public contact positions, would
work an undue hardship). Largely because the duty
to accommodate has been substantially diluted by
judicial construction, § 701(j) has survived challenge under the First Amendment's Establishment

Clause. Protos v. Volkswagen of America, Inc. (3d Cir.1986).

2. PARTICULAR PRACTICES GIVEN SPECIAL STATUTORY TREATMENT

a. Restrictions Relative to Pregnancy and Abortion

The Pregnancy Discrimination Act of 1978, or "PDA," added to Title VII a new § 701(k). This amendment defines the sex discrimination prohibited by § 703 to include distinctions "on the basis of pregnancy, childbirth or related medical conditions. . . ." The PDA, in other words, effectively equates pregnancy discrimination with discrimination "because of sex" within the meaning of § 703. Refusing to hire (or firing) someone because she is pregnant therefore violates § 703. Such a violation is a form of facial or express gender discrimination, defensible in a refusal to hire case only by establishing a BFOQ. The PDA thus accomplishes the objective that principally motivated its enactment, overturning the Court's conclusion in General Electric Co. v. Gilbert (1976), that discrimination based on pregnancy is not based on gender.

The PDA does not require an employer to provide leaves or benefits for pregnancy that it does not provide to male employees for "comparable" conditions. The amendment prohibits private employers from discriminating based on pregnancy-related conditions but does not command preference on that basis. See California Federal Savings & Loan

Ass'n v. Guerra (1987); Armstrong v. Flowers Hosp., Inc. (11th Cir.1994). Thus PDA does not even require an employer to provide any leaves or benefits for pregnancy if it treats similar disabilities the same. Barrash v. Bowen (4th Cir.1988) (per curiam). But see "EEOC: Policy Guidance On Parental Leave," 405 FEP Man. 6885 (8/27/90). A circuit court has recently expressly approved use of the neutral practice/disproportionate adverse impact proof mode in a case under PDA. Garcia v. Woman's Hospital of Texas (5th Cir.1996). But the Act does not require more indulgence for absence or tardiness occasioned by pregnancy than for absences or tardiness attributable to any other ailment or medical condition. Bush v. Commonwealth Edison Co. (7th Cir.1993).

The Act does not preempt state legislation that treats pregnant employees preferentially by affirmatively requiring employers to offer leaves to pregnancy-disabled employees that the employer does not offer to others. *Guerra.* And an employer is not forbidden from offering greater health insurance benefits for pregnancy than for other medical conditions. Aubrey v. Aetna Life Ins. Co. (6th Cir.1989). On the other hand, an employer may not give mothers child care leaves if fathers are denied leave under similar circumstances, unless the leaves are keyed to actual pregnancy-related disability. Schafer v. Board of Public Educ. (3d Cir.1990).

The plaintiff has the burden of showing the employer's knowledge of her pregnant status. Geraci v. Moody–Tottrup Int'l Inc. (3d Cir.1996). Where the plaintiff produces evidence that adverse action was based on pregnancy, and the employer fails to offer comparative evidence involving the disabilities of nonpregnant employees, PDA treats distinctions based on pregnancy as unlawful discrimination "because of sex." See, e.g., Byrd v. Lakeshore Hospital (11th Cir.1994); Tamimi v. Howard Johnson Co. (11th Cir.1987).

No liability has been found when pregnancy played a part in decisions not to hire a plaintiff, to place her on involuntary disability leave, or even to terminate her, where the adverse action was taken in accordance with a neutral, evenly applied disability rule that would have disqualified similarly disabled men or other women. See respectively Marafino v. St. Louis County Circuit Court, (1983), Boyd v. Harding Academy of Memphis, Inc. (6th Cir. 1996), EEOC v. Detroit–Macomb Hospital Corp. (6th Cir.1992). Similarly, the PDA does not confer immunity on a pregnant employee from the ordinary consequences of employer decisions taken for reasons unrelated to her pregnancy. Smith v. F.W. Morse & Co. (1st Cir.1996). But a position-elimination defense may be overcome by evidence that management considered replacing plaintiff well before her leave commenced and interviewed a nonpregnant woman for her job. Quaratino v. Tiffany & Co. (2d Cir.1995).

The Supreme Court has held that PDA prohibits employer-sponsored health insurance provisions that exclude spousal pregnancies and thereby offer male employees inferior total coverage than their female co-workers. Newport News Shipbuilding and Dry Dock Co. v. EEOC (1983). PDA expressly proscribes discriminating against an employee for undergoing an abortion, either by terminating her employment or, apparently, denying her sick leave available for other medical disabilities. But the statute also explicitly relieves employers from subsidizing abortions through health insurance benefits, except in cases of "medical complications" or "where the life of the mother would be endangered if the fetus were carried to term."

Courts are still exploring the full reaches of the pregnancy related medical conditions to which the PDA applies. The Supreme Court held violative of PDA employer policies precluding fertile women from holding certain jobs in which their fetuses would be exposed to workplace environment health risks. International Union, U.A.W. v. Johnson Controls (1991). In effect the Court treated a woman's *capacity* to become pregnant as pregnancy itself or one of the "related medical conditions" that triggers PDA protection. *Johnson Controls* therefore provides some support for treating childrearing within the broad concept of "related medical conditions." The decisions are divided as to whether PDA therefore condemns discrimination against a woman absent from work because of treatments for infertility, a condition related to "potential or intended pregnancy." See Krauel v. Iowa Methodist Medical Center (8th Cir.1996). Similarly, a circuit court has held that PDA protects employees from termination not only for exercising the right to have an abortion, but for contemplating an abortion. Turic v. Holland Hospitality, Inc. (6th Cir.1996). Where an employer discharged a woman because of the high medical costs of caring for her child, however, no liability was found because, the court reasoned, "related medical conditions" as used in PDA refers to conditions of "pregnant women, not conditions of the resulting offspring." *Fleming v. Ayers & Associates.* And an employer's exclusion of benefits for the pregnancy-related medical expenses of relatives, as distinct from spouses, would not violate PDA, because only the denial of benefits to spouses would have adverse impact on the members of a particular gender, i.e., males.

b.   Fetal Vulnerability Rules

Because fetal vulnerability rules are treated as a form of express gender discrimination under PDA, they are theoretically defensible as a "bona fide occupational qualification" or "BFOQ." That, however, is unlikely under traditional BFOQ standards, since protection of employees' offspring would not normally be essential to the operation of any employer's business. The Supreme Court has held that the safety of an employee's fetus, as distinct from the safety of plant visitors or customers, is not essential to the operation of the employer's business and therefore fails as a BFOQ. *Johnson Controls.* More broadly, the decision elaborates dual requirements for any BFOQ. Not only must the employer's gender-, religion- or national origin-based exclusion substantially relate to the plaintiff's ability to perform her particular job; it must also go to the "essence" or "central mission" of the employer's business.

c. *Seniority Systems*

Two neutral practices are singled out for special treatment by the text of Title VII. Section 703(h) provides that "notwithstanding any other provision" of Title VII, an employer does not commit an unlawful employment practice by imposing different terms or conditions of employment pursuant to a bona fide seniority or merit system. The employer is immune from liability even if the effect or impact of these systems falls more heavily on the plaintiff's protected group. Judicial construction of these provisions, however, has afforded far greater protection for seniority and merit systems than for professionally developed ability tests.

Unless the plaintiff is able to prove that a seniority system was initially adopted or maintained with a specific discriminatory purpose, and is thus not "bona fide," a seniority system cannot be the basis of employer liability. International Brotherhood of Teamsters v. United States (1977). And such a system is lawful even though it was first *adopted* after the enactment of Title VII. American Tobacco Co. v. Patterson (1982); United Air Lines, Inc. v. Evans (1977). Absent proof of discriminatory purpose by the employer and union in adopting or maintaining such a system, § 703(h) insulates a bona fide seniority system from being declared an unlawful employment practice notwithstanding that it perpetuates underlying hiring, assignment or promotion discrimination that took place before or even after the effective date of Title VII. Thus a bona fide system may not be dismantled wholesale by declaratory judgment or injunction. But where other, primary unlawful employment practices are proved—hiring, assignment, or promotion discrimination, for example—courts have the remedial authority in effect to adjust the system's seniority ladder incrementally by awarding retroactive seniority for bidding or other competitive purposes to proven victims of discrimination. See Franks v. Bowman Transportation Company (1976), as modified by *Teamsters*.

A seniority system does not forfeit its status as bona fide merely because it has the effect of disproportionately "locking in" minority employees to lower paying or less skilled positions—for example, by discouraging them from transferring to better jobs in separate bargaining units where they might forfeit accumulated seniority with the company. *Teamsters*. Factors in assessing a system's bona fides include whether it discourages different protected groups equally from transferring between units; whether, if the seniority units are in separate bargaining units, the bargaining unit structure is rational and conforms to industry practice; whether the system has its "genesis" in prohibited discrimination; and whether subsequent negotiations that have maintained the system were tainted by unlawful motivation. James v. Stockham Valves & Fittings (5th Cir.1977).

The Court has broadly interpreted the kinds of collectively bargained arrangements that qualify as "seniority systems" entitled to the special protection of § 703(h). For example, a requirement that an employee work for a specified time *before* entering the permanent employee seniority ladder has itself been held to constitute part of a protected seniority system. California Brewers Association v. Bryant (1980). On occasion, however, a plaintiff has succeeded in sidestepping § 703(h) by framing the challenged employer decision as distinct from the functioning of a seniority system. See, e.g., Council 31, American Federation of State, County and Municipal Employees v. Ward (7th Cir.1992).

In response to a plaintiff's prima facie evidence that a facially neutral system had disproportionate adverse impact, the employer need only prove that the personnel decision in question was made pursuant to that system. To overcome the defense the *plaintiff* must then prove that the system is *not* bona fide. And trial court determinations about the adopters' intent—the ultimate issue on the bona fides of a seniority system—are unmixed findings of fact, reversible under Federal Rule of Civil Procedure 52(a) only if "clearly erroneous." Pullman–Standard v. Swint (1982).

Section 112 of the Civil Rights Act of 1991 overrules a restrictive Supreme Court decision by providing that the limitations period on a claim challenging the lawfulness of a seniority system begins to run either when the plaintiff became subject to the system's challenged provision or at the later time that provision was first applied to the plaintiff. 42 U.S.C.A. § 2000e–5(e).

d. *Professionally Developed Ability Tests*

Section 703(h) also permits employers to act upon the results of a "professionally developed ability test." But in sharp contrast to the great deference shown seniority systems, the judicial protection accorded these tests has been inconsistent. In many cases it has proven even *more* difficult for an employer to defend the adverse impact of a paper-and-pencil test than to avoid liability for other neutral practices. This is because, soon after Title VII became effective, the EEOC issued "guidelines" on employee selection procedures that require employers to conduct highly technical and demanding "validation" studies of ability tests to demonstrate that they reliably pinpoint desired employee traits essential to a particular job. The Supreme Court's deferral to those guidelines required employers to incur considerable expense in validation efforts before they could safely hinge employment decisions on the results of tests having significant differential adverse impact. Albemarle Paper Co. v. Moody (1975).

But lower courts have subsequently somewhat eased validation requirements, holding that employers need not slavishly adhere to the difficult and complex EEOC guidelines. Instead employers may defend more generally with evidence that tests are "predictive of or significantly correlated with important elements of work behavior ... relevant to the job ... for which candidates are being evaluated." See Contreras v. City of Los Angeles (9th Cir.1981). By its terms the Civil Rights Act of 1991, in an effort to restore the rigor of the defense, requires employers to justify the adverse impact of a particularly identified neutral practice by demonstrating the practice to be "job related for the position in question and consistent with business necessity...." If the courts should abandon the relaxed scrutiny delineated by *Contreras* and hold professionally developed ability tests either to the new statutory standard or to strict compliance with the EEOC guidelines, employers would once again find it considerably more difficult to justify those tests than § 703(h) apparently intended.

The 1991 amendments do not address validation standards in particular, but add a prohibition against the practice known as "race norming." Tests have long been held unlawful when they disproportionately screen out applicants or employees on the basis of race, sex, religion or national origin and the employer cannot justify their use through a job-relatedness or business necessity defense. As a remedy for such violations, courts sometimes ordered employers not to fill vacancies on a rank-order basis but instead to fill them from among candidates with examination scores that fell within specified "bands" or ranges, in order to minimize the differential impact. See, e.g., Bridgeport Guardians, Inc. v. City of Bridgeport (2d Cir. 1991). Section 116 of the 1991 Civil Rights Act specifically reaffirms "court-ordered remedies, affirmative action, or conciliation agreements, that are in accordance with the law." But Section 106 prohibits an employer from adjusting the scores of, using different cutoff scores for, or otherwise altering the results of employment related tests because of race or another prohibited ground of discrimination. Apparently, then, it is now specifically unlawful for an employer to do directly what a court may order it to do in order to offset the discriminatory effects of an employment related test. In between are cases where an employer adopts banding on its own initiative but does so in order to achieve goals set forth in a consent decree. See Officers for Justice v. Civil Service Commission of San Francisco (9th Cir.1992).

3.   RETALIATION

To protect employees who seek to vindicate their rights under § 703, a separate provision, § 704(a), broadly prohibits retaliation. Two basic species of conduct are protected: 1) participation in any administrative or judicial investigation, proceeding, or hearing to enforce Title VII rights; and 2) less formal, but good faith opposition to practices that an employee reasonably believes to be prohibited by the Act.

Once conduct is characterized as protected, the prima facie case is straightforward. (1) The plaintiff must produce evidence of her participation in proceedings authorized by Title VII or her opposition to one or more *apparently* prohibited practices. The practice opposed must be one "made an unlawful employment practice by" Title VII, although the plaintiff may prevail even if the employer was not in fact violating the statute. It is settled that the practice the § 704 plaintiff opposed need not have actually violated Title VII in order for her opposition to it to be protected. See Jennings v. Tinley Park Community Consolidated School District No. 146 (7th Cir.1988). While the plaintiff need not demonstrate that the conduct she protested was an unlawful employment practice, her belief that the conduct was unlawful must be reasonable. Trent v. Valley Elec. Ass'n Inc. (9th Cir.1994). Some but not all courts have held that the plaintiff's own activity, not that of someone associated with her, must be the predicate for protection against retaliation. See Holt v. JTM Industries, Inc. (5th Cir.1996).

The plaintiff must also show (2) her employer's awareness of her protected participation or opposition; (3) an adverse term or condition of employment she sustained thereafter; and (4) a causal connection between the adverse employment action and the protected opposition or participation. See, e.g., EEOC v. Crown Zellerbach Corp. (9th Cir. 1983). Evidence that the adverse action was taken shortly after the protected participation or opposition fortifies or perhaps suffices to show the required causal link. The passage of several years between the protected conduct and the act of alleged retaliation may defeat, but not conclusively, the inference of retaliatory motive. See respectively

Chavez v. Arvada (10th Cir.1996) and Shirley v. Chrysler First, Inc. (5th Cir.1992).

Once plaintiff makes the prima facie showing, the employer must produce evidence of a legitimate nondiscriminatory reason for the challenged employment action. If it does, the plaintiff bears the ultimate burden of persuading that the employer's reliance on that reason is pretextual. Zanders v. National Railroad Passenger Corp. (6th Cir.1990). Several circuit courts have held that an employer can limit its liability for retaliation under Section 706(g), Title VII's "mixed motives" provision. That section, which is silent about its applicability to retaliation, expressly relieves an employer that has unlawfully taken race, gender or another prohibited ground into account from liability for reinstatement and monetary relief (other than attorney's fees) if it can demonstrate that it would have taken the same action for an independent, lawful reason.

The "opposition" right has been subject to fact-sensitive qualifications concerning the lawfulness or reasonableness of the manner and means of opposition. The Supreme Court wrote that employers are not required to "absolve" employees who engage in "unlawful activity against it." McDonnell Douglas Corp. v. Green (1973). Even some lawful protests may be unprotected if they violate established, legitimate work rules. When a court adjudges an employee's manner of opposition to have gone beyond what is reasonable or necessary for effective protest—when, for example, she gratuitously embarrasses a superior—employee discipline will likely be upheld.

The court balances the legislative goal of protecting reasonable opposition to arguably discriminatory employer conduct against the countervailing goal of preserving maximal managerial control. Jennings; Wrighten v. Metropolitan Hosp., Inc. (9th Cir.1984). See O'Day v. McDonnell Douglas Helicopter Co. (9th Cir.1996). But an employer's unilateral sense of diminished loyalty resulting from the opposition will not by itself be considered a legitimate, nondiscriminatory reason for discipline. *Jennings; EEOC v. Crown Zellerbach Corp.* (9th Cir.1983).

By contrast, the "participation" protection, designed to assure free access to the administrative and judicial bodies empowered to investigate and adjudicate Title VII violations, is virtually unlimited. Just as the plaintiff's underlying informal protest need not have been in fact well founded under § 703 to support a claim of unlawful "opposition" under § 704, so a "participation" plaintiff need not have prevailed in the proceeding she was disciplined for initiating. An employer's unilateral view that an employee lied in the EEOC charge documents cannot justify retaliatory action. Pettway v. American Cast Iron Pipe Co. (5th Cir.1969). Further, a plaintiff asserting that he was retaliated against for having filed an EEOC charge generally need not file a distinct retaliation charge with EEOC or otherwise exhaust administrative remedies before suing for retaliation in federal court. Such retaliation is actionable even if it occurs after dismissal of the plaintiff's EEOC charge. Malarkey v. Texaco, Inc. (2d Cir.1993).

Although § 703 protects "any individual," Section 704 protects only "employees or applicants." But the Supreme Court has concluded that even a former employee may, under this language, maintain a claim of retaliation, even for post-employment conduct. Robinson v. Shell Oil Company (1997). The classic example would be negative references or "blacklisting" by a former employer advising a prospective employer that the plaintiff had filed an EEOC charge against it. But the retaliation against the ex-employee must somehow impair an existing or prospective employment relationship. Nelson v. Upsala College (3d Cir.1995).

Retaliation charges may be based on the manner in which an employer defends a charge or complaint of discrimination. Yet the "after-acquired evidence" doctrine that limits a plaintiff's relief when an employer discovers after-the-fact information that would have led it to terminate the plaintiff (see *McKennon*, Ch. 19B.3., *infra*) encourages employers to investigate plaintiff misconduct during employment after a charge or complaint has been filed. Despite language in § 704 that appears to limit protection to those who have opposed or participated personally, a retaliation claim by an employee whose co-employee protested on his behalf has been upheld. EEOC v. Ohio Edison Co. (6th Cir.1993). A claim was upheld by a plaintiff who was required by his employer to discriminate against others. Moyo v. Gomez (9th Cir.1994). Courts are divided over the standing of plaintiffs to complain of retaliation based on discrimination practiced against members of racial minorities or other protected persons with whom the plaintiffs are associated or wish to associate. Compare Maynard v. City of San Jose (9th Cir.1994) with *Childress*.

4.   CONSTRUCTIVE DISCHARGE

Closely related to but distinguishable from environmental harassment and retaliation is the doctrine of constructive discharge. In essence, the claim avails an employee whose departure is in form voluntary but who in fact was virtually compelled to quit as the result of discriminatory job terms or harassment extreme in significance, duration or offensiveness. The consequence of establishing the claim is a broader remedy: the plaintiff who succeeds will be eligible for an order directing reinstatement as well as available monetary relief.

At a minimum the claim requires the standard showing that the plaintiff's involuntary resignation was caused by differential treatment unlawful because based on her race, sex, religion, national origin or age. Evidence that the plaintiff would have resigned for independent personal reasons or work-related reasons unconnected with aggravated unlawful discrimination breaks the causal connection and defeats the constructive discharge claim. See Henson v. Dundee (11th Cir.1982).

The decisions are uniform that an employee has been constructively discharged when his termination results from intolerable working conditions that the employer created with the specific intent of forcing the employee to resign. Some circuits consider indispensable evidence of subjective employer intent to force a resignation. See Allen v. Bridgestone/Firestone, Inc. (8th Cir.1996); Martin v. Cavalier Hotel Corp. (4th Cir.1995). Others require "aggravating circumstances." Dashnaw v. Pena (D.C.Cir.1994) (case under ADEA) More, however, subscribe to an "objective" test, requiring only that the complained of conduct would have the foreseeable result of creating working conditions sufficiently unpleasant or difficult that a reasonable person in the employee's position would feel compelled to resign. See, e.g., Burks v. Oklahoma Publishing Co. (10th Cir.1996).

Most acts of discrimination are such that a "reasonable" employee should stay on the job; oppose the employer practice informally or by filing a charge; and trust in the efficacy of the § 704 protection against retaliation. Classic instances include wage discrimination, nonpromotion, or assignment to less attractive or lucrative positions. See Bourque v. Powell Electrical Mfg. Co. (5th Cir.1980).

At the other end of the spectrum, where the prospects of proving constructive discharge are much improved, are cases showing that the plaintiff endured repeated slurs, was assigned especially demeaning work for unlawful discriminatory reasons, or subjected to egregious, unrelenting, and unremedied harassment. Sexual harassment claims have served as a predicate for constructive discharge. See, e.g., Steiner v. Showboat Operating Co. (9th Cir.1994). But the harassment must be sufficiently severe to meet a particular circuit's test. See Landgraf v. USI Film Products (5th Cir. 1992). On occasion, a serious "single non-trivial incident of discrimination" may suffice to make resignation reasonable. Schafer v. Board of Public Educ. (3d Cir.1990). But subjecting an employee to "unreasonably exacting standards of job performance" has been held presumptively not sufficiently adverse to warrant a reasonable employee to resign, lest the courts undermine employer insistence on high standards. Clowes v. Allegheny Valley Hospital (3d Cir.1993).

The employee must therefore make a critical decision, usually without benefit of counsel, concerning how to respond to varied employer actions. If racial slurs are so offensive or repeated that an employee who quit over them would later be deemed by a court to have acted reasonably, the employee could safely quit or take the lesser measure of remaining on the job and demanding an apology. If he keeps working but his demand leads to his discharge, he might well have a claim for retaliation in violation of § 704. See Walker v. Ford Motor Co. (11th Cir. 1982). But if he overestimates the seriousness or offensiveness of the employer's discrimination and quits, he may find that his only remedy is backpay from the time of the underlying discrimination until the date of his "voluntary" termination.

5. UNION LIABILITY

Labor unions are not excluded from the general definition of "employer," and consequently may be liable for violations of § 703(a) on the same terms as any other employer. In addition, § 703(c) declares distinct unlawful practices applicable to labor organizations alone. One, found in § 703(c)(3), is to "cause or attempt to cause an employer" to discriminate in violation of § 703. Another, declared by § 703(c)(2), is to rely on prohibited grounds in segregating or classifying union members or applicants, or in failing to refer individuals for employment, so as to deprive them of employment opportunities. Finally, wholly apart from any effect on employment opportunities, labor organizations are prohibited by § 703(c)(1) from excluding applicants from membership or otherwise discriminating against them. Construing this last prohibition quite broadly, the Supreme Court has held that a union commits an unlawful employment practice by refusing to file race-bias grievances presented by black members. This is so even when the union's refusal is to avoid antagonizing the employer and in turn to improve its chances of success on other collective bargaining issues, and even though the percentage of all types of grievances filed on behalf of black members is proportional to their representation in the union. Goodman v. Lukens Steel Co. (1987).

Unions may also be liable for retaliation under § 704. For example, a union that refused to process race discrimination grievances under a collective bargaining contract whenever the would-be grievant had a charge pending against the union with a state or federal anti-discrimination agency was found to have violated Title VII. Liability attached even though the union processed other grievances as fairly for black as for white members and claimed that its policy was compelled by the employer. Johnson v. Palma (2d Cir.1991).

CHAPTER 19

TITLE VII MODES OF PROOF, ADMINISTRATIVE PROCE-DURES, AND REMEDIES

There are two generic forms of employer conduct actionable under Title VII. First there is express or nonexpress but still intentional discrimination or "disparate treatment." More controversial is employer liability for "neutral," that is facially non-discriminatory, work practices that have greater statistical "disproportionate adverse impact" on members of the plaintiff's protected group than on others. Particular employer practices may implicate two or more modes of proof.

A. INDIVIDUAL DISPARATE TREATMENT—"DIRECT" EVIDENCE

1. IN GENERAL

The most obvious way of showing an unlawful employment practice is to offer "evidence that can be interpreted as an acknowledgment of discriminatory intent by the defendant or its agents...." Troupe v. May Department Stores Company (7th Cir.1994). Examples include epithets or slurs uttered by an authorized agent of the employer in connection with the challenged decision; or, even more clearly, an employer policy framed in terms of race, sex, religion, or national origin. When produced, such "direct" evidence will ordinarily suffice to show that an adverse employment condition, or limitation on an employment opportunity, was imposed "because of" the plaintiff's protected group characteristic. But evidence is treated as "direct" only when, if believed, it would prove the existence of the fact in issue without inference or presumption. Thus statements other than slurs that merely suggest discriminatory motive, for example by identifying neutral or positive traits commonly associated with the group in question, may by viewed as circumstantial rather than direct evidence, probative only as part of the inferential *McDonnell Douglas* proof mode described below. Evans v. McClain of Georgia, Inc. (11th Cir.1997)

Neutral practices that operate to exclude 100% of the plaintiff's protected group are sometimes analyzed as instances of disparate treatment. Thus the Pregnancy Discrimination Act of 1978 equates pregnancy discrimination with gender discrimination; and the Supreme Court views the practice of excluding fertile women from working in areas where they will encounter sufficient lead exposure to endanger a fetus or potential fetus as expressly gender discriminatory, because the adverse effects of the practice fell 100% on women. International Union, UAW v. Johnson Controls, Inc. (1991). Similarly, an employer or union requirement that a new applicant be related by blood or marriage to an existing employee or union member, while neutral in form, may result in the continued absolute exclusion of members of a protected group that historically was systematically excluded through intentional discrimination; it will therefore be viewed as an instance of express discrimination. See, e.g., E.E.O.C. v. Enterprise Association Steamfitters Local No. 638 (2d Cir.1976). By contrast, employer practices that correlate with age to a high degree are not necessarily unlawful disparate treatment under ADEA. Hazen v. Biggins (1993).

Outside the slur, formal policy, and 100% exclusion cases, there are few smoking-gun exemplars of "direct" evidence. The Supreme Court has, however, treated employers' agents' statements reflecting stereotypical views of women as direct evidence of gender discrimination, even when the views expressed bear somewhat tangentially on the plaintiff's capacity to perform the core elements of the position. Price Waterhouse v. Hopkins (1989) (plurality opinion and opinion of O'Connor, J.).

Justice O'Connor's concurring opinion sets out three prerequisites for employer speech to constitute "direct" evidence: the remarks must be by the applicable decision maker, be related to the decision process, and not "stray." Stereotypical attitudes become "direct" evidence only when extrinsic evidence gives reason to believe that the decisionmaker who voices them is motivated by a factor made unlawful by Title VII. The difficulty lies in differentiating gender- or age-related comments or conduct that amount to "direct" evidence of discrimination from merely "stray" remarks or "isolated" incidents. Compare Radabaugh v. Zip Feed Mills, Inc. (8th Cir.1993) with Davis v. Chevron U.S.A., Inc. (5th Cir.1994). Further, even though slurs and stereotypes are sometimes treated as "direct" evidence of discriminatory intent, their real meaning or purpose may be equivocal. See Gray v. University of Arkansas (8th Cir.1989). And a "same actor" doctrine permits the inference that the employer did not discriminate when the same employer agent hired as well as fired the plaintiff. Buhrmaster v. Overnite Transp. Co. (6th Cir.1995).

Even if comments derogatory of plaintiff's group are accepted as "direct" evidence of discrimination, the plaintiff may also have to prove that the attitudes they reflect played at least a motivating part in the employment decision under challenge. Discrimination "in the air" must be brought to ground, lest Title VII be used as a mechanism for controlling pure thought or speech. To do so the plaintiff must show first that a discriminatory attitude was to some degree actually relied on by the relevant decisionmaker. See, e.g., Trotter v. Board of Trustees of University of Alabama (11th Cir.1996). Discrimination is not preference or aversion; it is acting on the preference or aversion. Therefore an employer who preferred to exclude members of national origin groups other than his own did not violate Title VII even where the employment practice in question (word-of-mouth hiring) brought about that result, so long as the practice was motivated only by other reasons, e.g., efficiency. EEOC v. Consolidated Service Systems (7th Cir.1993). Similarly, a statement attributable to management or even a sign on the employer's premises expressing a disinclination to hire members of a protected group probably does not by itself violate Title VII, although it would violate the fair employment laws of some states and municipalities. Finally, to make a prejudicial statement actionable the plaintiff must also show that the difference in treatment adversely affected a term or condition of the plaintiff's employment. See Crady v. Liberty National Bank & Trust Co. (7th Cir.1993).

The proximity in time and pertinence between a disparaging comment and an adverse term of employment often determines liability. Compare O'Connor v. Consolidated Coin Caterers Corp. (4th Cir.1995) with Haynes v. W.C. Caye & Co. (11th Cir.1995).

2. THE "BFOQ" AFFIRMATIVE DEFENSE

Section 703(e)(1) affords an employer its only defense to policies or work rules that expressly or facially discriminate in hiring; and the defense is available only to discrimination on the basis of gender, religion or national origin. It authorizes the employer to "hire and employ," and a labor organization or joint labor management committee to "admit or employ" to membership or apprenticeship or retraining programs, on the basis of gender, religion or national origin, when that group status is a "bona fide occupational qualification ['BFOQ'] reasonably necessary to the normal operation" of the enterprise. It does not excuse discrimination in post-hire terms and conditions of employment— compensation, promotion, discipline, harassment or discharge. See EEOC v. Fremont Christian School (9th Cir.1986). Nor does it defend against any discrimination on the basis of race. ADEA contains a similarly worded BFOQ defense, and the Court has construed the corresponding provisions of the two statutes virtually identically. See, e.g., Western Air Lines, Inc. v. Criswell (1985).

As its text would suggest, BFOQ is a true affirmative defense which the employer therefore has the burden of pleading and proving by a preponderance of the evidence. Still, the language of § 703(e)(1) would appear satisfied if an employer could show that a refusal to hire based on religion, sex, or national origin is reasonably necessary to the normal operation of the defendant's overall business. Yet in order to prevent the exception from virtually eliminating an applicant's protection against these forms of express discrimination, the Supreme Court has required the employer to show that its discriminatory rule relates to a trait that goes to the "essence" of the enterprise, *and* that the rule bears a "high correlation" to the plaintiff's ability to perform her particular job. *Johnson Controls.*

The two basic elements of the defense derive from a pair of decisions of the former Fifth Circuit, Diaz v. Pan American World Airways, Inc. (5th Cir.1971) and Weeks v. Southern Bell Telephone & Telegraph Company (5th Cir.1969). *Diaz* insisted that the job qualification or employee trait for which the employer's practice or policy screens must be closely related to the "essence" of the business. Thus the psychological reassurance or sexual titillation ostensibly afforded airline passengers by a requirement that flight attendants be female could not justify the exclusion of males once the court defined the essence of the business as safe transportation rather than maximum profit. And employers may not define the essence of their business as maximizing profit, because then customer preference—often the embodiment of the very kind of accumulated prejudice or stereotype Title VII seeks to overcome— could be invoked to justify a vast range of expressly discriminatory rules. Fernandez v. Wynn Oil Co. (9th Cir.1981).

Weeks added the second layer. Even if an exclusion of members of a particular protected group is designed to enhance execution of a function critical to the business, the employer's evidence must demonstrate that "all or substantially all" members of the excluded group lack the required trait and would therefore be unable adequately to perform the job in question. The defense would therefore still work for the positions of sperm donor and wet nurse. But the *Weeks* test will doom many BFOQ defenses rooted in the assertion that only members of a particular gender have the strength or endurance required by the job.

An early Supreme Court decision, still good law on its extreme facts, upheld the exclusion of women from contact positions as guards in unusually dangerous maximum security prisons in Alabama, even though the state failed to offer evidence that substantially all of the women who would seek those jobs would be incapable of maintaining order and safety. The Court merely hypothesized that women guards would be attacked because they were women—skipping over the fact that *all* guards in the Alabama maximum security system were targets simply because they were despised authority symbols. Dothard v. Rawlinson. (1977).

But the Court's more recent decision in *U.A.W. v. Johnson Controls* confirms the narrowness of the BFOQ defense. The employer's rule barred all still-fertile women of any age, marital status, or childbearing inclination from holding a job in which they would likely be exposed to levels of lead that endangered the health of a fetus they might be carrying. Relying on the "occupational" limitation in § 703(e)(1), the Court concluded that the defense fails unless the employer demonstrates objectively that the exclusion is not only "reasonably necessary" to the "normal operation" of the "particular" business but also relates to "job-related skills and aptitudes." The Court rejected the defense because, so far as the record revealed, "Fertile women . . . participate in the manufacture of batteries as efficiently as anyone else." Distinguishing *Dothard*, the Court wrote that third-party safety concerns had figured in the BFOQ analysis there only because inmate safety "went to the core of the employee's job performance"—something demonstrably not the case with batterymaking.

Johnson Controls appears also to have restricted the employer's option to skirt *Weeks* by showing only that some, rather than "substantially all" members of the excluded group lack traits essential to the job and business when it is "impracticable" to ascertain the other members of the group who do. When the two BFOQ requirements, refined by *Johnson Controls*, are combined, the defendant faces a formidable task: "An employer must direct its concerns about a woman's ability to perform her job safely and efficiently to those aspects of the woman's job-related activities that fall within the 'essence' of the particular business."

Given the stringency of the BFOQ defense, its principal remaining utility may lie in resisting claims of age discrimination, especially where an employee's deteriorating physical capabilities correlate strongly with aging and would impair safe hands-on performance. See Usery v. Tamiami Trail Tours, Inc. (5th Cir.1976). It is unlikely that the BFOQ defense could justify a slur, as opposed to an employer policy. Lower courts have, however, upheld relaxed applications of the defense to accommodate a legitimate business need to assure customer privacy. Healey v. Southwood Psychiatric Hosp. (3d Cir.1996). Moreover, EEOC guidelines relax the rules where employers have an interest in the gender-authenticity of such employees as actresses, actors, strippers, and food and drink servers

at restaurants or bars where a primary job and
business function is the projection of a sexually
provocative display. See 29 C.F.R. § 1604.2 (1979)
(actors and actresses). Finally, the Supreme Court
has dispensed altogether with the necessity of a
BFOQ showing to justify otherwise permissible "benign," "voluntary" employer affirmative action programs favoring women. Johnson v. Transportation
Agency (1987).

B. INDIVIDUAL DISPARATE TREATMENT—INFERENTIAL PROOF

1. IN GENERAL

Because direct evidence of intent is so rare, courts
have recognized alternative ways of establishing
unlawful discrimination circumstantially. First
there is suspicious timing, ambiguous statements,
or other "behavior toward or comments directed at
other employees in the protected group ... from
which an inference of discriminatory intent might
be drawn." Second is evidence, statistical or anecdotal, that persons outside the plaintiff's protected
group, otherwise similarly situated to the plaintiff,
were better treated with respect to the relevant
terms and conditions of employment. This of course
is the essence of disparate treatment, but plaintiffs
should take care that their "comparator" is in fact
similarly situated from the standpoint of status and
conduct. See, e.g., Hargett v. National Westminster
Bank, USA (2d Cir.1996).

A third indirect mode, involving proof of "pretext," is named after the decision that described it, McDonnell Douglas Corp. v. Green. (1973). See also Texas Dept. of Community Affairs v. Burdine (1981), and St. Mary's Honor Center v. Hicks (1993). The plaintiff makes a *McDonnell Douglas prima facie* case—and thereby survives a Federal Rule of Civil Procedure 41(b) involuntary dismissal motion, or, in a jury trial authorized by the Civil Rights Act of 1991, a Rule 50(a)(1) motion for judgment as a matter of law at the close of her case in chief—by offering evidence that she (1) belongs to a protected group; (2) applied for or continued to desire the position in question; (3) met minimum uniform qualifications to receive or retain the position; and (4) was rejected. This evidence, the Court has explained, eliminates several of the most common nondiscriminatory reasons for the plaintiff's rejection, nonpromotion, discipline or discharge and thus makes it more likely that the employer's real reason, or one of them, was a status protected by Title VII.

A final element, sometimes relaxed or waived by lower courts, is evidence that the employer, after rejecting the plaintiff, continued to seek applicants with her general qualifications or selected a person from outside her protected group. In rehiring cases, the plaintiff need not show that he was identically situated with others of a different race who resigned or were terminated at the same time; it suffices that the plaintiff's former position was filled by a member of a different race, or simply that plaintiff was qualified for the new job for which he was rejected. Richardson v. Leeds Police Dep't (11th Cir.1995); Talley v. Bravo Pitino Restaurant, Ltd. (6th Cir.1995). And even if a replacement is of the same race as plaintiff, she may still show that the decision to terminate her was unlawfully based on race. Carson v. Bethlehem Steel Corp. (7th Cir. 1996).

The four basic elements may be flexibly adapted to the facts of a given case. The first of the numbered prima facie elements is pro forma—anyone, even a white male, can claim protected group status by contrasting himself in racial, religious, national origin, or gender terms to the group he claims was preferred. But some courts deny white race discrimination claimants the use of *McDonnell Douglas'* inferential mode of proving intentional discrimination. Hill v. Burrell Communications Group, Inc. (7th Cir.1995). Or they may require special "background circumstances," like the white plaintiff's superior qualifications relative to a selectee, "to support the suspicion that the defendant is the unusual employer who discriminates against the majority." See Parker v. Baltimore & Ohio R.R. (D.C.Cir.1981).

An employee complaining of promotion denial need not show element (2), that she applied for the higher position, if it was the employer's routine practice to offer promotions to persons with her seniority and position. Loyd v. Phillips Bros., Inc. (7th Cir.1994). The third element, qualifications, has the greatest practical importance, as it eliminates the most common nondiscriminatory reason for rejection where an application has been made. The Supreme Court has declared that this showing refers to minimal or absolute rather than relative or comparative qualifications. Patterson v. McLean Credit Union (1989).

After the Civil Rights Act of 1991 paved the way for jury trials and legal relief in disparate treatment cases, the Court has indicated that the requisite quantum of evidence the plaintiff must adduce to survive this prima facie stage of the case is "infinitely less than what a directed verdict demands." *St. Mary's Honor Center.* This suggests that the trial should advance to the next stage, defendant's evidence, even if reasonable jurors might not find for the plaintiff by a preponderance of the evidence on one or more of the prima facie elements.

If the plaintiff carries the prima facie case, a judicially created presumption makes the resulting inference of discrimination conclusive unless the defendant offers evidence that it had one or more "legitimate, nondiscriminatory reasons" for an employment decision. *McDonnell Douglas.* The preliminary question whether plaintiff established a *prima facie* case loses all significance once defendant presents its proof. Put otherwise, the definition of the prima facie case merely aids the court in determining whether to grant a defendant's motion for judgment as a matter of law under FRCP 50(a) (or "directed verdict" as it is still known in most state courts) at the close of plaintiff's case. But once both sides rest, the trier of fact must evaluate all admitted evidence, including but not limited to the plaintiff's *prima facie* evidence, to decide if plaintiff has carried the ultimate burden of demonstrating intentional discrimination. United States Postal Service Bd. of Governors v. Aikens (1983).

Where the trial court makes the ultimate determination about discriminatory intent—whether shown through direct or indirect evidence—the issue is one of fact and may therefore be overturned on appeal only if "clearly erroneous." Anderson v. City of Bessemer (1985); Federal Rule of Civil Procedure 52(a).

Traditionally, most courts have viewed as "legitimate" virtually any reason distinct from race, gender, religion or national origin that the employer shows it actually relied on. Turnes v. AmSouth Bank (11th Cir.1994). This view is evidently driven by deference to the employer's superior knowledge of its own productivity, safety and efficiency requirements. See Furnco Construction Corp. v. Waters (1978). Factors highly but incompletely correlating with age, e.g., pension status or years of service, are factors other than age not expressly prohibited by the Age Discrimination in Employment Act, rather than unlawful proxies for intentional age discrimination. Hazen Paper Co. v. Biggins (1993).

Although the opinion in *McDonnell Douglas* suggested that the employer need only "articulate" a legitimate, nondiscriminatory reason, perhaps simply in an argument or brief, the Court ultimately determined that the employer's burden may be discharged only through evidence that clearly explains its proffered reason or reasons. But the Court has insisted that the defendant's burden is one of production only; the burden of persuading about intentional discrimination resides with the plaintiff throughout. Accordingly, like the presumptions described in Federal Rule of Evidence 301, the *McDonnell Douglas* presumption of unlawful discriminatory intent that arises from a successful prima facie case disappears and has no further force in the litigation if the employer discharges its modest burden of producing evidence of a legitimate, nondiscriminatory reason for the challenged employment action—the bubble bursts.

A plaintiff can nevertheless prevail by persuading the court, by the standard preponderance of the evidence, that the defendant's purported legitimate reason is a smokescreen or "pretext" for intentional discrimination. It bears emphasis, however, that the plaintiff does not encounter this burden until after the defendant has produced evidence of one or more specific legitimate nondiscriminatory reasons. Thus in making the prima facie case the plaintiff need only show that she possessed the base, minimum qualifications the employer uniformly required for attaining or retaining a job. She need not do more at that stage of the case—for example, rebut employer assertions that she engaged in misconduct or show that she possessed qualifications equal to or superior to the employee retained or selected in her stead. Such a requirement would in effect prematurely demand that she prove that the employer's reason is pretextual before the employer is called on to identify, through evidence, its legitimate nondiscriminatory reason. That, in turn, would prematurely force the plaintiff to turn to the ultimate issue in the case, intentional discrimination. See, e.g., *Patterson v. McLean Credit Union.*

The plaintiff may make the pretext showing in either of two generic ways: by demonstrating through her own affirmative evidence, including her prima facie evidence, that the employer, in reaching its decision, explicitly relied on plaintiff's protected group status rather than on its proffered legitimate reason; or, less directly, simply by convincing the judge or jury to disclose that the employer's proffered reason was its actual reason for the challenged decision. The Supreme Court recently held, in *St. Mary's Honor Center*, that the latter showing permits but does not mandate a judgment for the plaintiff. In jury-triable, intentional discrimination cases authorized by the Civil Rights Act of 1991, therefore, the jury may be charged accordingly.

Despite some language in the *St. Mary's* majority opinion to the contrary, it appears that the plaintiff's prima facie case, coupled with convincing evidence of the falsity of the employer's proffered nondiscriminatory explanation, suffice to prove unlawful discrimination, provided the fact finder further determines that the disbelieved reason was offered as a pretext to mask prohibited race, gender, religious or national origin discrimination rather than something else. See *St. Mary's*. Most circuits

are in accord with this view. See Binder v. Long
Island Lighting Co. (2d Cir.1995). A recent EEOC
Enforcement Guidance explicitly confirms this conclusion. Enforcement Guidance on St. Mary's Honor
Center v. Hicks (1993). Nevertheless, a few circuit
opinions read St. Mary's to require the plaintiff to
offer affirmative evidence, beyond that produced
during the prima facie case, that the defendant's
agents discriminated against her at least in part
because of her protected group status. See Jiminez
v. Mary Washington College (4th Cir.1995).

There is greater uncertainty about applying *St.
Mary's* to motions for summary judgment or directed verdict. Certainly judgment for the employer is
warranted where the employee rests solely on her
McDonnell Douglas prima facie case and fails to
offer any kind of "pretext" evidence refuting the
employer's evidence of a legitimate, nondiscriminatory reason. Pritchard v. Southern Co. Services
(11th Cir.1996); Wallis v. J.R. Simplot Company
(9th Cir.1994). This is so even though, under *St.
Mary's,* the trier of fact may take the prima facie
evidence into account in assessing whether plaintiff
has shown the falsity of defendant's asserted legitimate reason or has proven that the employer's
reason was a pretext for discrimination on a prohibited ground.

But what if the plaintiff, in resisting summary
judgment or before resting at trial, offers evidence
tending to refute the employer's proffered reason,
but fails to offer "affirmative" evidence that the
employer's real or motivating reason was discrimi-

nation on a ground prohibited by Title VII or ADEA? The *St. Mary's* majority observed, if only in passing, that "it is not enough to disbelieve the employer." Citing this language, a number of circuits have required the plaintiff to produce independent evidence of unlawful motivation in order to survive defendant's motion for summary judgment or, before or after verdict, for judgment as a matter of law. See Hoeppner v. Crotched Mountain Rehabilitation Center (1st Cir.1994); Bodenheimer v. PPG Industries (5th Cir.1993).

Most circuits, however, have squarely rejected the argument that the plaintiff must produce affirmative, independent evidence of discriminatory animus in addition to the prima facie evidence coupled with the evidence that the employer's proffered explanation was false. For these courts, evidence raising a genuine question about falsity, coupled with the still surviving (but no longer presumption-raising) prima facie *McDonnell Douglas* proof, is enough to warrant a trial, submit a case to the jury, or support a jury verdict under instructions consistent with *St. Mary's*. See Combs v. Plantation Patterns (11th Cir.1997); Barber v. CSX Distribution Servs. (3d Cir.1995).

The Supreme Court has placed no categorical limitations on the types of affirmative evidence that may establish pretext in the *McDonnell Douglas/Burdine/St. Mary's* indirect disparate treatment case. For example, a plaintiff is not required to demonstrate that she was better qualified than a successful applicant, but may alternatively or additionally present evidence, including statistical evidence, that the employer had previously practiced unlawful discrimination against her or her group. *McDonnell Douglas; Patterson.*

On the other hand, a plaintiff's demonstration in a non-promotion case that he was in fact the most qualified applicant is not necessarily tantamount to a showing that the employer understood or agreed with that assessment and promoted another as a pretext for discrimination. The employer's explanation, in other words, may be ill founded in fact or misguided in judgment or policy but credible and therefore nonpretextual in the sense intended by *St. Mary's.* Hughes v. Brown (7th Cir.1994). Similarly, EEOC's enforcement guidance on *St. Mary's* observes that while the decision "does not, as a matter of law, require a plaintiff to produce additional evidence of intent to discriminate where the employer's explanation for its actions is found not to be credible, it does, as a practical matter, permit a fact finder to require such affirmative evidence."

2. THE PROBLEM OF "MIXED MOTIVES"

The *McDonnell Douglas* matrix assumes that an employer acted *entirely* for a prohibited reason or a legitimate one. In fact, courts often conclude that an employer relied on one or more lawful reasons as well as a reason condemned by Title VII.

In Price Waterhouse v. Hopkins (1989), a Supreme Court plurality concluded that when an employer makes a challenged employment decision for more than one reason, and the reason that is unlawful under Title VII is a "motivating," or "substantial motivating" factor in the employer's decision, liability will attach unless the employer can prove by a preponderance of the evidence that it would have reached the same decision for one or more independent, lawful reasons. The plurality insisted that the employer, to be relieved of liability, must have known of and *acted* on the basis of a lawful reason when it denied a benefit to or imposed a detriment on the plaintiff. If an employer carries this "same-decision" persuasion burden, the plurality wrote, it should be found not to have committed an unlawful employment practice, despite the evidence of partial unlawful motive.

Section 107 of the Civil Rights Act of 1991, codified as new Title VII Section 703(m), declares that an unlawful employment practice is established when the plaintiff demonstrates that employer reliance on protected group status was a "motivating factor" for "any" employment practice, "even though other factors also motivated the practice." The "motivating" factor language, derived from the plurality opinion in *Price Waterhouse,* appears significantly less burdensome than the counterpart requirement under ADEA that the plaintiff prove age discrimination was a "determinative" factor. And by omitting any reference to the kind of "direct" or "substantial" plaintiff's evidence of unlawful discrimination that the *Price Waterhouse* concurers would have required before imposing the "same-decision" burden on the employer, the Act apparently requires the Title VII defendant to bear that burden regardless of whether plaintiff's case is built on "direct," anecdotal, or *McDonnell Douglas* inferential evidence. See Kerr–Selgas v. American Airlines, Inc. (1st Cir.1995). But see Fuller v. Phipps (4th Cir.1995).

The employer then has the opportunity, and burden, to demonstrate "that it would have taken the same action in the absence of the impermissible motivating factor." Section 107(b) (amending Title VII § 706(g), 42 U.S.C.A. § 2000e–5(g) (1972)). This "demonstration" places on the employer the burden of persuasion as well as production. Section 104 (adding subsection 701(m) to Title VII, 42 U.S.C.A. § 2000e–m). The court's charge to the jury should allow for the possibility that the employer's decision was the product of more than one consideration, and should instruct that at a minimum the plaintiff has the burden of demonstrating that a prohibited consideration had a motivating (Title VII) or determinative (ADEA) influence on the outcome. Miller v. CIGNA Corp. (3d Cir.1995).

An employer who carried the "same-decision" burden under *Price Waterhouse* would have been relieved of all liability. By contrast, the 1991 Act provides in new Title VII Section 706(g)(2)(B), that the defendant who makes the required demonstration is relieved only of the duty to reinstate the plaintiff and of monetary liability—i.e., back and front pay and compensatory and punitive damages. So long as unlawful discrimination was a "motivating" factor in the challenged employment decision, the employer has committed a law violation remediable by prospective relief and attorneys' fees even if it proves it would have taken the same challenged action for independent lawful reasons.

There are several key implications of the fact that Sections 703(m) and 706(g)(2)(B) of the 1991 Act do not amend ADEA, only Title VII. First, thanks to Section 703(m), the Title VII plaintiff's ultimate burden is only to demonstrate that an unlawful ground was "motivating", rather than "determinative," in the employer's imposition of an employment detriment or denial of an employment benefit. Second, where the Title VII plaintiff attempts to meet this burden through the indirect *McDonnell Douglas* formula, judges ruling on summary judgment and FRCP 50 motions will apply the *St. Mary's* requirements for "pretext" less stringently than in corresponding litigation under ADEA. Third, a Title VII plaintiff who takes the *McDonnell Douglas* path and presents evidence sufficient under *St. Mary's* to survive a Rule 50 motion at the close of all the evidence may be entitled under Section 703(m) to an instruction imposing on the employer the burden of demonstrating that it would have reached the same decision independent of the unlawful reason. It is not at all clear that an ADEA plaintiff who presents only such indirect evidence of age discrimination is eligible for such an instruction under *Price Waterhouse*. See *Miller v. CIGNA Corporation*, Fourth, under Section 706(g)(2)(B), the Title VII defendant who carries the "same-decision" showing is nevertheless liable and subject to declaratory and injunctive relief and attorneys' fees; the ADEA defendant who carries that showing per *Price Waterhouse* is probably relieved of liability altogether. *Id*.

3. "AFTER–ACQUIRED EVIDENCE": A LIMITATION OF EMPLOYER LIABILITY

Suppose an employer has committed an unlawful employment practice and cannot sustain the *Price Waterhouse*/703(m) "same-decision" showing; but that after committing the violation, the employer discovers evidence of plaintiff misconduct (resume fraud, theft, or other serious misconduct during employment) that would have led the employer to terminate the plaintiff if the employer had possessed that information at the time of the offense. Even though the tardily discovered lawful reason for the employer's challenged decision was not a substantial part of its motivation when it failed to hire or promote or demoted or terminated the plaintiff, its showing of "after-acquired evidence" will limit its liability. As the doctrine is codified in the 1991 Civil Rights Act, the employer who acted with mixed lawful and unlawful motives is relieved of liability for reinstatement or monetary remedies, remaining potentially liable only for appropriate declaratory or injunctive relief and attorneys' fees. The after-acquired evidence showing likewise avoids a reinstatement order, but ordinarily leaves the employer liable for retroactive, monetary relief through the date the plaintiff's misconduct was discovered.

In a decision under the Age Discrimination in Employment Act, applicable as well to Title VII claims, the Supreme Court steered a compromise course among the widely varying approaches taken by the circuits. McKennon v. Nashville Banner Publishing Co. (1995).

The Court specifically distinguished mixed-motive situations; after-acquired evidence matters only after the factfinder has determined that the employer's sole or motivating basis for the challenged employment decision was unlawful and that the employer would not have reached the same decision on lawful grounds. To capitalize on subsequently discovered employee misconduct, the employer bears the burden of proving "that the wrongdoing was of such severity that the employee *in fact would* have been *terminated* on those grounds alone if the employer had known of it...." A mere possibility or speculation that the employer would have terminated the plaintiff based on the subsequently discovered evidence will not suffice; the employer must show that it would have discharged the plaintiff had it known of the misconduct. Ricky v. Mapco, Inc. (10th Cir.1995). On the other hand, the court need not agree that the employee's misconduct is "serious" or "pervasive," so long as the employer can prove that under its own established rules, applied without discrimination, it would have discharged the employee had it known of such conduct when it occurred. The employer must carry this burden by the normal "preponderance of the evidence" quantum. O'Day v. McDonnell Douglas Helicopter Co. (9th Cir.1996).

The employer must show that had it known of plaintiff's misconduct at the relevant time, it would have *fired* her, not merely failed to *hire* her. Shattuck v. Kinetic Concepts, Inc. (5th Cir.1995) (post-McKennon ADEA case). In deciding that question the EEOC first looks to the employer's handling of past comparable incidents. Failing those, it considers such criteria as whether the misconduct is criminal or "compromised the integrity of the employer's business...." EEOC Enforcement Guidance on After Acquired Evidence, No. 915.002 (Dec.14, 1995). Although McKennon involved misconduct during employment, one circuit court has clarified that its limitation on liability applies equally to an employee misrepresentation in the application process. Wallace v. Dunn Constr. Co. (11th Cir.1995). By contrast, post-employment misconduct cannot serve as the predicate for the *McKennon* limitation. Sigmon v. Parker Chapin (S.D.N.Y.1995).

The employer that demonstrates sufficient misconduct gains a limitation on liability, not a complete defense. While acknowledging that the relevant equitable considerations will vary from case to case, the Supreme Court nevertheless concluded in *McKennon* that "here, and as a general rule in cases of this type, neither reinstatement nor front pay is an appropriate remedy. It would be both inequitable and pointless to order the reinstatement of someone the employer would have terminated, and will terminate, in any event and upon lawful grounds.'' The Court also suggested that the normal monetary remedy should be backpay calculated from the date of an unlawful discharge to the date the information about misconduct was discovered. See Russell v. Microdyne (4th Cir.1995). In Ricky v. Mapco (10th Cir.1995), the court permitted the jury to award back pay not just through the date of the employer's discovery of the plaintiff's misconduct, but through the date it determined the employer would have fired him. So unlike the ''mixed-motive'' employer—who establishes that it would have taken the challenged action even absent reliance on a motivating factor forbidden by Title VII—the employer who carries the persuasion burden on after-acquired evidence will likely sustain some monetary liability.

EEOC and circuit court decisions after *McKennon* have opined that Title VII compensatory and punitive damages and ADEA liquidated damages, if otherwise appropriate, are available notwithstanding after-acquired evidence. *Russell v. Microdyne; Wallace v. Dunn Constr. Co.,*; EEOC Enforcement Guidance on After Acquired Evidence. Further, according to EEOC, protecting the employer's interest in severing the employment relationship does not warrant placing a time limit on compensatory damages for emotional harm. Rather, the after-acquired showing limits only those out-of-pocket losses that are analogous to backpay or front pay. Nor does EEOC see in *McKennon* a ban or limitation on punitive damages, provided the plaintiff proves the employer's malice or reckless indifference.

C. SYSTEMIC DISPARATE TREATMENT

Intentional discriminatory treatment may also be demonstrated in the aggregate, typically by a group of plaintiffs suing as a class or joined under Federal Rule of Civil Procedure 20. Such "systemic disparate treatment" may be visualized as the statistical bottom line of multiple, discrete intentionally discriminatory decisions. The plaintiff must prove that the employer, through a variable mix of policies, practices, and individual decisions by its agents, discriminated against members of the protected group in general. All members of the protected group rejected for hire or promotion during any period that the group is found to have been expressly discriminated against or grossly underrepresented are presumptively entitled to relief—regardless of which particular employer policies or practices or individual agents' decisions led to their rejection. Franks v. Bowman Transp. Co. (1976). By contrast, relief in the "impact" case (see section "D." immediately below) is limited to those plaintiffs who suffered an employment detriment as the result of a particular practice shown to have had disproportionate adverse impact on the plaintiff's group.

Occasionally plaintiffs can establish systemic treatment with evidence of an employer policy that on its face distinguishes on the basis of a prohibited characteristic. See, e.g., Los Angeles Department of Water & Power v. Manhart (1978). More typically, plaintiff groups will have to rely on statistical evidence showing a substantial disparity or "underrepresentation" between the lesser number of their members whom the defendant actually hired or promoted during a given time period (the "observed" number), and the greater number of such persons having the requisite interest and qualifications who theoretically would have been hired or promoted if the employer's decisions had been made random (the "expected" number). The theory is that, "absent explanation, it is ordinarily to be expected that nondiscriminatory hiring practices will in time result in a work force more or less representative of the racial and ethnic composition" of the relevant pool. International Brotherhood of Teamsters v. United States (1977). Anecdotal evidence of particular instances of individual disparate treatment fortifies the inference of systemic disparate treatment raised by statistical disparities; but statistical disparities alone may prove intentional discrimination where they are sufficiently gross.

To show legally significant gross underrepresentation of the protected group through statistics, the plaintiff must calculate the number of its members "expected" to be hired or promoted by reference to the relevant pool from which the selection will be made. That pool must be limited to those with the minimum qualifications, including geographic proximity, for the job in question. See Hazelwood School District v. United States (1977). Protected group representation in a recruiting-zone population or local workforce may suffice where the jobs in question are largely unskilled. *Teamsters.* The percentage of protected group members employed by other area employers is a better measure for jobs that are moderately skilled. But fair assessment of a disparity between expected versus actual representation of the plaintiff group in highly skilled positions demands refinement for availability, interest, and, especially, specialized qualifications. *Hazelwood.* In such cases the court may measure the group's representation in the defendant's workforce against a nationwide pool of candidates with particular educational or experience credentials.

Courts have on occasion dispensed with refined evidence of pool characteristics when the disparities are extreme. The classic example is where the protected group in question constitutes what has been termed the "inexorable zero"—no representation at all in the employer's workforce. *Teamsters;* EEOC v. O & G Spring & Wire Forms Specialty Co. (7th Cir.1994). But see Carter v. Ball (4th Cir.1994). In the case of promotions historically made exclusively or primarily from within, the pool would consist of lower-level employees in the employer's own workforce who meet the base requirements for promotion.

In addition to using a legally significant pool, plaintiff must establish a statistically significant "gross" disparity between observed and expected protected group representation. The magnitude of the disparity must be sufficient to show that discrimination was an employer's routine operating procedure, so that relief should presumptively be granted to the entire underrepresented class. This generally requires expert testimony concerning the statistical technique of binomial distribution and its key measure, standard deviation. The actual and expected numbers of protected group members, together with the total number of persons hired for or promoted to the job during the liability period alleged in the complaint, are fed into the binomial distribution formula, which is designed to gauge the degree to which an "under-representation" departs from hypothetical "random" or "chance" hiring or promotion.

Statisticians have conventionally ruled out chance as the likely cause of a negative deviation from the norm when the formula shows that the observed number falls more than 1.95 standard deviations below the expected number; this convention holds that there is then less than a 5% chance that the under-representation is itself the result of chance. To avoid "false positives"—implicating an innocent employer—the Supreme Court has written somewhat vaguely that unlawful discrimination may be suspected as the cause of an underrepresentation only "if the difference between the expected value and the observed number is 'greater than two or three [negative] standard deviations.'" That is a level at which statisticians would exclude chance as the explanation with overwhelming confidence.

Because the law requires an underrepresentation of such great magnitude, a court may rely solely on statistical evidence to find an employer liable for systemic disparate treatment discrimination in violation of § 703(a) without running afoul of § 703(j). Section 703(j) provides that Title VII shall not be

> "interpreted to require any employer to grant preferential treatment ... because of race, color, religion, sex, or national origin ... on account of an imbalance which may exist with respect to the total number or percentage of persons of any race, color, religion, sex or national origin employed by any employer ... in comparison with the total number or percentage of persons of such race, color, religion, sex, or national origin in any community ... or in the available work force in any community...."

Holding an employer liable for systemic treatment discrimination upon proof of a gross statistical underrepresentation is not tantamount to a requirement, condemned by § 703(j), "that a work force *mirror* the general population." *Teamsters*. Many employee complements will fail to mirror the protected group's percentage in a surrounding population or work force without falling short *enough* to exceed the "two or three [negative] standard deviation" test and therefore violate § 703(a).

A more sophisticated statistical technique, multiple regression analysis, will usually be required to establish the requisite disparity when variations in the particular term and condition of employment at issue—for example, compensation—are explainable by reference to a large number of factors. The Court has indicated, however, that a plaintiff's multiple regression analysis need not eliminate all potential nondiscriminatory explanations of disparity, only the most significant. Bazemore v. Friday (1986).

Once the plaintiff group adduces express or statistical evidence of systemic disparate treatment, the employer has an opportunity to defend by offering what *Teamsters* termed a nondiscriminatory "explanation" for the disparity. The employer's principal defense in these cases is to present evidence that casts doubt on the logical, statistical, or legal probative value of plaintiff's evidence. For example, an employer may avoid the force of evidence of disparity by showing infirmities in the plaintiff-defined pool that exaggerate the availability of qualified members of the protected group. Or it may challenge the validity of the statistical conclusions drawn by plaintiff's expert, including objections to insufficient sample size. See Mayor of Philadelphia v. Educational Equality League (1974); Birkbeck v. Marvel Lighting Corp. (4th Cir.1994). Or it might demonstrate that a protected group's under-representation is attributable largely to then-lawful, discriminatory hiring that took place before the employer became subject to Title VII. *Hazelwood.*

In the alternative, the employer may present statistical counter-comparisons. A more restrictively refined availability pool, for example, may generate negative disparities too small (less than two or three standard deviations) for liability. Indeed, the employer may refute the existence of any negative disparity by offering data suggesting that it hired or promoted a *greater* number of protected group members than their availability in the employer-advocated pool would predict: in that instance, the standard deviation would be positive. Most powerfully, an employer that has maintained applications or records differentiating its applicants by race, religion, national origin or gender may be able to offer "applicant flow" statistics to establish that it hired at least as great a percentage of protected group applicants as of others. The EEOC's record-keeping regulations do not require employers to keep records differentiating applicants by their protected group status, and indeed many state fair employment laws prohibit employers from asking applicants to indicate their race or gender. The regulations only require employers to keep applications for one year. 29 C.F.R. § 1602.14 (1994). The employer that has such records may compare the percentage of protected group members selected (from among protected group members who applied) with the corresponding percentage of nonprotected group members selected.

Because applicant flow evidence tends to show the defendant's actual treatment of persons interested enough to apply, it is generally accorded greater probative value than standard deviation evidence drawn from a hypothetical pool. But to be probative the employer's statistics must correspond to the same time periods and kinds of workers whose availability is measured by the plaintiff's prima facie showing. EEOC v. American National Bank (4th Cir.1981). Moreover, a plaintiff may re-

but employer-favorable applicant flow data by showing a preexisting extreme and notorious employer
reputation for discrimination against the group in
question that made it seem "futile" for other members of that group to apply. And of course applicant
flow figures may reinforce the *plaintiff's* showing of
gross statistical under-representation if employer
records show that it hired a significantly lower
percentage of qualified protected group applicants
than of others. See EEOC v. Olson's Dairy Queens,
Inc. (5th Cir.1993).

An employer unable to counter a finding of gross
statistical underrepresentation must nevertheless
be permitted to defend with a nondiscriminatory
"explanation" for the disparity. *Teamsters.* One
such controversial explanation accepted by some
courts is that, relative to others, the particular
protected group lacked interest in or qualifications
for the job in question. A highly publicized Seventh
Circuit decision so held with respect to women
seeking positions as commissioned salespersons.
EEOC v. Sears, Roebuck & Co. (7th Cir.1988). The
court seemed to consider it irrelevant whether, the
relative lack of interest or qualifications was "inherent" in women or a product of stereotyping in
American history or culture. In particular, the
court did not consider it important to examine the
"employer's [own] role in shaping the interest of
applicants." The "lack of interest" explanation has
lesser force when the court views the statistical underrepresentation as overwhelming, and particularly when there are no protected group members in

the job in question. *EEOC v. O & G Spring and Wire Forms Specialty.*

An employer may also explain an adequate prima facie showing of gross statistical underrepresentation by offering evidence that the disparity is partly or wholly attributable to a neutral employment practice that had disproportionate adverse impact on the protected group. See, e.g., Griffin v. Carlin (11th Cir.1985). This puts the employer in the odd position of becoming its own accuser, since such a neutral practice may independently give rise to Title VII liability even without proof of discriminatory intent. In effect, the employer argues that one unlawful employment practice explains another.

If it carries this showing, the employer limits its liability to those members of the protected group who were personally affected by the neutral practice. The court might even conclude that the neutral practice is itself justified because it is "job related for the position in question and consistent with business necessity" within the meaning of § 703(k)(1)(A)(i), added by § 105(a) of the Civil Rights Act of 1991. If so, the employer would be relieved of liability altogether. Courts that have permitted employers to defend a gross underrepresentation by pointing to such a neutral practice have required them to bear the burden of persuasion on the neutral practice justification. *Griffin.*

It is unclear whether this neutral-practice defense to groupwide intentional discrimination will survive a companion amendment, also part of § 105(a), which provides: "A demonstration that an employment practice is required by business necessity may not be used as a defense against a claim of intentional discrimination under this title." Title VII, § 703(k)(2). At a minimum this provision confirms the Court's position that a facially discriminatory practice may be excused, if at all, only under the stringent BFOQ defense, and not merely by a showing of job relatedness and business necessity. *Johnson Controls* (1991). But read broadly, § 703(k)(2) could also be applied to cases where the prima facie evidence of intentional discrimination consists of gross statistical disparities sufficient to establish systemic disparate treatment; if so, it would appear to deny the employer the neutral-practice defense previously recognized by case law.

D. THE RELIEF STAGE OF THE BIFURCATED SYSTEMIC DISPARATE TREATMENT ACTION

Systemic treatment trials are conducted in distinct liability and remedial phases. If the court determines that the employer has intentionally discriminated against the plaintiff's protected group, individual members of the plaintiff class who apply or reapply for the job or promotion in question become presumptively eligible for the full panoply of all otherwise appropriate Title VII remedies: declaratory and injunctive relief, reinstatement, back and front pay, retroactive seniority and, since the violation involves intentional discrimination, the capped compensatory and punitive damages made available by the Civil Rights Act of 1991.

The Supreme Court has substantially eased the individual plaintiff's burden of demonstrating entitlement to relief at the remedy stage of the systemic treatment case. Even if the prima facie case consists only of statistical evidence, that evidence, if believed by the factfinder and not successfully rebutted with a nondiscriminatory explanation, gives rise to a presumption that each plaintiff who unsuccessfully sought hire, promotion, or retention during the established liability period was rejected because of his or her protected group status. *Franks.* So long as the individual shows she applied for the position in question during the established liability period, she need not even produce evidence of her minimum qualifications. Proof of a broad-based policy of unlawful discrimination, in other words, generates "reasonable grounds to infer that individual hiring decisions were made in pursuit of the discriminatory policy and to require the employer to come forth with evidence dispelling that inference." *Teamsters.* Although the prima case does not "conclusively demonstrate that all of the employer's decisions were part of the proven discriminatory pattern and practice," it creates "a greater likelihood that any single decision was a component of the overall pattern." The employer is now a "proven wrongdoer," and must bear the burden of showing nondiscriminatory reasons for rejecting any individual plaintiff.

To rebut the presumption, the employer may avoid liability to individual plaintiffs or plaintiff class members by persuading a court that they were not in fact victims of discrimination. For example, the employer may demonstrate that there were no vacancies in the pertinent position at the time a particular class member applied, that the plaintiff lacked minimum qualifications that the employer insisted upon at the time of the plaintiff's rejection, or that a successful applicant was better qualified. Franks and *Teamsters*. Even class members who did not apply for a position during the proven liability period may sometimes receive individual relief; but they carry the heavy burden of persuading that it was futile for them to apply because of an employer's notorious reputation for egregious discrimination against their protected group and that they would have applied otherwise. It does not suffice for nonapplicants to show only that they are interested in obtaining a job at the time of judgment. This is because proven discriminatees may be awarded retroactive seniority for the period they would have accrued seniority had the employer not discriminated, so the job available through court order may be far more attractive than it was originally. Further, they, unlike "applicant" plaintiff class members, bear the burden of showing their own minimum qualifications at the time that, but for futility, they prove they would have applied. *Teamsters*.

E. HOW THE INDIVIDUAL AND SYSTEMIC DISPARATE TREATMENT CASES INTERRELATE

Given the relative ease of establishing a prima facie case of individual disparate treatment under *McDonnell Douglas/Burdine,* and the expense and difficulty of gathering and analyzing the data necessary to establish a case of systemic disparate treatment, solo plaintiffs usually proceed with "direct" or inferential evidence alone. Nevertheless, there is a complementary relationship between evidence of individual and systemic disparate treatment. A well financed individual plaintiff may fortify the individual disparate treatment case with evidence of statistically discriminatory patterns. Similarly, a plaintiff class may, and as a practical matter is well advised, to bolster a case of systemic discriminatory treatment with anecdotal evidence of discrimination against its individual members. The advocate should bear in mind that statistical systemic treatment evidence merely suggests that the employer routinely discriminated, but by itself does not suggest how. Counsel may fill the gap for skeptical judges by offering "direct" or inferential evidence that individual plaintiffs were discriminatorily treated. In both *Teamsters* and *Hazelwood* the Supreme Court observed that the plaintiffs had breathed life in the statistical evidence by offering evidence of individual disparate treatment.

On the other hand, the failure of a systemic treatment class action—or of the government plaintiff equivalent, a "pattern or practice" action by the U.S. Attorney General under Section 707—does not imply lack of merit to the individual disparate treatment case of any particular member of the plaintiff class. Cooper v. Federal Reserve Bank of Richmond (1984) Nor does that failure negate the employer's potential liability to an individual member of a plaintiff class for harm caused by a neutral employment practice. A given practice may disproportionately adversely impact those members of the plaintiff group who encounter it even though the group as a whole fares well at the "bottom line" of all policies, practices and decisions by employer agents. Connecticut v. Teal (1982).

F. NEUTRAL PRACTICES WITH DISPROPORTIONATE ADVERSE IMPACT

Writing for a unanimous Court in Griggs v. Duke Power Co. (1971), Chief Justice Burger wrote that practices fair in form but discriminatory in effect may violate Title VII even though the employer's motivation in adopting the practice is neutral or benign. The early cases developing this theory considered the lawfulness of "objective" employer practices such as educational requirements or standardized aptitude or psychological tests, see *Griggs* and Albemarle Paper Co. v. Moody, (1975); height and weight requirements, *Dothard;* or rules prohibiting the employment of drug addicts, New York City Transit Authority v. Beazer (1979); arrestees, Gregory v. Litton Systems, Inc. (9th Cir.1972); convicts, Green v. Missouri Pacific R.R. Co. (8th Cir.1975); or debtors whose wages have been frequently garnished, Wallace v. Debron Corp. (8th Cir.1974).

Consider a labor union's requirement that an applicant for membership must be sponsored by an existing member, and all of them are white. When none of the 30 members admitted under this policy during a six-year period were African-Americans or Hispanic, the plaintiff had proven prima facie that this "neutral" practice had a disproportionate adverse impact on members of the protected group. E.E.O.C. v. Steamship Clerks Union, Local 1066 (1st Cir.1995). The Supreme Court has also approved the use of impact analysis to scrutinize "subjective" promotion decisions. Watson v. Fort Worth Bank and Trust (1988).

A one-time employer practice—for example, a layoff—may trigger disproportionate adverse impact analysis; the practice need not be a repeated or customary method of operation to be subject to impact scrutiny. Council 31, American Federation of State, County and Municipal Employees v. Ward (7th Cir.1992). Yet even after the 1991 Act, which codified the *Griggs* proof mode, there are decisions ruling out the use of disparate impact evidence when, in the court's view, the plaintiff fails to specify a particular aspect of an employer's subjective decision making process that is allegedly responsible for an underrepresentation of the plaintiff class. See, e.g., Anderson v. Douglas & Lomason Company (5th Cir.1994). Contra, Thomas v. Washington County School Board (4th Cir.1990).

A single component of an employer's multi-stage selection process may have unlawfully discriminatory adverse impact on the particular protected group members it screens out even if the protected group as a whole fares better than a non-minority group in the overall process. *Connecticut v. Teal.* This follows, the Court explained, because even though a plaintiff is not "discriminated against" in the disparate treatment sense intended by § 703(a)(1), neutral practices may, in the language of § 703(a)(2), "deprive or tend to deprive ... [the] individual of employment opportunities...." Section 703(a)(2) is accordingly not concerned with individual discriminatory decisions or the plaintiff group's success at the statistical "bottom line," but with particular "limitations" or "classifications" that limit the opportunity of individual members of the group to advance. So a racially balanced workforce—even one that results from affirmative action in favor of the plaintiff's protected group—does not immunize an employer from liability for a specific act of discrimination, intentional or neutral.

How to measure whether an employer's neutral practice has a "disproportionate" adverse impact on a protected group is addressed only vaguely by the Court's cases and remains unresolved by the 1991 Act. Some courts have adopted as a measure of disproportion the "eighty percent rule" from EEOC's Uniform Guidelines on Employee Selection

Procedures. These provide that a protected group's selection rate that is less than 80 percent of the rate for the group with the greatest success will be regarded by the Commission for enforcement purposes as evidence of adverse impact. 29 C.F.R. § 1607.4. *See Connecticut v. Teal,*.

But the 80% rule does not take sample size into account and thus may fail to detect statistically significant adverse impact on large samples. Further, its comparison of group pass rates may not measure the magnitude (as opposed to mere statistical significance) of a disparity as well as other techniques. Justice O'Connor, writing for a plurality in *Watson v. Fort Worth Bank & Trust,*, observed that EEOC's 80% test, while perhaps appropriate as a rough administrative guide for allocating agency prosecutorial resources, was not binding on judges. Insisting that the plaintiff should have to produce evidence that the challenged practice had a "significantly discriminatory impact," Justice O'Connor alluded to the need for a more rigorous and reliable measure of intergroup disparity. Justice O'Connor hinted that a better measure of whether a practice has legally and not just statistically significant adverse impact is the binomial distribution analysis approved by the Court for cases of systemic disparate treatment. A majority of the Court later appeared to agree with this approach. Wards Cove Packing Co. v. Atonio (1989).

Similar uncertainty has surrounded the employer defense if the plaintiff succeeds with the prima facie case. The Court wrote in *Griggs* that an employer could avoid liability if it could show that the challenged requirement was "related," either "demonstrably" or "manifestly," to the job in question, or was required by business "necessity". In *Albemarle Paper Co. v. Moody,*, the Court explained in dictum that even if an employer justifies the adverse effect of its practice by reference to a business reason, the plaintiff may still prevail by demonstrating that the employer could to some degree have satisfied the business reasons underlying its chosen practice by adopting a "less discriminatory alternative." But logically, if the plaintiff can show such an alternative, how could the employer's original challenged have been a matter of strict necessity? In *Wards Cove*, a 1989 decision, the Court required more rigorous prima facie evidence that a particular employment practice caused a specified disproportionate adverse impact on plaintiff's group; relaxed the nature and quantum of the employer's defense; and demanded that in rebuttal the plaintiff propose an alternative practice that would have fully, rather than partly, served the employer's legitimate goals with less adverse impact on plaintiff's group.

The Civil Rights Act of 1991 overrules significant aspects of *Wards Cove*. It unequivocally declares that the employer's justification to a prima facie case is an affirmative defense consisting of separate elements of job relatedness and business necessity; and it reaffirms that the employer must persuade as well as produce evidence on that defense. But it fails to clarify the magnitude of the required prima facie case of disproportionate impact; it procedurally complicates that showing by requiring the plaintiff to disentangle the effects of bundled employer practices; and it carries forward the seemingly unworkable *Wards Cove* innovation that the employer may avoid liability by adopting an alternative practice after the fact, perhaps even at the eleventh hour in the middle of a trial.

The central provision, § 703(k)(1)(A), declares that an impact-based unlawful employment practice is proved when:

(i) a complaining party demonstrates [defined in Section 701(m) as a burden of persuasion as well as production] that a respondent uses a particular employment practice that causes a disparate impact [of unspecified statistical magnitude] on the basis of race, color, religion, sex, or national origin and the respondent fails to demonstrate that the challenged practice is job related for the position in question and consistent with business necessity; or

(ii) the complaining party makes the demonstration described in subparagraph (C) with respect to an alternative employment practice and the respondent refuses to adopt such alternative employment practice.

Wards Cove had required the plaintiff to isolate the single practice among several that produces an alleged adverse impact. New § 701(k)(1)(B)(i) relieves the plaintiff who is attempting to demonstrate adverse impact under § 703(k)(1)(A)(i) from having to disentangle bundled practices, but only if she can "demonstrate" "that the elements of a respondent's decision making process [a 'process' is apparently a package of 'practices'] are not capable of separation for analysis." Section 105(a) (adding Title VII § 703(k)(1)(B)(i)). Otherwise she must show that "each particular challenged employment practice causes a disparate impact...."

A related provision, § 703(k)(1)(B)(ii), is apparently intended to apply when the plaintiff has been allowed, by virtue of § 703(*l*), to attack an entire selection process without demonstrating the adverse impact of each particular component practice. In such a case subdivision (ii) relieves the employer of showing the business necessity of any particular practice that *it* can demonstrate does not cause a disparate impact on plaintiff's group.

Wards Cove held the employer's required justification established if the defendant merely produced some evidence that the challenged practice serves, "in a significant way, the legitimate goals of the employer." *Wards Cove.* An opaque compromise in the 1991 Act somewhat stiffens this easily satisfied version of the "business necessity" prong of the defense, while also requiring the employer to show "job relatedness," a link between its chosen practice and the needs of the particular job. Once the plaintiff demonstrates that a specific practice causes a disparate impact, the employer must now "demonstrate that the challenged practice is job-related for the position in question and consistent with business necessity...." Section 105(a) (adding Title VII § 703(k)(1)(A)(i), 42 U.S.C.A. § 2000e–2(k)(1)(A)(i)) (emphasis added). The requirement to "demonstrate" these elements re-imposes on the employer, as was generally held before *Wards Cove,* the burden of persuasion on this defense.

But what do job-relatedness and business necessity now mean? A preliminary provision on legislative purpose, Section 3 of the 1991 Act, expresses the intention of codifying those concepts as they were defined by *Griggs* and in subsequent Supreme Court disparate impact decisions before *Wards Cove.* Congress adds in § 105(b) that only one specified interpretive memorandum may be "relied upon in any way as legislative history in construing or applying ... any provision of this Act that relates to *Wards Cove*–Business necessity/cumulation/alternate business practice." Unfortunately, the referenced memorandum, dated October 25, 1991, merely repeats virtually verbatim Section 3's statement that the new versions of business necessity and job relatedness are akin to those developed by the Supreme Court before *Wards Cove.*

The problem is that there was real variation in the Supreme Court's post-*Griggs,* pre-*Wards Cove* descriptions of the defense. After *Griggs,* the Court in dictum demanded a "manifest relation" between the neutral practice and requirements of the job in question. It also insisted that the neutral practice be "necessary to safe and efficient job performance...." *Albemarle Paper Co.* and *Dothard.* Later decisions, still pre-*Wards Cove*, used much looser language: the employer need only show that the challenged practice measures "skills related to effective performance" of the job in question. *Teal.*

No dimension of performance was specified, nor did the Court require any level of linkage between the employer's requirement and "effective" performance. Subsequently, in dictum or alternative holding, the Court deemed a "manifest relationship" standard met if the employer's general "legitimate employment goals of safety and efficiency" are "significantly served by—even if they do not require" the practice in question. New York City Transit Authority v. Beazer (1979). *Watson, Wards Cove's* immediate precursor, repeats the lenient *Beazer* formulation of the defense. Yet *Watson* was only a plurality opinion, and therefore may not qualify as one of the opinions of the Supreme "Court" that Section 3 identifies as authentic interpretive sources.

This chronology affords the current Court latitude to return to a relatively mild standard for the "business necessity" defense. If so, the outcome of many impact cases will ultimately hang on the fate of the plaintiff's rebuttal.

The Act appears to reject the *Wards Cove* requirement that the plaintiff show a less discriminatory alternative practice to be "equally effective," by directing a return to "the law as it existed on June 4, 1989," the day before the *Wards Cove* decision. But it also leaves open the possibility that the courts will continue to adhere to the *Wards Cove* insistence on equal effectiveness, with its focus on avoiding additional cost to the employer, because that notion was embraced by the plurality opinion in *Watson*.

Finally, even if the plaintiff meets whatever new standards the Court may ultimately demand, this rebuttal may ultimately fail because the Act carries forward another innovation of *Watson* that also attracted a majority of the Court in *Wards Cove*. Under Section 105(a)(ii), adding Title VII § 703 (k)(1)(A)(ii), there is no law violation, even if the plaintiff does demonstrate a less discriminatory alternative, unless "the respondent refuses to adopt such alternative employment practice."

It is unclear when such an employer refusal must take place to fasten liability on the employer. The provision uses the words "respondent" and "complaining party" rather than "defendant" and "plaintiff," perhaps suggesting that the employer's last chance to trump a showing of violation is during state, local or EEOC proceedings rather than at trial. But the section in which the refusal-to-adopt provision is found prescribes for the entire "title" how to establish an "unlawful employment practice" based on disparate impact. This implies that an employer may defeat the plaintiff's newly relaxed showing of a less discriminatory alternative as late as the trial on the merits. That construction is supported by the present-tense verbs in Section 703(k)(1)(A)(ii): the violation is established if the respondent "refuses to adopt" an alternative practice. The refusal, in turn, occurs only after the complaining party "makes the demonstration" of the less discriminatory alternative; and a "demonstration," as elsewhere defined in the 1991 Act, refers to a persuasion burden met during a judicial trial.

G. ADMINISTRATIVE PREREQUISITES AND PROCEDURES

1. IN GENERAL

Although 1972 amendments to Title VII gave the U.S. Equal Employment Opportunity Commission ("EEOC") the right to seek judicial relief in the first instance, most judicial action takes the form of private suits in federal district court.

The complainant must first file a written charge with the EEOC, Section 706(b), 42 U.S.C.A. § 2003–5(b). The charge must be "sufficiently precise to identify the parties and to describe generally the action or practice complained of." 29 C.F.R. § 1601.12(b) (1992). But this EEOC regulation has been construed liberally to require only the bare minimum there specified. See Downes v. Volkswagen of America, Inc. (7th Cir.1994); Waiters v. Robert Bosch Corp. (4th Cir.1982). Contra Diez v. Minnesota Mining and Manufacturing Co. (8th Cir. 1996).

In the few states that do not have statewide or local fair employment practices legislation and enforcement agencies, or where such a law does not provide jurisdiction over a particular violation, the potential Title VII plaintiff need only file a charge with EEOC within 180 days of an alleged unlawful employment practice. Section 706(e), 42 U.S.C.A.

§ 2000e–5(e). But the great majority of states do have laws prohibiting discriminatory practices that also violate Title VII and establishing one or more agencies with authority to grant or seek relief concerning those practices. In those states, Title VII requires "deferral" to the state or local agency, which must be given 60 days in which to attempt to resolve the dispute before EEOC may proceed. Section 706. The charge must be filed with EEOC within the earlier of 300 days of the alleged violation, or 30 days after the charging party receives "notice that the state or local antidiscrimination agency has terminated" proceedings under state or local law. Section 706(e), 42 U.S.C.A. § 2000e–5(e). So the scheme as a whole suggests not only that the state filing must precede a filing with EEOC, but also (subtracting 60 from 300), that the charge must ordinarily be filed with a state or local "deferral" agency within 240 days of the alleged unlawful employment practice. See Mohasco Corp. v. Silver (1980).

Nevertheless, a state or local filing later than 240 but within 300 days of the alleged unlawful practice will be considered timely—even though this would leave less than 60 days before day 300 for state or local administrative deferral—if the state or local agency "terminates" its proceedings before day 300. Moreover, the plaintiff gets the benefit of the 300–day period for filing with EEOC, and may use the 240-day "plus" schedule for filing with the state or local agency, even if the latter filing is untimely under the applicable state or local antidiscrimination law. EEOC v. Commercial Office Products (1988).

These requirements by their terms contemplate that the complainant file a charge "with" the state or local agency and then "with" EEOC. But informal administrative agreements between EEOC and many state and local deferral agencies have altered these requirement so that a filing with one can constitute a filing with the other, and the EEOC filing may even precede the local one. For example, the state or local administrative filing will be considered adequate even where the complainant has filed a charge only or initially with EEOC, if EEOC itself refers the charge to the local agency and suspends its proceedings for the required 60 days or the earlier date when local proceedings terminate. Love v. Pullman (1972). Conversely, a "work sharing" agreement may specify that where the complainant files first with a state or local agency, that agency becomes EEOC's agent for receiving the charge, even if it never forwards the charge to EEOC. See, e.g., Williams v. Washington Metropolitan Area Transit Authority (D.C.Cir.1983).

In fact, state or local agency waivers in worksharing agreements of the right to process the charge initially, or to proceed if the charge is filed more than a specified time after the occurrence of an alleged unlawful practice, have been held to constitute a "termination" of state or local proceedings that authorizes the EEOC to begin its investigation without affording the local agency 60 days. See Ford v. Bernard Fineson Dev. Ctr. (2d Cir.1996). In such jurisdictions the complainant need never file with the state or local agency and can wait to file a charge with EEOC until day 300. If it chooses, however, the state or local agency may retain jurisdiction to process the charge thereafter. *EEOC v. Commercial Office Products*. And where the state or local agency does make a determination, the statute directs EEOC to give its findings "substantial weight" in determining whether there is reasonable cause to support the charge. Section 706(b), 42 U.S.C.A. § 2000e–5(b).

There is authority that federal employees, unlike employees of private, state or local government employers, must actually *exhaust* and not just initiate their administrative remedies. Accordingly they may lose the right to sue if they reject what a court later determines to have been an offer of full relief at the agency level. Francis v. Brown (5th Cir.1995). Wrenn v. Secretary, Dept. of Veterans Affairs (2d Cir.1990).

The 180-day or 300-day charge-filing deadline periods are triggered only when the alleged unlawful employment practice is complete and when the applicant or employee knows or should know of the facts that support a claim under the statute. The accrual date is usually the date on which the complaining applicant or employee should be aware of the probable consequences and unlawfulness of employer conduct, not later when those consequences come to pass. Delaware State College v. Ricks (1980). This approach may start a charge-filing clock well before a termination is consummated, as in *Ricks;* or it may stop a clock from running until an employee learns the facts that suggest a termination was unlawful. See, e.g., E.E.O.C. v. City of Norfolk Police Dept. (4th Cir.1995). Pursuing a grievance under a collective bargaining agreement will not toll the time to file a charge with EEOC. International Union of Electrical Workers v. Robbins & Myers (1976).

The 300-day (or 180-day) EEOC charge-filing deadline, although critical, is not technically jurisdictional. Rather it is a procedural precondition to suit, analogous to a statute of limitations, and thus may be waived, estopped, or equitably tolled. Zipes v. Trans World Airlines, Inc. (1982). Active deception will toll the running of the charge-filing period until the facts that would support a charging party's allegations become or should be apparent to a person having a reasonably prudent regard for her rights. Oshiver v. Levin, Fishbein, Sedran & Berman (3d Cir.1994). Yet tolling does not necessarily require positive misconduct on the part of the employer.

Some courts have equitably tolled the 300-day EEOC filing deadline when an unrepresented claimant receives misleading or incomplete advice about filing from a state deferral agency. See, e.g., Anderson v. Unisys Corp. (8th Cir.1995). Still, plaintiff's own due diligence is a prerequisite for equitable tolling, which will not save the untimely filing of a claimant who simply waits until others similarly situated complete a successful challenge to the policy affecting them all. Chakonas v. City of

Chicago (7th Cir.1994). Further, there is no general doctrine that allegations of constructive discharge will equitably toll the relevant deadlines. Hulsey v. K-mart, Inc. (10th Cir.1994) (case under ADEA). But most circuit courts confronting the question have held that the charge-filing period is triggered in constructive discharge cases only when the plaintiff resigns, not during the antecedent course of harassment or denigration that plaintiff claims caused the resignation.

2.   CONTINUING VIOLATIONS

The judicially created continuing violations doctrine aids attacks on discriminatory acts that occurred "outside," that is, before the beginning of, the applicable Title VII charge-filing deadline. Because that deadline is 180 or at most 300 days, but the Act permits back pay to accrue as far back as two years (i.e., roughly 730 days) before the filing of an EEOC charge, Congress may have envisioned continuing remediable violations that existed prior to the running of the period. But the courts have generally limited the employer's liability to discriminatory acts that occur within the charge-filing period. Adverse *effects* of pre-period discriminatory conduct do not ordinarily revive the statute on that conduct even when those effects are felt within the period. United Air Lines, Inc. v. Evans. (1977). Ordinarily the "present consequence of a one-time violation" does not extend the period, and so the EEOC charge must be filed within 300 (or 180) days of that discrete act. See EEOC v. Westinghouse Electric Corp. (3d Cir.1983).

The relatively permissive use of the doctrine under the Equal Pay Act is explained by the fact that the sole EPA violation, discrimination in compensation, is an ongoing practice. Title VII, by contrast, also reaches a variety of employer decisions that may be deemed complete at one moment in time. For example, the Supreme Court, rejecting a simple "last day of work" rule, held that a college professor's claim of discriminatory discharge accrued when he was notified of the employer's decision to deny him tenure, not later when his appeals or grievances were denied or his contract expired. Delaware State College v. Ricks (1980). It is clear, however, that some Title VII violations are subject to the continuing violations doctrine. In Bazemore v. Friday (1986), plaintiffs challenged a public employer's pay system as racially discriminatory. The employer argued that the statute's charge filing period should run from the dates it adopted and first applied the system. But the Court held that "[e]ach week's pay check that delivers less to a black than to a similarly situated white is a wrong actionable under Title VII." And the Court also observed that even where the doctrine is inapplicable, *evidence* of past, out-of-time discrimination may be admissible because it "might in some circumstances support the inference that such discrimination continued [into the 180-day or 300-day charge-filing period], particularly where relevant aspects of the decisionmaking process had undergone little change.''

Aside from salary discrimination, continuing violations have been found respecting some ongoing denials of promotion and racial or sexual harassment that consists not of one dramatic episode but of a series of less aggravated acts that in the aggregate alter the plaintiff's conditions of employment or create a hostile or abusive work environment. Gonzalez v. Firestone Tire & Rubber Co. (5th Cir. 1980); Galloway v. General Motors Service Parts Operations (7th Cir.1996). Provided, therefore, that at least one alleged act of harassment occurred within the charge-filing period, courts will admit related evidence, antedating the beginning of that period, that constitutes part of the same general pattern of conduct. Decisions differ, however, in the required degree of nexus between the harassing conduct occurring before, and that occurring within, the charge-filing period.

The Civil Rights Act of 1991 has made resort to the continuing violation doctrine unnecessary with respect to Title VII violations caused by the unlawful adverse impact of unlawful, non-bona fide seniority systems. Overruling a Supreme Court decision, the Act provides that such violations occur not only when the system is adopted, but subsequently when a person is injured by it. Section 706(e)(2). This provision illustrates that claims alleging that an employer's neutral practice has unlawful discriminatory impact do not even accrue until the plaintiff's protected group experiences adverse effects and the plaintiff herself is denied an employment benefit through the implementation of that practice.

It is often difficult to distinguish between an ongoing unlawful practice and the delayed consequence of a single discriminatory act that took place more than 180 or 300 days before an EEOC charge was filed. The circuits are split, for example, on when the limitations period begins to run on challenges to hiring lists compiled from discriminatory test results. Compare Bouman v. Block (9th Cir. 1991) with Bronze Shields, Inc. v. New Jersey Dep't of Civil Serv. (3d Cir.1981). While a challenge to a subjective employment evaluation has been held timely if filed within a limitations period running from the date the evaluation resulted in adverse effect, another court deems the limitations period triggered by a denial of training, not the subsequent layoff resulting from the lack of training. See, respectively, Johnson v. General Electric (1st Cir. 1988) and Hamilton v. Komatsu Dresser Indus., Inc. (7th Cir.1992).

3.   FROM EEOC TO FEDERAL OR STATE COURT

The EEOC investigation ultimately arrives at one of two basic conclusions. After investigation, the Agency may find "reasonable cause" to believe that the Act has been violated, and must then undertake conciliation. Alternatively, EEOC may find "no reasonable cause" and issue a notice of dismissal. 42

U.S.C.A. § 2000e–5. In either event, a complainant is entitled upon demand to receive a "right-to-sue" letter from EEOC no later than 180 days after the effective date of the filing of a charge with the agency. Since EEOC frequently takes years to process charges, the question has arisen how long a prospective Title VII plaintiff may wait beyond 180 days before demanding a right-to-sue letter. Courts have occasionally barred Title VII actions in these circumstances on grounds of laches, when a delay of several years in demanding a suit letter was deemed unreasonable and caused tangible prejudice to the defendant. An appellate court has recently reached the opposite conclusion under ADEA, reasoning that laches cannot be a bar under a federal statute that contains a statute of limitations. Miller v. Maxwell's International, Inc. (9th Cir.1993). On the other hand, if EEOC is willing to issue the right to sue notice before the end of its 180–day period of presumptive exclusive jurisdiction, the plaintiff may proceed to court, provided she files within 90 days of receiving the notice. Sims v. Trus Joist MacMillan (11th Cir.1994).

Title VII affords plaintiffs a liberal federal venue choice among the districts where the alleged unlawful employment practice occurred; where records pertaining to the practice are maintained; or where the plaintiff allegedly would have worked but for the unlawful practice. Title VII § 706(f)(3), 42 U.S.C.A. § 2000e–5(f)(3). When the prospective defendant cannot be "found" in any of the above districts, the statute provides as a default the district where it has its principal office. The text also indicates that each of these districts is a suitable place for the action to be transferred under 28 U.S.C.A. §§ 1404 and 1406. It has been held that in considering a motion for transfer under Title VII, the court should apply the same considerations of party and witness convenience that ordinarily apply under those sections, rejecting the argument that the special Title VII venue choices are intended to give plaintiff the last word on forum selection. Ross v. Buckeye Cellulose Corp. (11th Cir.1993).

Although the vast majority of Title VII actions are brought in federal court, state courts have concurrent jurisdiction. Yellow Freight v. Donnelly (1990). A complainant who wishes to sue in either state or federal court must commence an action by filing a complaint within 90 days after receipt of the EEOC "right-to-sue" letter or notice of dismissal. That deadline is generally strictly enforced, although it, like the administrative charge-filing deadline, is apparently amenable to equitable tolling, estoppel, or waiver. See Baldwin County Welcome Center v. Brown (1984). Related actions under the Reconstruction Civil Rights Acts, notably § 1981, may be commenced even before Title VII charges have been administratively processed; but the limitations periods and administrative deadlines of the respective statutes must be satisfied independently. Johnson v. Railway Express Agency, Inc. (1975).

The right to bring a judicial lawsuit does not turn on EEOC's evaluation of the probable merits of a charge. The judicial action may be commenced even if EEOC concludes that there is no reasonable cause to believe that the employer has violated Title VII. *McDonnell Douglas*. The case may proceed even if EEOC believes that an employer offer of settlement affords the charging party full relief. An EEOC determination of no reasonable cause to believe that race discrimination allegations are true may be admissible under the public record exception to the hearsay rule in a private action for employment discrimination. Barfield v. Orange County (11th Cir.1990). Similarly, an EEOC or state agency determination that there is reasonable cause is also admissible, at least in bench trials. Heyne v. Caruso (9th Cir.1995); Gilchrist v. Jim Slemons Imports (9th Cir.1986). But see Walker v. NationsBank (11th Cir.1995). In any event, the agency's determination of "reasonable cause" or "no reasonable cause" will be given only such weight at trial as the federal court believes it deserves. If EEOC certifies to the court that a case initiated by a private party is of "general public importance," it may intervene as of right in the proceeding. Section 706(f)(1), 42 U.S.C.A. § 2000e–5(f)(1).

4. ARBITRATION AS PRECLUDING THE CIVIL LAWSUIT: THE POTENTIAL OF THE GILMER DECISION

A plaintiff subject to a collectively bargained grievance or arbitration procedure is not barred from proceeding to court under Title VII even after an unfavorable arbitral award. Alexander v. Gardner–Denver Co. (1974). But the Supreme Court, relying on the Federal Arbitration Act ("FAA"), has ruled that a securities industry employee who "voluntarily" agreed to arbitrate could not proceed to court until he had first arbitrated a claim under the Age Discrimination in Employment Act ("ADEA"). Gilmer v. Interstate/Johnson Lane Corp. (1991). The Court implied that an adverse arbitration award would bar the plaintiff's subsequent ADEA action. The Court distinguished the agreement to arbitrate in *Gardner–Denver* as (1) the product of collective bargaining rather than individual assent and (2) extending only to claims concerning the interpretation and application of the terms of the union contract, rather than claims of statutory employment discrimination.

Some federal appellate courts, relying on § 118 of the Civil Rights Act of 1991, have incrementally extended *Gilmer* beyond ADEA by compelling arbitration of claims asserted under Title VII against employees who had agreed to arbitrate as a condition of employment. See, e.g. Seus v. John Nuveen & Co. (3d Cir.1998). § 118 provides that, "to the extent authorized by law," arbitration and other "alternative" dispute resolution procedures are encouraged "to resolve disputes arising under the Acts or provisions of Federal law amended by this title"—including Title VII, ADEA, § 1981, and ADA. These courts have found that the individual employee's agreement to arbitrate evidences a voluntary personal commitment to arbitrate all claims related to that employment—a commitment enforceable under *Gilmer* and the FAA. In contrast, a recent circuit opinion reads Section 118 as precluding the compulsory arbitration of Title VII claims; it treated as compulsory rather than voluntary an agreement to arbitrate statutory claims demanded by a securities industry employer as a condition of employment. Duffield v. Robertson Stephens & Co. (9th Cir.1998).

The extent to which the federal judiciary will enforce individual employees' agreements to arbitrate discrimination claims outside the securities industry setting depends in part on how broadly the courts interpret the § 1 exception to FAA's enforcement powers. That provision excludes from FAA's reach arbitration agreements in "contracts of employment of seamen, railroad employees, or any other class of workers engaged in foreign or interstate commerce." Federal circuit courts have followed a narrow, "transportation-only" interpretation of § 1, applicable only to employment contracts of seamen, railroad workers, and other classes of workers engaged in moving goods through interstate commerce, or, somewhat more broadly, to agreements to arbitrate reached through collective bargaining. They have therefore enforced agreements to arbitrate both Title VII and ADEA claims where those agreements are found in individual employment contracts not involving transportation employees. See Patterson v. Tenet Healthcare, Inc. (8th Cir.1997).

When the agreement to arbitrate is contained in a collectively bargained agreement, most post-*Gilmer* decisions have continued to apply *Gardner–Denver,* permitting the plaintiff to pursue a statutory claim unless he individually agrees to arbitrate after a dispute has arisen. See, e.g., Brisentine v. Stone & Webster Engineering Corp. (11th Cir.1997). But one circuit court construes *Gilmer* as overriding *Gardner-Denver.* The court wrote broadly that as long as an agreement to arbitrate is voluntary, it is valid whether contained in "a securities registration application, a simple employment contract, or a collective bargaining agreement." Austin v. Owens–Brockway Glass Container, Inc. (4th Cir.1996). The Supreme Court agreed to review the Fourth Circuit's idiosyncratic approach, but in the end dodged the major issue. In Wright v. Universal Maritime Serv. Corp., 1998 U.S. Lexis 7270 (Nov. 16, 1998), the Court declined to decide if a union-negotiated, pre-dispute waiver of a judicial forum for the resolution of federal statutory employment discrimination rights could ever be validly enforced against the individual union member. Instead it held that such a waiver was not entitled to any presumption of arbitrability and must at a minimum be clear and unmistakable. Because neither the arbitration clause nor the collective bargaining agreement at issue specifically required the employer to adhere to or arbitrate claims respecting the ADA, the Court's "clear statement" requirement was not met and the grievant could not be required to arbitrate as a precondition of filing suit.

Even if *Gilmer* continues to be applied beyond ADEA to individual Title VII claims, the § 1 FAA exception remains narrow, and *Gardner–Denver* is overruled, a plaintiff may present special circumstances justifying her in bypassing arbitration or ignoring an arbitral award and proceeding to court. She could do this by showing that her particular agreement to arbitrate was not knowing and voluntary, as where it is insufficiently specific about the statutory claims the parties agreed to arbitrate. See Renteria v. Prudential Ins. Co. (9th Cir.1997). Or she may show the agreement was contained in a contract of adhesion. See Doctor's Associates, Inc. v. Casarotto (1996). Or she may show that the particular arbitration system to which she assented lacks procedural protections or remedies adequate to meet the standards of the employment discrimination statute in question. See Cole v. Burns Int'l Sec. Services (D.C.Cir.1997).

5. SUIT BY EEOC

The EEOC has an option other than issuing a determination of reasonable or no reasonable cause, followed by a notice of right to sue. It may initiate suit in its own name against private employers. See §§ 706(f)(1) and 707, 42 U.S.C.A. §§ 2000e–5(f)(1) and 2000e–6. EEOC's authority to bring "pattern or practice" suits on behalf of a class affected by an unlawful employment practice enables it to assert claims on behalf of large numbers of employees whose diverse claims might not withstand a typicality or representativeness attack under Federal Rule 23 in a private class action. EEOC v. Mitsubishi Motor Mfg. of America, Inc. (C.D.Ill.1998).

Unlike individual plaintiffs, the agency faces no fixed deadlines within which it must file suit. There is even authority that it may commence an action based on a charge filed by an employee whose own judicial action was dismissed as untimely. See EEOC v. Harris Chernin, Inc. (7th Cir.1993). Thus only a delay long enough to invoke the defense of laches serves as a check on EEOC's promptness in bringing suit. See Occidental Life Ins. Co. of California v. EEOC (1977).

But unlike private litigants, who need satisfy *only* charge-filing and action-commencement deadlines in order to sue, EEOC has other pre-suit responsibilities. It must notify the charged party within 10 days after it receives a charge and attempt during the administrative process to eliminate unlawful employment practices through "conference, conciliation, and persuasion." §§ 42 U.S.C.A. § 2000e–5(b).

If EEOC files suit before one can be commenced by a private charging party, the private party is limited to intervention in EEOC's action and may not file her own. See Behlar v. Smith (8th Cir.1983). And EEOC may attempt to preserve its suit priority by rescinding a previously issued notice of right to sue before the private action is commenced. Lute v. Singer Co. (9th Cir.1982). If, however, the charging party commences an action under Title VII before EEOC does, EEOC may only exercise its statutory right to intervene. Johnson v. Nekoosa–Edwards Paper Co. (8th Cir.1977). There is authority under the ADEA, however, that EEOC may either intervene or commence an independent action even if the complainant has filed first. EEOC v. G–K–G, Inc. (7th Cir.1994).

It has been held that a person potentially affected by an action brought by EEOC must intervene to avoid being bound by a judgment against EEOC. Adams v. Proctor & Gamble Mfg. Co. (4th Cir. 1983). But it is unclear whether this authority survives a Supreme Court decision holding that private plaintiffs must join such persons, who need not intervene and who remain free to attack judgments in actions in which they were not joined as parties. Martin v. Wilks (1989). A provision of the 1991 Act responds to *Wilks* by barring actions challenging employment practices authorized or commanded by litigated judgments or consent decrees if the challenger failed to intervene after receiving notice of the proceedings or was adequately represented in them by another party—e.g., EEOC. Section 108 (adding subsection 703(n)(1) to Title VII, 42 U.S.C.A. § 2000e–2(n)(1)).

6.   PLAINTIFF JOINDER AND CLASS ACTIONS

Title VII actions in federal court are limited by statutory requirements concerning parties and allegations. The EEOC charge which forms the predicate for a Title VII action may be filed either "by or on behalf of" a person who is "aggrieved." Section 706(f)(1). Thus named plaintiffs who have filed charges may prosecute the action on behalf of class members in a Federal Rule 23 class action, and those class members need not themselves have filed individual EEOC or state agency charges if the class is certified. *Albemarle Paper Co. v. Moody*.

Rule 23 requires:

(1) a sufficient number of class members that ordinary joinder under Rule 20 would be impracticable;

(2) questions of law or fact common to the class;

(3) claims (or, in a defendant class action, defenses) of the representative parties that are "typical" of those of the class as a whole; and

(4) a likelihood that the representative parties will fairly and adequately protect the interests of the class.

The first two requirements are usually easily met in employment discrimination class actions. Numerosity is seldom a problem, with plaintiff classes containing as few as 18 members having been certified. Cypress v. Newport News Gen. & Nonsectarian Hospital Ass'n (4th Cir.1967). And so long as the named plaintiffs assert that disparate treatment on a prohibited ground is classwide, or that one or more neutral practices has classwide impact on a protected group, the commonality requirement is also rarely a barrier. Employment discrimination by its very nature partakes of classwide discrimination.

The Supreme Court has strictly applied the third and fourth factors, typicality and representativeness. For a putative class to comply with Rule 23's requirement that the claims of the named plaintiffs be "typical" of those of the class, the complement of named plaintiffs in a private Title VII class action must usually include at least one representative who complains not only on the same prohibited ground of discrimination (e.g., race or sex) as the

putative class, but also of each discriminatory practice the class proposes to attack. General Telephone
Co. of Southwest v. Falcon (1982). The Court did
recognize an exception that permits certification,
despite diversity in the practices challenged by the
representative plaintiffs and class members, where
those practices are the product of a common device
(e.g. a test) or common decisionmaker applying the
same subjective criteria. See, e.g., Carpenter v. Ste-
phen F. Austin State University (5th Cir.1983).

Courts have read *Falcon* to require at least one of
the named plaintiffs to have allegedly suffered the
same detrimental term or condition of employment—failure to hire, unequal pay or discipline,
nonpromotion, on-the-job harassment, discharge—
as the members of each class or subclass sought to
be represented. One plaintiff response is to narrow
the attack to one or two terms and conditions of
employment (e.g., hire or promotion) or one or two
employer practices. To mount broader challenges
after *Falcon,* the named plaintiffs must assemble
diverse groups of representative plaintiffs—representing applicants, employees, and former employees; subordinates and superiors; unsuccessful test
takers and victims of discriminatory discipline;
women sexually harassed and those suffering unequal pay; persons discharged and persons not promoted. Defendants have then successfully asserted
that these diverse groups are rife with internal
conflicts, so that, in Rule 23's terms, the named
plaintiffs are not fairly "representative" of the class
members whose fate will ride with them if the class

is certified. See, e.g., Watson v. Fort Worth Bank & Trust (5th Cir.1986); Briggs v. Anderson (8th Cir. 1986).

By effectively requiring the formation of a large and diverse group of named plaintiffs, *Falcon* has more sharply put into focus the ethical concerns associated with the solicitation of additional named plaintiffs. The Court has been rather lenient about permitting plaintiff class counsel, directly or through the original clients, to encourage others similarly situated to join the named plaintiff group, particularly when the class action is serving a "private attorney general" function in combating race discrimination. Gulf Oil Co. v. Bernard (1980). *Falcon* has also spurred more elaborate and expensive motion practice about the propriety of class certification, as well as limitations on precertification discovery.

To alleviate such conflicts, plaintiffs or district courts have sometimes subdivided the class into "subclasses" that one or more of the named plaintiffs can fairly represent. On occasion, however, the result of forming subclasses is that each is smaller than the approximately 30 or so that the courts have generally required before a plaintiff group is sufficiently numerous to warrant class action certification. In this way a challenge to typicality generates a challenge to representativeness that in turn generates a challenge to numerosity. By their nature these challenges invite early consideration of the merits of the class members' claims, although the court is formally prohibited from considering those merits in determining whether to certify. Eisen v. Carlisle & Jacquelin (1974).

The rejection on the merits of class claims of systemic treatment does not bar the claims of individual class members alleging disparate treatment a la *McDonnell Douglas/Burdine.* Cooper v. Federal Reserve Bank of Richmond (1984). Moreover, when a court denies class action certification, the claims of individual class members who have not filed a charge with EEOC or commenced a judicial action may still be timely. That is, the filing of a class action tolls, until the denial of certification, both the 90–day period for filing suit and the applicable deadline (180 or 300 days) for filing a charge with EEOC. See, e.g., respectively, Crown, Cork & Seal Co. v. Parker (1983) and Griffin v. Singletary (11th Cir.1994). Even when a class is decertified because no class representative has standing to assert the claim subsequently brought by individual plaintiffs, those plaintiffs have been allowed to "piggyback" on the timely filed EEOC charges of the class action plaintiffs. But rejection of class claims on the merits has preclusive effect under federal common law in subsequent actions asserting the same pattern claims. And the pendency of a class action in which class status is denied or a class is decertified does not toll the charge-filing or action-commencement deadlines for class members who bring a subsequent *class* action—otherwise there would be "endless rounds of litigation ... over the adequacy of successive named plaintiffs to serve as class representatives."

A "single-filing" rule recognized by at least five federal circuits outside the class action context permits plaintiffs who have not filed their own EEOC charge to piggyback on a charge or charges filed by coplaintiffs. The plaintiffs are relieved of filing their own charges if the claims of all parties are based on a common employer practice or practices during the same rough time frame, and the filed charge or charges timely and adequately alerted the employer to the alleged illegality of all the practices ultimately challenged in court. EEOC v. Wilson Metal Casket Co. (6th Cir.1994) (citing cases). It is not a prerequisite to single filing that the foundation claim allege classwide discrimination. Howlett v. Holiday Inns Inc. (6th Cir.1995). The rule has also been applied to permit the plaintiff who has not filed an EEOC charge to intervene in an action brought by the plaintiff who has, or to join that action as coplaintiff after an unsuccessful attempt at intervention. See Calloway v. Partners National Health Plans (11th Cir.1993).

7. RELATION OF FEDERAL LAWSUIT TO EEOC INVESTIGATION

Since the EEOC charge is the necessary foundation for a Title VII action, the issues that may be litigated in federal court will be tied to some degree to the contents of the charge. But recognizing that EEOC charges are often drafted by unrepresented employees ill-equipped to craft them technically, courts have permitted Title VII plaintiffs to try claims "like or related to allegations contained in the charge and growing out of such allegations during the pendency of the case before the Commission." Sanchez v. Standard Brands, Inc. (5th Cir. 1970).

The widespread adoption of the Sanchez rule gives defendants an incentive to try to limit the scope of EEOC proceedings. Generalizations about the meaning of "like or related" are hazardous. But allegations in a Title VII judicial complaint that add a new *ground* of discrimination (race or sex, for instance) are less likely to be entertained than are allegations that touch on additional *terms or conditions of employment* or implicate other potential plaintiffs in different departments or divisions. Even then, plaintiffs whose administrative charges complained of adverse treatment respecting limited terms and conditions of employment will be permitted to target in court only those other terms and conditions of employment that EEOC could reasonably have been expected to investigate based on the charge. See Park v. Howard Univ. (D.C.Cir.1995).

The Seventh Circuit appears to be moving to an alternative, and apparently stricter, standard: whether the claims in the judicial action are "fairly encompassed" within or "implied" by the charge the plaintiff filed with EEOC. Decisions applying the new standard have precluded allegations by the same plaintiff, on the same prohibited ground, if they attack different terms and conditions of employment or implicate different individuals from those targeted by the EEOC charge. Chambers v.

American Trans Air, Inc. (7th Cir.1994); Kirk v. FPM Corp. (7th Cir.1994).

An especially liberal application of the charge-filing requirement permits a plaintiff to press a retaliation claim under § 704, without having filed a separate EEOC charge of retaliation, where that claim grows out of a properly filed charge of discrimination violating § 703. See, e.g., Malarkey v. Texaco, Inc. (2d Cir.1993). But that liberality is extended only when the underlying charge of primary discrimination was itself timely. Jones v. Runyon (10th Cir.1996). Some circuits have limited the federal court's ancillary jurisdiction in such cases to charges of alleged retaliation occurring after, and not before, the filing of the underlying charge. McKenzie v. Illinois Department of Transportation (7th Cir.1996).

8. EMPLOYER RECORDKEEPING REQUIREMENTS

Pursuant to Section 709(c),EEOC has promulgated regulations requiring employers to maintain records pertinent to a wide range of employment decisions. These require employers to retain all personnel records for six months after they are created and, when a charge is filed, to retain all records relevant to that charge "until final disposition of the charge or action." 29 C.F.R. § 1602.14 (1994). In employment discrimination actions, the employer has custody of virtually all records critical to resolution of the disputed claim; hence in the reported decisions it is the employer that allegedly violated the Title VII recordkeeping requirements.

But judicial enforcement of employer recordkeeping violations has generally been conspicuously lenient. Typically the courts of appeals that have found employers to have destroyed documents in violation of the EEOC regulation give the plaintiff the benefit of a "presumption that the destroyed documents would have bolstered her case." See, e.g., Favors v. Fisher (8th Cir.1994). But then they either assume or conclude that the presumption was "overcome"—the evidence for which may simply be an innocent explanation by an authorized employer agent, coupled with his assertion that he had not been instructed to preserve records in accordance with the government regulation. And sanctions have typically been mild: requiring the defendant to bear the costs of record reconstruction; limiting its production of evidence on the matters reflected in the destroyed documents; or invoking the presumption that the records would have supported plaintiff's case. See EEOC v. Jacksonville Shipyards, Inc. (M.D.Fla.1988).

H. TITLE VII REMEDIES

1. REINSTATEMENT AND BACK PAY

The range of judicial remedial authority is prescribed by § 706(g). This section provides for injunctions and "such affirmative action as may be appropriate," including orders directing reinstatement or hire, back pay, and other equitable relief. It also "limits" a defendant's back pay liability retrospectively to no earlier than two years before the filing of a charge with EEOC. "Limits" is placed in quotation marks because a complainant need only file a charge with EEOC within 180 days, in the handful of states that do not have their own local antidiscrimination laws and agencies, or 300 days in the majority of states that do. Thus in effect the 2-year "limit" on back pay authorizes its award earlier than the "trigger" date that starts the running of Title VII's administrative charge-filing deadlines.

Prevailing plaintiffs are routinely awarded injunctions against ongoing violations. Where disparate treatment has been proved, reinstatement may be ordered; if there is no position available at the time of judgment, the plaintiff may receive priority in filling vacancies. Anderson v. Phillips Petroleum Co. (10th Cir.1988). Reinstatement may be denied, however, where the discriminatee, although qualified when unlawfully rejected, is no longer qualified for the position in question at the time of judgment. See, e.g., *McKennon*; Kamberos v. GTE Automatic Electric, Inc. (7th Cir.1979).

Back pay is also awarded almost as a matter of course. This is because, as the Supreme Court has explained, back pay serves both of the Act's remedial goals: to restore discrimination victims to the approximate status they would have enjoyed absent discrimination, and to deter employer violations. Accordingly, the Court, while recognizing that federal judges enjoy some discretion to withhold any

Title VII remedy in particular circumstances, held in *Albemarle Paper Co. v. Moody* that back pay may be denied only for unusual reasons which, if applied generally, would not impede those remedial objectives. For example, the "neutral practice/disproportionate adverse impact" case dispenses with evidence of discriminatory intent. Accordingly, a general good faith exception to back pay liability would seriously erode the advantages of that mode of proof. The Court has consequently rejected such an exception. *Albemarle.* The presumption in favor of back pay has been overcome where a ruling was a "marked departure from past practice" and the brunt of the requested remedy would fall on innocent third parties—pensioners or current employees. Los Angeles Dep't of Water and Power v. Manhart (1978). The Court also held that the states' ordinary Eleventh Amendment immunity from federal court monetary awards is overridden in Title VII actions because Congress enacted the statute in at least partial reliance on its Fourteenth Amendment power to enforce the Equal Protection Clause. Fitzpatrick v. Bitzer (1976).

Back pay is the compensation the employee has lost as a result of defendant's violations from the date of the adverse employment decision through the date of final judgment. The plaintiff must make efforts to mitigate her losses. Back pay awards are reduced by amounts the plaintiff earned, or with reasonable diligence could have earned, since the date of a discharge or failure or refusal to hire. Booker v. Taylor Milk Co. (3d Cir.1995). Self-employment is an acceptable form of mitigation for this purpose. Smith v. Great American Restaurants, Inc. (7th Cir.1992). The back pay clock should stop when "the sting" of discriminatory conduct has ended. Syvock v. Milwaukee Boiler Mfg. Co. (7th Cir.1981).

The requirement of filing suit within 90 days after receipt of the EEOC's notice of right to sue means that most Title VII judicial actions will be commenced well before two years have expired after the filing of the EEOC charge. Title VII nevertheless authorizes the award of back pay for violations that occurred up to two years before that charge was filed. This sometimes makes back pay recoverable for "continuing violations" that began before the last event that triggers Title VII's 300-day (or, in nondeferral states, 180-day) "statute of limitations." See, e.g., Palmer v. Kelly (D.C.Cir.1994)

Although the 1991 Act adds compensatory and punitive damages as "legal" remedies to the Title VII plaintiff's arsenal, it does not change the "equitable" character of the pre-existing remedies like back pay. Determination of eligibility for back pay, although virtually automatic under the *Albemarle* presumption, is therefore formally for the court, not the jury, as is the critical calculation of the back pay amount. Yet at least one circuit has held that "the issue of reasonable mitigation is ultimately a question of fact for the jury." *Smith*. EEOC Guidelines recognize a "no-injury" defense but require the employer to prove by "clear and convincing" evidence that, despite its discriminatory conduct, the plaintiff suffered no harm as a result. 29 C.F.R. §§ 1614.203, 1614.501(b), (c).

Because each species of Title VII relief before the 1991 Civil Rights Act was considered equitable, jury trials were not available unless a Title VII claim was joined with a claim for legal relief—for instance, a claim under § 1981. There clearly is a jury trial right under § 1981. *Johnson v. Railway Express Agency, Inc.* Where an action presents claims under both statutes, the right to jury trial under § 1981 may not be estopped by the prior bench trial of an equitable claim. Rather, prior jury determinations of facts reached in deciding the legal, § 1981 claims should be adopted by the trial court when it later determines any equitable claims under Title VII. Cf. Lytle v. Household Manufacturing, Inc. (1990).

Before the 1991 amendments, the "equity" characterization also limited the available monetary relief under Title VII to back pay and attorney's fees, precluding more generous measures such as emotional distress or punitive damages. Some courts also denied nominal damages, viewing them as compensatory in nature. But prejudgment interest, as well as the standard post-judgment interest allowed by 28 U.S.C.A. § 1961 "on any money judgment in a civil case recovered in a district court," is integrally related to back pay. It is therefore routinely awarded in Title VII actions; and its denial may be an abuse of discretion. Sellers v. Delgado Community College (5th Cir.1988), absent unusual reasons.

Any prevailing party, plaintiff or defendant, is also eligible for an award of "costs" under Federal Rule of Civil Procedure 54(d). These are limited, however, to items specified by 28 U.S.C.A. § 1920: clerk and marshal fees, fees by court reporters for transcripts "necessarily obtained for use in the case"; printing disbursements and witness fees; specified docket fees; and fees for court-appointed experts and certain interpreters. Most important, "costs" as used in Rule 54(d) do *not* include the prevailing party's attorneys' fees. But § 701(k) of Title VII separately provides that a prevailing party may recover a reasonable attorney's fee as part of "costs." See Chapter 20 Section E. For purposes of calculating postjudgment interest, these statutorily shifted attorneys' fees shall be included as part of the judgment. Carter v. Sedgwick County, Kansas (10th Cir.1994). Section 113 authorizes the court to include the fees of experts, without a specific cap, as part of the award of attorneys' fees to prevailing Title VII plaintiffs.

2. COMPENSATORY AND PUNITIVE DAMAGES FOR TITLE VII AND AMERICANS WITH DISABILITIES ACT VIOLATIONS AFTER NOVEMBER 20, 1991

Section 102 of the Civil Rights Act of 1991, codified at 42 U.S.C.A. § 1981a, authorizes jury trials and compensatory and punitive damages for claimants alleging intentional discrimination in actions under, among other statutes, Title VII and the Americans With Disabilities Act. These remedies are "in addition to any relief authorized by" § 706(g) of Title VII. Section 102 (adding § 1977A(1) to the Revised Statutes, 42 U.S.C.A. § 1977A(1)), 42 U.S.C.A. § 1981a(a)(1). The compensatory portion of an award "shall not include backpay, interest on backpay, or any other type of relief authorized under" § 706(g) of Title VII—in other words, the equitable relief available before the Civil Rights Act of 1991. 42 U.S.C.A. § 1981a(b)(2). In terms the Act provides that compensatory and punitive damages are available only if the "complaining party cannot recover under 42 U.S.C.A. 1981." But the EEOC and some courts have interpreted the latter restriction to bar only double recovery under Title VII and § 1981, not to interfere with administrative or judicial processing of claims under either statute prior to judgment. See EEOC Policy Guide on Compensatory and Punitive Damages Under 1991 Civil Rights Act, July 7, 1992, BNA Fair Employment Manual 405:7091, 7092 (1992)(hereinafter, "EEOC Damages Guidance").

The Act expressly denies compensatory or punitive damages to challengers of facially neutral practices. Title VII plaintiffs who prevail only by demonstrating the disproportionate adverse impact of neutral practices, or ADA plaintiffs who demonstrate only a failure to reasonably accommodate by an employer who "demonstrates good faith efforts," are still limited to the preexisting equitable Title VII remedies of prospective relief and back and front pay. See 42 U.S.C.A. § 1981a(a)(1) and 42 U.S.C.A. § 1981a(a)(3).

Section 1981a also makes compensatory, but not punitive, damages available to plaintiffs who prosecute intentional discrimination claims successfully against a government agency or subdivision. Compare § 102(b)(2) with § 102(b)(1). Punitive damages are authorized against nongovernmental defendants who are proven to have engaged in an unlawful discriminatory practice "with malice or with reckless indifference to the federally protected rights of an aggrieved individual." 42 U.S.C.A. § 1981a(b)(1). Although the precise standards governing jury awards of punitive damages will require considerable case law explication by analogy to punitive damages in tort, it has already been held that, as under §§ 1981 and 1983, compensatory damages are not a prerequisite to a punitive award. See Smith v. Wade (1983) (case under § 1983).

Section 1981a(b)(3) places dollar caps, varying with employer size, on the *sum* of "compensatory" and "punitive" damages "for each complaining party." These caps are set at $50,000 for businesses that employ between 15 and 100 persons; $100,000 where the employer has between 101 and 200 employees; $200,000 where the employer has between 201 and 500 employees; and $300,000 for all employers with 501 or more employees. Section 102(b)(3), 42 U.S.C.A. § 1981a(b)(3). EEOC has concluded that "all covered employment agencies and labor organizations with 100 or fewer employees are subject to the $50,000 cap on damages." EEOC Damages Guidance, at 405:7093. A plaintiff's argument for recovering up to the cap separately for compensatory and punitive damages has been rejected; the cap defines the maximum amount available for both kinds of harm defined. Hogan v. Bangor and Aroostook R.R. (1st Cir.1995). On the other hand, where there are multiple parties who have joined together under FRCP 20 or 23 to assert common claims, "Each complaining party may receive (to the extent appropriate) up to the cap amount." EEOC Memorandum on Computation of Compensatory and Punitive Damages (April 18, 1995). § 1981a(c)(2) further provides that "the court shall not inform the jury" about the statutory damages caps. This stricture has been held also to preclude counsel from referring to the caps, for example during closing argument. Sasaki v. Class (4th Cir.1996).

Capped "compensatory damages" are defined by § 1981a(b)(3) to include monetary relief for "future pecuniary losses, emotional pain, suffering, inconvenience, mental anguish, loss of enjoyment of life, and other nonpecuniary losses...." "Pecuniary" losses include "quantifiable" losses such as moving and job search expenses and psychiatric, physical therapy, and other medical expenses. EEOC Damages Guidance, at 405:7095. "Nonpecuniary losses" include damages for "intangible injuries of emotional harm such as emotional pain, suffering, inconvenience, mental anguish, and loss of enjoyment of life," as well as injury to professional standing, character, reputation, credit standing, or health. 405:7096. Traditional authority to the effect that an award for emotional distress might rest on the plaintiff's own testimony, without specific evidence of the economic value of that loss, see, e.g., Bolden v. SEPTA (3d Cir.1994) (collecting cases), is being tested by recent decisions that insist on corroborating testimony by a spouse, co-workers, friends, relatives and perhaps even treating or other medical experts. See Fitzgerald v. Mountain States Telephone and Telegraph Co. (10th Cir.1995).

Read in isolation, Section 1981a(b)(3) caps future pecuniary losses and all "claims that typically do not lend themselves to precise quantification, i.e., punitive damages . . . and [past or future] nonpecuniary losses." EEOC Damages Guidance at 405:7094. In other words, only *past pecuniary* losses like backpay and interest on backpay are uncapped by § 1981a(b)(3) standing alone. But the immediately preceding subsection, § 1981a(b)(2) provides, "Compensatory damages awarded under [and capped by] this section *shall not include* backpay, interest on backpay, *or any other type of relief authorized under section 706(g) of the Civil Rights Act of 1964.*" So if the "compensatory damages" capped by subsection (3) take into account the exclusions in the final phrase of subsection (2), *all* Title VII relief that was traditionally available before the 1991 amendments, not just backpay, is excepted from the caps. EEOC Damages Guidance, 405:7094.

The two subsections collide on the remedy of "front pay," a discretionary monetary remedy granted by the court if reinstatement is impossible, impracticable or inequitable. Front pay is awarded in an amount that estimates the total future salary, pension and other benefits the plaintiff, absent an unlawful discriminatory discharge, would have earned with the employer from date of judgment until probable loss of job or date of retirement. Because it is calculated on the basis of highly speculative assumptions about the health of the business, the health of the plaintiff, the plaintiff's future satisfactory work performance and prospects for advancement, front pay is devilishly difficult to measure. Regardless of whether front pay is viewed as compensating for "nonpecuniary" or "future pecuniary" loss, it represents "compensatory damages" within the meaning of § 1981a(b)(3). See Hudson v. Reno (6th Cir.1997).

But front pay was frequently, although not invariably, held available under Title VII before the 1991 Civil Rights Act amendments first authorized legal relief. Accordingly, EEOC considers it a type of equitable relief previously "authorized under Section 706(g) of the Civil Rights Act of 1964"; therefore excluded from the § 1981a(b)(2) definition of "compensatory damages"; and consequently not part of the "compensatory damages" that are subject to the § 1981a(b)(3) cap. EEOC Damages Guidance, at 405:7094. The Sixth Circuit disagrees. *Hudson.*

On its face the "malice ... or reckless indifference" required by § 1981a(b)(1) for punitive damages in Title VII or Americans with Disabilities Act cases seems indistinguishable from the standard the Supreme Court announced for punitive damages under §§ 1983 or 1981: juries may assess punitive damages "when the defendant's conduct is shown to be motivated by evil motive or intent, or when it involves reckless or callous indifference to the federally protected rights of others." *Smith v. Wade.* This Reconstruction Act standard has sometimes but by no means always been construed to permit a jury to award punitive damages based solely on the evidence that establishes an intentional violation, with no necessary additional showing of any particular state of mind on the part of the defendant. See, e.g. Barbour v. Merrill (D.C.Cir.1995). But see Jackson v. Pool Mortgage Co. (10th Cir.1989). But in Title VII and ADA cases governed by § 1981a(b)(1), almost all circuit courts considering the question have adopted a two-tiered structure that demands not only conduct constituting an intentional violation, but also a judicial finding of egregious or willful conduct before a jury may award punitives. See e.g. Kolstad v. American Dental Association (D.C.Cir.1998). But see Luciano v. Olsten Corp. (2d Cir.1997).

Punitives are clearly available where there is evidence of malice or ill will directed against the plaintiff. See, e.g., Soderbeck v. Burnett County (7th Cir.1985). Malice will normally be found where there is proof of retaliation for opposing at least well founded complaints of unlawful activity. See, e.g., Hunter v. Allis–Chalmers (7th Cir.1986). EEOC suggests that the following additional unweighted factors should be taken into account: egregiousness of the conduct, as where it shocks or offends the conscience; the nature, extent and severity of the harm suffered by the complaining party; duration of the discriminatory conduct; whether the respondent engaged in similar conduct in the past; evidence of conspiracy or cover-up; and the employer's response after notice to discriminatory conduct by its agents. EEOC Damages Guidance, at 405:7100–7101.

Absent one or more of these probative factors, there is a wide range of circumstances in which the propriety of punitives is uncertain. At one extreme, it seems clear that mere proof of an intentional violation does not warrant a punitive award in a variety of situations analogous to the ADA defendant that is expressly exempt from punitives if it makes a good-faith but ultimately inadequate effort to reasonably accommodate an employee's disability. For example, the employer may have been unaware of a statutory prohibition, reasonably believed that its conduct was not reached by the prohibition, or relied plausibly on an affirmative defense that privileged its conduct. See, e.g., Hazen Paper Co. v. Biggins (1993). At the other extreme, a trial court's instructions were held to authorize punitive damages in a Reconstruction Act case when, in addition to proof of an intentional wrong, it advised the jury that such awards were designed to punish the defendant for "outrageous conduct" and "to deter him and others like him from similar conduct in the future." *Rowlett v. Anheuser–Busch*.

Courts have particularly struggled with establishing reasonable limits on the amount of a punitive award. In general, the award should "bear some relation" to the nature of defendant's conduct and the harm it caused. *Id.* One circuit, for example, has held that a punitive award may not be given in the maximum amount permitted by an applicable cap unless the violation was egregious. Hennessy v. Penril Datacomm Networks, Inc. (7th Cir.1995). Compare Emmel v. Coca–Cola Bottling Co. of Chicago (7th Cir.1996). Taking defendant's resources into account, the award should "sting" rather than "destroy." Keenan v. City of Philadelphia (E.D.Pa. 1991). EEOC has summarized a number of factors relevant to ascertaining the defendant's financial position for this purpose. EEOC Damages Guidance, at 405:7101–7102. But the agency takes the position that in general punitive awards under Title VII and ADA should rarely be found grossly excessive, because the sum of punitive damages together with future pecuniary and all nonpecuniary losses (like punitive damages) must stay within the caps of § 1981a(b)(3). EEOC Damages Guidance, at 405:7101 n.18.

3. TAX TREATMENT OF SETTLEMENT OR JUDGMENT PROCEEDS IN EMPLOYMENT DISCRIMINATION CASES

On August 20, 1996, President Clinton signed the Small Business Job Protection Act, which made the following underlined additions to the text of Section 104(a)(2) of the Internal Revenue Code:

(a) .... gross income does not include-

(2) the amount of any damages (*other than punitive damages*) received (whether by suit or agreement . . .) on account of personal *physical* injuries or *physical* sickness;

The Act also added to Section 104(a):

For purposes of paragraph (2), emotional distress shall not be treated as a physical injury or physical sickness. The preceding sentence shall not apply to an amount of damages not in excess of the amount paid for medical care . . . attributable to emotional distress.

The English translation? *Physical* injury is the ordinary precondition for exclusion from gross income under Section 104(a)(2). Accordingly, in the usual Title VII or ADEA case, where the employer's conduct does not cause "physical" injury or sickness, the great bulk of any judgment or settlement will be ineligible for exclusion—i.e., will be fully taxable. Because the first sentence of the addendum specifically excludes emotional distress from the Section 104(a)(2) definition of "physical" injury or sickness, the part of any settlement or judgment representing recovery for the intangible harms of emotional distress will also be nonexcludable, except where there is separate tangible physical injury. The only excludible portion of a settlement or judgment in a non-physical case would be the relatively minor component that represents reimbursement of medical expenses for treatment of emotional distress. But where an employment discrimination plaintiff does suffer some "physical" injury as the result of the defendant's conduct, he may exclude "any damages" received in respect of those injuries, including those awarded for intangible emotional distress. Finally, because of the "(other than punitive damages)" language, punitive damages will now almost never be eligible for exclusion in employment discrimination cases, even when awarded in cases of *physical* injury.

I. RETROACTIVE SENIORITY FOR PROVEN VICTIMS OF DISCRIMINATION: A FIRST LOOK AT THE PROBLEM OF "REVERSE DISCRIMINATION"

More complex and controversial than the availability of back pay in Title VII actions are awards of retroactive "remedial" seniority to victorious discriminatees who secure orders directing their hire, promotion or reinstatement. Remedial seniority helps restore proven victims or "discriminatees" to their "rightful place"—the rung on the ladder to which they likely would have climbed between the date of discrimination and date of judgment—by providing them the level of economic benefits (e.g. vacations, rate of pay) they probably would have received had they remained in the employ of the defendant. Because the benefits geared to retroactive seniority are paid by the adjudicated wrongdoer (the employer), the award serves both Title VII remedial objectives, deterrence and compensation.

In Franks v. Bowman Transportation Co. (1976), the Supreme Court held that retroactive remedial seniority for benefits purposes is presumptively available on the same, virtually universal terms as back pay. The Court rejected the argument that § 703(h)—which insulates bona fide seniority systems from being declared unlawful, and therefore protects them from *wholesale* dismantling by injunction—prohibits the *incremental* adjustment of the seniority ladder that results when judges award discriminatees fictional, retroactive seniority as a remedy for discrimination in hiring, assignment or promotions. The Court also agreed that an award of retroactive seniority, because it is essential to redress proven discrimination, is also not a "preference" prohibited by § 703(j).

"Competitive" unlike "benefits" retroactive seniority serves the additional purpose of improving the discriminatees's position relative to other employees in competing for scarce job resources—better-paying positions, more favorable hours, or protection against demotion or layoff. Unlike seniority for benefits purposes, retroactive "competitive" seniority is not paid for by the defendant, it therefore furthers only the goal of compensation, not employer deterrence. In *Franks,* the Court recognized that retroactive competitive seniority is not preferential and is necessary to make a proven victim of discrimination whole; without it, she is vulnerable to layoff, termination or simply poorer job assignments without any of the seniority protection that she would almost surely have earned absent the employer's unlawful conduct. It therefore held, following *Albemarle Paper Co. v. Moody*, that the "competitive" as well as the "benefits" brand of retroactive fictional seniority is presumptively available.

But only a year later the Court drew back from authorizing the automatic or immediate implementation of retroactive seniority for competitive purposes. *International Brotherhood of Teamsters v. United States.* Unlike the situation in *Franks,* immediate implementation of retroactive competitive seniority in *Teamsters* would have immediately and visibly, rather than only potentially harmed incumbent employees; restoring the discriminatees to "their" rung on the seniority ladder would have delayed the recall date of incumbent employees who were already out on recall. Without formally disturbing the *Franks* presumption, the Court took its cue from Justice Powell's concurring opinion in that decision. It directed trial judges to exercise "qualities of mercy and practicality" to decide "when" and "the rate at which" discriminatees may receive retroactive competitive seniority. The unweighted equities thrown in the balance include the number of protected and non-protected group persons interested in the scarce resource, the number of current vacancies, and the economic prospects of the industry. *Teamsters* left undisturbed the *Franks* holding that seniority for *benefits* purposes should be implemented uncontingently and immediately after issuance of a judgment.

Although the Supreme Court has implied that § 706(g) provides limited discretion to "bump" an incumbent employee in order to reinstate a "discriminatee," lower courts have displayed great reluc-

tance to do so. See, e.g., Walsdorf v. Board of
Commissioners (5th Cir.1988). They have instead
sometimes awarded discriminatees "front pay."
Front pay is a discretionary remedy granted by the
court as a substitute for reinstatement if reinstatement is impossible, impracticable or inequitable. It
may be the only feasible way to make a victim of
discrimination whole where there is no available
position in which to reinstate her, or where, as in a
constructive discharge or other harassment case,
reinstatement would be unsuccessful or unproduc-
tive because of the workplace hostility that either
prompted the claim or resulted from its prosecution. See, e.g., Robinson v. Southeastern Pennsylvania Transportation Authority (3d Cir.1993).

Circuit courts, before the 1991 Act, typically held
front pay available under Title VII. See, e.g., Weav-
er v. Casa Gallardo, Inc. (11th Cir.1991). The principal argument against front pay revolved around
the fact that all Title VII remedies were then equitable, and some judges characterized front pay as
"legal." Now that the 1991 Act adds legal remedies
to the menu of relief under Title VII, the Supreme
Court, in dictum, has noted the availability of front
pay with approval. United States v. Burke (1992).

Front pay leaves the incumbent in place and,
beginning at final judgment, orders the employer to
pay the discriminatee an amount equivalent to what
he would earn if actually reinstated. See *American
Tobacco Co. v. Patterson*. Because of the uncertain
duration of the period during which the victim of
discrimination may remain employed after judg-

ment, or at what level and pay, the front pay remedy is fraught with computational difficulties and entails "predicting the future." See Griffin v. Michigan Dept. of Corrections (6th Cir.1993).

Front pay will not necessarily terminate when plaintiff quits subsequent, substitute employment; on the other hand, in recognition of the duty to mitigate, the employer need only pay such a plaintiff the difference between the amount she would have received had she remained employed (or secured substantially equivalent employment) and the amount she could have continued to receive in the *lesser*-paying substitute job that she quit. Shore v. Federal Express Corp. (6th Cir.1994). It appears that courts also enjoy equitable discretion to reduce the front pay award by amounts received from "collateral sources," a question on which the circuits are split as applied to backpay. All that can be said with confidence is that purely arbitrary limits on front pay may be overturned as an abuse of the trial court's discretion. See, e.g., Carter v. Sedgwick County, Kansas (10th Cir.1994). On occasion, awards of as long as 25 years have been made when that represents plaintiff's first eligibility for a full pension. Padilla v. Metro–North Commuter Railroad (2d Cir.1996).

Lower courts have divided over how to allocate front pay issues between judge and jury. The First Circuit, for example, appears to allow juries to determine not only the amount of front pay but the threshold question of its availability. Sinai v. New England Telephone & Telegraph Co. (1st Cir.1993).

By contrast, the Sixth Circuit insists that the propriety of any front pay is an equitable question for the court that "must ordinarily precede ... submission of the case to the jury." Roush v. KFC National Management Co. (6th Cir.1993). The Ninth Circuit agrees that the jury decides only the appropriate amount, and must reduce the amount of a front pay award to the extent it finds the plaintiff failed reasonably to mitigate damages. In computing an appropriate amount, the jury may rely on lay testimony about future earnings and other compensation, as well as appropriate inflation and discount rates. Cassino v. Reichhold Chemicals, Inc. (9th Cir.1987).

J. AFFIRMATIVE ACTION BY "VOLUNTARY" PROGRAMS AND JUDICIAL DECREES

"Voluntary," "benign" employer affirmative action, and reverse discriminatory remedies imposed by court order or consent decree, raise similar yet legally distinct questions of fairness as between minority and majority group employees. Strictly speaking, employer affirmative action in the form of self-imposed quotas or goals does not really implicate the judiciary's remedial authority under § 706(g) at all. An employer simply institutes racial or gender preferences, without court compulsion, typically to avoid lawsuits by the group benefiting from the preference or to preserve federal contracts that require affirmative action. Such a plan is unlawful, if at all, because it operates to prefer members of defined minority or female groups or classes, rather than individuals proven to have suffered discrimination at the hands of the defendant employer. As a result, these preferences are suspect under § 703 as ordinary unlawful employment practices directed against any majority group members or males who are denied employment opportunities by the plan. See, e.g., Billish v. City of Chicago (7th Cir.1992). The jeopardy would seem considerable because the Court has regularly emphasized that the statute seeks to protect individuals from discrimination on the basis of group characteristics, rather than groups as such. See, e.g., *Teal, McDonald v. Santa Fe Trail, Manhart.*

But the Supreme Court, in a landmark 1979 opinion that expressly exalted assumed legislative "spirit" over statutory text, gave qualified approval to "voluntary," "benign" racial preferences. United Steelworkers v. Weber (1979). A majority held that the employer there had lawfully taken race into account in preferring black employees as a group for admission to an on-the-job training program—a preference that on its face violated the specific terms of § 703(d). The Court acknowledged that the white race of Brian Weber was the factor that resulted in his denial of the employment benefit, in apparent violation of that section. But it concluded from the spirit animating Title VII that Congress would not have intended § 703 to apply in the context of the "benign" program at issue. The Court relied instead on a weak negative pregnant from § 703(j), which provides that nothing in Title VII shall "require" employers with work forces racially imbalanced vis-a-vis surrounding local population percentages to grant minorities preferential treatment in order to redress such imbalances.

It appeared from the *Weber* opinion that an employer could justifiably adopt race-conscious programs of this type whenever it found a manifest underrepresentation of blacks in a traditionally segregated job category; the employer need not first uncover evidence of its *own* prior discrimination in filling those positions. And the plan in *Weber* was approved despite being arguably involuntary; it was adopted after the Office of Federal Contract Compliance Programs had threatened the employer with debarment from federal contracts under Executive Order 11246 if it did not increase its skilled minority representation. The *Weber* majority listed a number of factors circumscribing the scope of such lawful "benign" discrimination. It observed that the employer plan before it did not require white employees to be discharged and therefore did not "unnecessarily trammel" their interests; that it did not absolutely bar white employees from the skilled positions, but merely limited their numbers; and that it was a temporary measure, intended not to maintain a racial balance but to eliminate a manifest imbalance in the skilled job categories.

The Court later extended the *Weber* principle by upholding an explicit *gender* preference for *promotions,* this time in the face of the apparently plain prohibition of § 703(a). Johnson v. Transportation Agency of Santa Clara County (1987). Justice Brennan for the majority confirmed that the employer need not itself have firm or indeed any evidence of its own prior discrimination against the group that benefits from the program. Instead, it is a sufficient predicate for instituting a race- or gender-based affirmative action program that the beneficiary group is underrepresented in a traditionally segregated job category for any reason—societal prejudice, self-selection, or discrimination by other businesses or unions. Further, "underrepresentation" may be measured in relation to that group's representation in the surrounding labor market, unrefined for interest or qualifications. And the Court even dispensed with the necessity of a specific end date for the program, because no specific number of slots were set aside for members of the beneficiary group.

Still, lawful race-conscious affirmative action must probably have the purpose of remedying the effects of someone's past discrimination. Cunico v. Pueblo School District No. 60 (10th Cir.1990). For example, in a highly-publicized reverse-discrimination case, a public school system's desire for racial diversity among its faculty was held not a permissible purpose justifying the severe harm of layoff to a nonminority employee under Title VII—even assuming that Title VII would permit more race-conscious preferential treatment than would the Supreme Court's current race-neutral concept of equal protection. United States v. Board of Education of Piscataway (D.N.J.1993).

Affirmative action plans have fared less well when challenged as violations of equal protection. For example, the Court has concluded that a public employer, before instituting such a program, must have "convincing evidence" of its own prior discrimination and must employ means narrowly tailored to rectify that conduct. Wygant v. Jackson Board of Education (1986). The collective bargaining agreement there required the layoff of nonminority teachers with greater seniority than minority teachers who were retained, a feature that might also have offended the *Weber* limit of "unnecessary trammeling." In any event, the *Wygant* plurality's approach subsequently commanded a majority when the Court struck down a municipal program that set aside a minimum amount of subcontracting work for minority business enterprises. The Court insisted that the Equal Protection Clause is violated whenever government takes race into account unless (1) it has a compelling justification and (2) the means adopted are narrowly tailored to go only so far as that justification requires. City of Richmond v. J.A. Croson Co. (1989). A circuit court, taking note of the first of these requirements, has observed that a local government will now be hard pressed to justify a race-based setaside program unless it can offer current statistical evidence demonstrating its own prior discriminatory practices and their ongoing effects. Associated General Contractors of Connecticut, Inc. v. New Haven, Connecticut (2d Cir.1994).

In public contracting and employment settings, redressing general societal or historical discrimination against African–Americans has not proven a sufficiently compelling justification for racial preferences. Race may now be a constitutional factor in distributing benefits only to redress a governmental unit's own prior discrimination, and only as long as and to the extent necessary to remedy the discriminatory injury that unit inflicted. See, e.g., *City of Richmond v. Croson,* supra (plurality opinion). But no formal, judicial determination of past discrimination by the governmental unit in question is necessary to show the requisite compelling governmental interest. See *Croson.* Still, the evidence of such discrimination must be "strong" or "convincing." United Black Firefighters Ass'n v. City of Akron (6th Cir.1992). For this purpose the plaintiff may rely on statistical evidence of the kind that establishes a prima facie case of systemic disparate treatment under Title VII—evidence reflecting a gross disparity between, on one hand, the number of protected group members one would "expect" to see selected based on their percentage representation in a qualified labor pool, and, on the other, the actual number of those persons selected.

Unlike "voluntary" affirmative action, judgments directing preferential treatment for a minority or gender group, issued after litigated findings of discrimination or upon the parties' consent, squarely test the limits of a court's remedial authority under § 706(g) of Title VII to "order such affirmative action as may be appropriate." In the case of public employers, these judgments may also deny the disfavored racial or gender groups equal protection. The justices have been deeply divided over the equitable propriety under § 706(g) of consent judgments that afford relief to minority group members who are not themselves proven victims of discrimination. The degree of "trammelling" appears important. An opinion that in dictum declared such relief beyond a court's authority concerned a consent judgment modification that would have required more senior non-minority firefighters to be laid off before their more junior minority counterparts. Firefighters Local Union No. 1784 v. Stotts (1984). Yet the Court subsequently upheld a district judge's authority to approve a consent judgment that established firefighters' promotion quotas but did not compel layoffs or terminations. Local No. 93, International Ass'n of Firefighters v. City of Cleveland (1986).

Although formal, judicial findings of past discrimination are not indispensable to the approval of group-based remedies, the Supreme Court has more often upheld programs that were judicially ordered after litigated findings of persistent, egregious discrimination. Local 28, Sheet Metal Workers' International Ass'n v. EEOC (1986); United States v. Paradise (1987). The judgment in *Local 28*, for example, absolutely excluded certain whites from union membership, in turn precluding their employment. But the goal was upheld in part because there was evidence of long-standing intentional discrimination and contumacious defiance of prior judicial orders. Moreover, as the Supreme Court had stressed in *Wygant,* the burdens of a hiring goal are "diffused to a considerable extent among society generally" and do not "impose the same kind of injury" as layoffs or even promotions. The Court has not, however, clearly articulated why the animus or stubborn litigiousness of an employer or union justifies imposing a race-based remedy on persons not responsible for the discriminatory practices of the adjudicated wrongdoer. The Court insists that Congressional racial preference programs meet the same "strict scrutiny" equal protection standards that the Court imposes on state and local governments under *Croson.* Adarand Constructors, Inc. v. Pena (1995).

The strict scrutiny approach to "benign" racial preferences reflected in the Supreme Court's recent equal protection decisions has since been applied to employment discrimination consent decrees involving government employers. And circuit decisions have held that a preference enjoys no greater protection because it is embodied in a judicial decree than when it is part of an employer's "voluntary" affirmative action plan. See, e.g., United Black Firefighters Ass'n v. Akron (6th Cir.1992); In re Birmingham Reverse Discrimination Employment Litigation (11th Cir.1987). It is therefore quite likely that an affirmative action plan or consent decree affecting a state or local government employer may pass muster under Title VII's *Weber/Johnson* standards yet run afoul of the Constitution. See, e.g., Brunet v. City of Columbus (6th Cir.1993).

In fact the new "race-neutral" constitutional guideposts seem to have heightened the circuit courts' scrutiny under Title VII of government employer affirmative action and consent decrees; the previously prevailing permissiveness appears to be waning. See, e.g., Ensley Branch v. Seibels (11th Cir.1994); In re Birmingham Reverse Discrimination Employment Litigation (11th Cir.1994) (*"Birmingham II"*). The Eleventh Circuit has written, for example, that its "application of the *Johnson* [i.e., Title VII] manifest imbalance test ... is informed by Croson's discussion of the necessity [under the Equal Protection Clause] for a government entity to identify with specificity the discrimination it seeks to remedy through race conscious measures." *Birmingham II.* The recent decisions have been particularly critical of government employer promotion preferences when they are not narrowly tailored to remedy prior discrimination by the government defendant. Aiken v. City of Memphis (6th Cir.1994); *Birmingham II.*

The question has arisen whether 1991 Civil Rights Act amendments to Title VII make voluntary affirmative action plans unlawful. Section 703(m) of Title VII, added by those amendments, provides that an unlawful employment practice is "established" when race or gender is shown to be "a motivating factor ... even though other [e.g., benign, compensatory] factors motivated the practice." Standing alone, that section would seem to condemn many if not all forms of affirmative action. But the preface to § 703(m) is qualified by the words "Except as otherwise provided in this title...."; and part of that title, § 116, also added in 1991, provides that the amendments shall not be construed to affect "court-ordered remedies, *affirmative action,* or conciliation agreements, that are in accordance with the law." (emphasis added). That text, in turn, raises the question whether affirmative action must be "court-ordered" to be saved by § 116. Viewing the "court-ordered" requirement as modifying only the first item on the list, "remedies," both EEOC and circuit courts have concluded that voluntary affirmative action programs and conciliation agreements are still lawful if they meet the pre-existing *Weber/Johnson* standards. See EEOC Enforcement Guidance dated July 7, 1992, Part IV; Plott v. General Motors Corp. (6th Cir.1995).

While employers face legal risks when they exceed the *Weber/Johnson* limits on voluntary affirmative action plans or, as in *Birmingham,* implement broad-based decrees beyond their underlying justifications, their employment decisions taken pursuant to a settlement of individual charges of discrimination are usually upheld. The settlement is treated as a legitimate, nondiscriminatory reason for the hiring or promotion decision under challenge. See Marcantel v. State of La., Dept. of Transportation (5th Cir.1994).

K. PROCEDURES AND REMEDIES IN AFFIRMATIVE ACTION CHALLENGES

When a white or male plaintiff challenges an employment practice as a form of intentional discrimination, the employer may defend by asserting that the practice was dictated by the provisions of a valid affirmative action plan. If the plaintiff's prima facie case is developed with the inferential *McDonnell Douglas* mode of proof, the employer may justify simply by producing evidence that its challenged decision was made pursuant to an affirmative action plan. It is then the plaintiff's burden to prove either that the decision was not made pursuant to the plan, or that the plan is invalid. Johnson v. Transportation Agency of Santa Clara County (1987). The Court has similarly held that when race-based government action is challenged under the Equal Protection Clause, "the ultimate burden remains with the employees to demonstrate the unconstitutionality of an affirmative-action program." *Wygant.* By contrast, some equal protection decisions place on the defendant the burden of producing evidence of a plan's constitutionality, leaving the plaintiff with the "ultimate burden of proving its unconstitutionality." See Aiken v. City of Memphis (6th Cir.), cert. denied sub nom. Brunet v. Tucker (1994).

Some courts have held that white plaintiffs who demonstrate that they were denied the right to compete on an equal basis because of their race are entitled to damages to the extent of any demonstrated economic loss or emotional distress, even if they fail to demonstrate that, but for the race-based preference, they would have been selected. See, e.g., Price v. City of Charlotte, N.C. (4th Cir.1996); Hopwood v. Texas (5th Cir.1996). Others, however, deem that failure of proof so fundamental as to deprive the plaintiffs of standing to sue at all, at least where they fail minimum eligibility requirements. See, e.g., Grahek v. City of St. Paul, Mn. (8th Cir.1996).

CHAPTER 20

OTHER FEDERAL ANTIDISCRIMINATION LAWS

A. THE CIVIL RIGHTS ACTS OF 1866, 1870, AND 1871

(42 U.S.C.A. §§ 1981, 1983, *Bivens* Claims and 1985(3))

1. IN GENERAL

The Civil Rights Acts of 1866, 1870, and 1871 are generally referred to as the Reconstruction Civil Rights Acts, and they were originally intended to enforce the 13th and 14th Amendments in the post-Civil War era. The most frequently invoked provisions are codified at 42 U.S.C.A. §§ 1981, 1983, and 1985(3). These acts remained dormant for many years but were resurrected in the 1960's. Plaintiffs proving a claim under any of these statutes may receive the open-ended, tort-like remedies available under a companion provision, 42 U.S.C.A. § 1988.

What is now § 1981 was first enacted in 1866 under authority of the 13th Amendment, and re-enacted in 1870, two years after ratification of the 14th Amendment. It prohibits race or ancestry discrimination in the making and enforcement of contracts, including employment contracts. The Supreme Court has relied on the 13th Amendment origins of § 1981 to apply these statutes to purely private defendants, including employers, at least respecting transactions open to the public. See Jones v. Alfred H. Mayer Co. (1968); Runyon v. McCrary (1976); Patterson v. McLean Credit Union (1989). Yet the Court has relied on the 14th Amendment origins of § 1981 to limit its reach to violations that reflect intentional race or ancestry discrimination General Building Contractors Ass'n v. Pennsylvania (1982).

Section 1983, the most used of these statutes, provides a remedy against persons or entities acting under color of state law for the violation of any federal constitutional right. Public employees with claims of discrimination based on race, gender, age, and other classifications protected by the Equal Protection Clause may prefer Section 1983 to applicable modern statutes like Title VII or the ADEA, because Section 1988's damages are uncapped.

Section 1985(3), like § 1983 and in contrast to §§ 1981 and 1982, creates no rights of its own. It provides damages for the conspiratorial deprivation of certain rights independently secured by the federal Constitution and, perhaps, other federal statutes. But when the conspiracy is among purely private actors, only two rights are protected; and even with at least one government or "state actor" conspirator, § 1985(3) offers no protection unless the conspirators act with a specific racial animus or

motive. See Bray v. Alexandria Women's Health
Clinic (1993).

2. SECTION 1981

Section 1981 secures equal contracting rights
without regard to race. It affords "all persons" in
the United States "the same right ... to make and
enforce contracts ... and to the full and equal
benefit of all laws ... as is enjoyed by white citizens...." Section 1981 has also been interpreted to
provide a civil damages remedy for racial discrimination arising from contracts of employment, even
though Congress has comprehensively addressed
employment discrimination much more recently in
Title VII. And § 1981, unlike Title VII, has no
minimum-employee numerical threshold for employer liability.

By its terms § 1981 also reaches a host of contracting relationships—with private schools, to
name just one—not reached by Title VII. Moreover,
the Court has held that § 1981 also reaches purely
private conduct. Runyon v. McCrary (1976). So private employers of any size are covered defendants.
Patterson v. McLean Credit Union (1989). Section
1981 therefore serves as a distinct and potentially
attractive alternative to Title VII against private
and most public employers. But the Supreme Court
has held that Title VII, where available, preempts
§ 1981 claims against *federal* employers. Brown v.
GSA (1976). And lower courts have consistently
held that § 1981 cannot support any claim of dis-

crimination under color of federal law—even, that is, where Title VII is not available. See Lee v. Hughes (11th Cir.1998).

The Supreme Court has construed the language that secures to all the same contracting rights as "white citizens" as referring only to the racial character of the prohibited discrimination, rather than as limiting the class of appropriate plaintiffs to non-whites. Accordingly, while the lower courts are in agreement that the statute does not prohibit discrimination because of gender, it is also settled that whites as well as blacks may assert contract denial claims under § 1981 on the basis of race. *McDonald v. Santa Fe Trail,*.

The Supreme Court has construed § 1981's ban on "race" discrimination to include discrimination on the basis of ancestry. The Court has understood ancestry, in turn, to mean membership in an "ethnically and physiognomically distinctive sub-grouping." St. Francis College v. Al–Khazraji (1987) and Shaare Tefila Congregation v. Cobb (1987). This somewhat vague formulation has generated predictable confusion among the lower federal courts. It is clear that § 1981 "ancestry" does not mean national origin, religion, or alienage status as such. On the other hand, these latter characteristics are often statistically correlated with a particular ancestry. Consider, for example, a case where a hiring supervisor disparaged the plaintiff's Israeli background and his prior sales experience in Israel by saying "Israel doesn't count." The appellate court ruled that the jury was entitled to treat these comments not just as discrimination on the basis of national origin-actionable under Title VII, but also as discrimination based on the plaintiff's Israeli ancestry and thus his "race" within the meaning of § 1981. *Sinai v. New England Telephone and Telegraph Co.,*.

Although § 1981, like Title VII, does not prohibit discrimination on the basis of alienage per se, a limited protection from employment discrimination on the basis of non-citizenship status is now provided by the Immigration Reform and Control Act of 1986, discussed below. But aliens, like other "persons within the jurisdiction of the United States," may use § 1981 to complain of race or ancestry and possibly alienage, i.e., non-citizenship. Compare Duane v. GEICO (4th Cir.1994) with Bhandari v. First National Bank of Commerce (5th Cir.1987). By contrast, under Title VII the plaintiff may complain of race, gender, religious, or national origin, but not ancestry or alienage discrimination. Espinoza v. Farah Mfg. Co. (1973).

Section 1981 contains no threshold numerical requirement for employer coverage. In the course of considering the amendments, Congress observed that § 1981 constitutes the only national protection against race or ancestry discrimination for those millions of applicants or employees whose employers are too small to be covered by Title VII. Despite this understanding, the amendments make no attempt to protect those applicants or employees against the other forms of discrimination prohibited by Title VII, that is, sex, religion, or national origin, or against race discrimination resulting solely from the effects of a neutral practice. It is well settled that § 1981 affords no protection against discrimination based on gender. See *McDonald v. Santa Fe Trail*; Runyon v. McCrary. *St. Francis* and *Shaare Tefila* suggest that it provides no protection against religious discrimination as such.

The federal judiciary began to place significant limitations on the utility of § 1981 in General Building Contractors Assn. v. Pennsylvania (1982). There the Supreme Court held that a showing of disparate impact does not suffice to prove a § 1981 employment violation, which requires instead a demonstration, directly or through statistical evidence, of discriminatory intent. Consistent with this ruling, the Court has also approved for use in § 1981 actions the inferential way of showing intentional disparate treatment outlined in *McDonnell Douglas Corp. v. Green* for cases under Title VII. *Patterson v. McLean Credit Union*. Yet at times the cases suggest that the showing of intent required in § 1981 cases by *General Building Contractors* in practice demands somewhat more "direct" evidence of discrimination than would usually be required under Title VII. See Durham v. Xerox Corp. (10th Cir.1994).

And it remains uncertain whether, in § 1981 "mixed motive" situations where the employer proves it would have reached its decision on entirely lawful grounds, the courts will follow: the no-liability approach used in First Amendment cases under § 1983, Mt. Healthy v. Doyle (1977); the limited liability approach mandated by the 1991 Civil Rights Act for post-November 21, 1991 employment practices that violate Title VII; or the no-liability approach applied by the Supreme Court in *Price Waterhouse v. Hopkins,* which governed Title VII cases before the 1991 amendments and may still govern cases under ADEA. The uncertainty is fueled by the fact that the 1991 Act, which in other respects expressly modifies § 1981, refers only to Title VII in the provisions that modify *Price Waterhouse.*

Section 1981 has also been read more narrowly than Title VII with respect to the standing of "testers" to challenge discriminatory referrals by employment agencies. Testers have been defined as persons of different races "equipped with fake credentials intended to be comparable...." who apply for employment to an agency or employer without an intention to accept an offer if one is forthcoming. See Fair Employment Council of Greater Washington, Inc. v. BMC Marketing Corporation (D.C.Cir. 1994). The typical ensuing claim is that the employment agency, on grounds of race, failed to refer the African–American (or female) tester but did refer the white or male. Title VII provides that any "person claiming to be aggrieved" by an unlawful employment practice may, after exhausting administrative remedies, sue such an agency in court. 42 U.S.C.A. §§ 2000e–5(b), (c), (f)(1). Although there is debate on the point in the circuit opinions, this language has sometimes been read to confer standing on testers to bring a Title VII claim despite their own lack of a bona fide interest in employment. *Fair Employment Council.*

By contrast, the text of § 1981 suggests that only a person deprived of what is otherwise a legal right to make or enforce a contract has standing. Reasoning that testers could not have enforced an employment contract offer because of the material misrepresentations of fact they made to the defendant employment agency about their intentions to secure employment, a panel of the District of Columbia Circuit has held that tester plaintiffs cannot state a claim for damages under § 1981: "the loss of the opportunity to enter into a *void* contract—i.e., a contract that *neither* party can enforce—is not an injury cognizable under § 1981, for a void contract is a legal nullity." Fair Employment Council. But cf. Watts v. Boyd Properties (11th Cir.1985).

On the other hand the courts have permitted the assertion of § 1981 claims where intimate or associational rights of the plaintiff are allegedly invaded by a defendant whose conduct was aimed at third parties. See, e.g., Alizadeh v. Safeway Stores, Inc. (5th Cir.1986). A related, but distinct question is whether the defendant must be the party with whom the plaintiff contracts or seeks to contract. Courts have answered this question in the negative, holding § 1981 violated by a racially motivated interference with a plaintiff's right to enter into contracts with others of a different race and by third parties' attempts to punish the plaintiff for making such contracts. See Des Vergnes v. Seekonk Water District (1st Cir.1979).

The accrual date for § 1981 claims is determined as a matter of federal law. But the Supreme Court has directed the lower federal courts to borrow analogous state limitations periods and tolling rules in § 1981 actions, and has held that pursuing Title VII administrative procedures does not toll the § 1981 statute of limitations. *Johnson v. Railway Express Agency, Inc.* The forum state's general or residual "personal injury" statute of limitations applies. Goodman v. Lukens Steel Co., (1987).

Title 42 U.S.C.A. § 1977A(a)(1), added by § 102 of the Civil Rights Act of 1991, provides that damages under Title VII are recoverable only if the complainant "cannot recover" under § 1981. But the EEOC has interpreted that language not to bar parallel proceedings under the two statutes, only double recovery for the same injury. Putative plaintiffs with intentional race discrimination claims against employers large enough to be covered by and not exempt from Title VII can therefore apparently choose whether to proceed under Title VII or § 1981 or both. That choice will be heavily influenced by the availability of unlimited compensatory and punitive damages under § 1981, free of Title VII's variable caps; and by the immediate access to court under § 1981, free of the Title VII state and federal administrative prerequisite requirements with their rather early filing deadlines.

Procedurally and remedially, the Reconstruction Civil Rights Acts, § 1981 in particular, usually hold several attractions over Title VII. For one, no administrative exhaustion is required. See Patsy v.

Board of Regents of the State of Florida (1982). Second, the applicable limitation periods borrowed from state law are normally longer than the 300-day or 180-day Title VII deadline for filing charges with federal or state agencies. Third, although jury trials are now available under either statute with respect to claims of intentional discrimination, the nineteenth-century statutes offer compensatory and punitive damages unlimited in amount. By contrast, even after the Civil Rights Act of 1991, Title VII plaintiffs who prove intentional discrimination are subject to caps on those damages that vary with the number of employees working for the defendant employer. Under § 1981, as under Title VII, punitive damages are not available against a defendant government entity. See Walters v. City of Atlanta (11th Cir.1986) and cases therein cited.

But a potential plaintiff with an intentional race discrimination claim actionable under both statutes may prefer Title VII if she cannot afford counsel and believes that state or federal agency administrative processing of her charge will induce her employer to settle. By statute the EEOC is expected to assist with investigation and conciliation. In addition, it remains possible, to an as yet uncertain extent, for a plaintiff who cannot prove intentional discrimination and would therefore fail under § 1981, to succeed under Title VII by establishing that an employer's neutral practice had a disproportionate adverse impact on her group and that the employer cannot justify the practice as a matter of job relatedness and business necessity.

In its 1988 Term, the Court held that discriminatory conduct directed against an employee after hire falls outside the right granted by § 1981 to "make" a contract free from racial discrimination. *Patterson v. McLean Credit Union,*. The 1991 Civil Rights Act overturns this decision and thereby restores 42 U.S.C.A. § 1981 as a forceful supplementary vehicle for redressing race or ancestry discrimination respecting the term of employment, at least when the defendant's conduct is shown to be *intentional.* The legislation provides that the right to "make" a contract extends beyond initial contract formation to include "performance, modification and termination." The sweeping text of this addition appears to equate the sphere in which § 1981 forbids contract discrimination with the wide range of terms and conditions of employment protected under Title VII. In particular, it now seems clear that claims of race-based harassment, nonpromotion, and discharge are once again actionable under § 1981. Retaliation may be as well. Andrews v. Lakeshore Rehabilitation Hospital (11th Cir.1998).

Courts commonly permit the showing of intent requisite under the Reconstruction Acts to be made inferentially, that is, through the *McDonnell Douglas/Burdine/St. Mary's* formula of shifting evidentiary burdens that is paradigmatic under Title VII. See, e.g., *Patterson v. McLean Credit Union*; *Barbour v. Merrill* (D.C.Cir.1995). Traditionally, such evidence has supported not only liability but also punitive damages. Fifteen years ago the Supreme Court announced that punitive damages may be assessed in an action under § 1983 "when the defendant's conduct is shown to be motivated by evil motive or intent, or when it involves reckless or callous indifference to the federally protected rights of others." *Smith v. Wade*. This standard, used alike in cases under all the Reconstruction Acts, has sometimes been construed to permit a jury to award punitive damages based solely on the evidence that establishes an intentional violation, with no necessary additional showing of any particular state of mind on the part of the defendant. See, e.g. *Barbour v. Merrill* (D.C.Cir.1995). But see Jackson v. Pool Mortgage Co. (10th Cir.1989).

3.   SECTION 1983

Section 1983 authorizes actions at law or suits in equity against any "person" for the deprivation of rights, privileges or immunities secured by the federal Constitution or laws, so long as the defendant acted "under color of" state law, custom or usage. For most employment discrimination claimants, § 1983 is of less utility than § 1981. First, it vindicates only rights, notably equal protection, protected by the U.S. Constitution or other federal statutes. Second, deprivations of those rights are actionable only if imposed "under color of" state law. Third, while the Supreme Court has held that municipalities and other local governments are "persons," and hence appropriate defendants, for purposes of § 1983, it simultaneously concluded that municipalities are not subject to liability vicariously, through *respondeat superior.* Monell v. Department of Social Services of City of New York (1978).

Instead, local government entities are responsible only for conduct composing a well established entity "custom"; for official policies or actions taken or approved by employees with "final policymaking authority," a question to be decided by the court before trial by reference to local law; or for omissions so likely to result in unconstitutional harm as to amount to "deliberate indifference." On the "final policymaking official" requirement, see Pembaur v. Cincinnati (1986) (plurality opinion); St. Louis v. Praprotnik (1988) (plurality opinion); and Jett v. Dallas Independent School District (1989) (5-member majority opinion).

Fourth, the § 1983 liability of individual government employees, state or local, has been sharply circumscribed by a series of Supreme Court rulings expanding the range of absolute immunity for government officials respecting conduct constituting a legislative, judicial or prosecutorial function, and by an increasingly generous brand of qualified immunity for discretionary executive or administrative acts. See generally Forrester v. White (1988) (judicial immunity); Burns v. Reed (1991)(prosecutorial immunity); Harlow v. Fitzgerald (1982) and Anderson v. Creighton (1987)(qualified immunity).

Despite these obstacles, § 1983 presents the tempting prospect of uncapped compensatory damages, as opposed to the capped compensatory damages under Title VII. And while Title VII does not support claims against individual employer agents like supervisors, § 1983 does; and it subjects them not only to uncapped compensatory damages but in appropriate cases to punitive awards as well. The United States Supreme Court has yet to decide whether Title VII provides the exclusive remedy for employment discrimination against state actors, thus impliedly preempting § 1983. But the federal circuit courts are largely in accord that the mere availability of a Title VII claim does not altogether preempt a § 1983 claim arising from the same facts. But see Hughes v. Bedsole (4th Cir.1995). Most, however, also hold that the § 1983 employment discrimination plaintiff cannot rest simply on the "and laws" branch of that statute, which provides a remedy for action under color of state law that violates a federal statutory right. See, e.g., Pontarelli v. Stone (1st Cir.1991). This means that in general § 1983 can be used to challenge only employment discrimination that violates the Equal Protection or Due Process Clauses of the Constitution, rather than Title VII alone. But see Wu v. Thomas (11th Cir.1989).

Discrimination actionable under Title VII's "disparate treatment" theory may be vindicated through § 1983, because that kind of intentional discrimination could also violate the Equal Protection Clause. By contrast, employer conduct that violates only the Title VII "neutral practice/disparate impact" theory fails to show the intentional discrimination requisite for a violation of the Equal Protection Clause. See Washington v. Davis (1976).

May the plaintiff prove the purposeful discrimination element of a § 1983 equal protection claim in the same variable ways she may establish purposeful discrimination under Title VII? The standard formula under Title VII for showing purposeful discrimination inferentially was set out in *McDonnell Douglas Corp. v. Green*, and later reaffirmed in *Texas Dept. of Community Affairs v. Burdine,*. The Supreme Court has assumed that "the *McDonnell Douglas* framework is fully applicable to racial-discrimination-in-employment claims under 42 U.S.C.A. § 1983." *St. Mary's Honor Center v. Hicks*. By satisfying the *McDonnell Douglas* formula for showing intentional discrimination under Title VII, or by showing intentional discrimination more directly, a plaintiff also establishes a Fourteenth Amendment violation and therefore is eligible to recover under § 1983. Boutros v. Canton Regional Transit Authority (6th Cir.1993).

Beyond proving intentional discrimination, the plaintiff must contend with the distinct additional requirements and defenses of § 1983. In suits against individual government officers, the plaintiff must overcome the formidable defense of qualified immunity. She confronts different obstacles in suing government entities. She may not sue a state in its own name, Will v. Michigan Department of State Police (1989); but by naming a state official in an official capacity she may secure prospective relief. *Id.* She may obtain damages by suing a state official in an individual capacity. Hafer v. Melo, (1991). But such a claim can be satisfied only from that official's own resources (including, if the plaintiff is fortunate, indemnity from the State) and in any event is subject to the defense of qualified immunity. To recover under § 1983 against a municipality or other local government, the plaintiff must show prima facie that the injury was caused by a well established "custom"; was inflicted or approved by a "final policymaking official" or was the result of official inaction amounting to the government's "deliberate indifference." See Lewis' Litigating Civil Rights and Employment Discrimination Cases (West 1996), as supplemented, for an extensive treatment of § 1983 claims, defenses and remedies.

4.   WHETHER § 1981 PLAINTIFFS SUING STATE AND LOCAL GOVERNMENT EMPLOYERS MUST MEET THE ADDITIONAL PROOF REQUIREMENTS OF § 1983

Title VII would appear to be the *only* remedy for race discrimination in federal employment, which has been held outside the reach of § 1981. Lee v. Hughes. In actions against state and local government employers, there is some doubt whether § 1981 is available on its own terms, or whether the plaintiff must also surmount the additional proof requirements and defenses available of § 1983. If the latter, then Title VII might once again become a more attractive option than § 1981.

The uncertainty stems from the Court's decision in Jett v. Dallas Independent School Dist. (1989). There the Court imposed the significant additional restrictions that confront § 1983 plaintiffs on plaintiffs seeking redress against state and local governments under § 1981. The Court held in Jett that "the express 'action at law' provided by Section 1983 ... provides the exclusive federal damages remedy for the violation of the *rights* guaranteed by Section 1981 when the claim is pressed against a state actor." Accordingly, the § 1981 plaintiff must show that the violation of his § 1981 "right to make contracts" was caused by a "custom" or "policy" or by "deliberate indifference" of the kind required by Section 1983. By engrafting § 1983 limitations on to actions enforcing § 1981 rights, *Jett* may also defeat any § 1981 claim against a State. This is because the Supreme Court has held that a state in its own name is not even a suable "person" under Section 1983. *Will v. Michigan Department of State Police.*

Yet the Civil Rights Act of 1991 casts doubt on the continued vitality of *Jett.* § 101 adds the following new subparagraph to § 1981:

> (c) The rights protected by this section are protected against impairment by nongovernmental discrimination *and impairment under color of state law.* (codified at 42 U.S.C.A. § 1981(c)) (emphasis added).

The early reported cases addressing the issue held or implied that this section effectively overruled

Jett. But the simple statement that § 1981 protects against "impairment under color of state law" does not really contradict *Jett,* which assumed that a plaintiff suing a state or local government employer could assert a claim under § 1981, not just § 1983. What *Jett* did demand was that the plaintiff bringing a § 1981 claim against a government entity satisfy § 1983's "policy" requirement for entity liability. Viewed this way, the language of new § 1981(c) arguably codifies, rather than overrules, *Jett.* Moreover, the legislative history of the 1991 Act lacks any stated intention to overrule Jett, despite the express statement found elsewhere in that history to overrule other Supreme Court rulings. Several recent decisions have therefore assumed or concluded that Jett is still vital notwithstanding § 1981(c). See, e.g., Federation of African American Contractors v. Oakland, Calif. (9th Cir. 1996).

4. *BIVENS* CLAIMS ASSERTED DIRECTLY UNDER U.S. CONSTITUTION

In limited circumstances the Constitution provides direct protection against certain forms of employment discrimination. The Fifth Amendment prohibits federal government deprivations of life, liberty, or property without due process; the Fourteenth Amendment prohibits the same deprivations by state and local governments. The Fourteenth Amendment also prohibits states from denying the equal protection of the laws; this prohibition has been judicially extended to federal action as part of the Fifth Amendment right of due process. See Bolling v. Sharpe (1954).

The Court has recognized an implied private right of action against individual federal agents for Constitutional violations. Bivens v. Six Unknown Named Agents of Fed. Bureau of Narcotics (1971), It has also upheld a "Bivens" claim for employment discrimination against a member of Congress under the equal protection component of the 5th amendment's due process clause. Davis v. Passman (1979) Individual federal officers sued under Bivens receive the same immunities available to individual state and local officers sued under § 1983. See, e.g., *Harlow,* 457 U.S. at 818 n.30, 102 S.Ct. at 2738 n.30; *Butz v. Economou,* (1978). The Supreme Court has declined to recognized a similar implied constitutional claim against federal agencies.

The Court has also crafted an exception to *Bivens*-based suits that radically reduces its utility as a remedy for employment discrimination. It has refused to imply a *Bivens* claim against a federal officer where the government action in question is subject to an elaborate statutory remedial scheme, even when the alternative does not afford as generous a remedy, or perhaps any remedy, against the offending agent. Schweiker v. Chilicky (1988); United States v. Stanley (1987). Most federal employees work for an agency that is a covered "employer" within § 717 of Title VII, 42 U.S.C. § 2000e–16, and therefore enjoy the protection against discrimination afforded by that statute. See Brown v. General Services Administration (1976). Accordingly, those employees may not maintain a *Bivens* claim alleging unconstitutional employment discrimination remediable by Title VII.

Even for employment claims other than discrimination, the Supreme Court has held that Congress' complete occupation of the federal personnel field is a "special factor" counseling against the *Bivens* damages remedy in matters related to "federal personnel policy." Bush v. Lucas (1983). After enactment of the Civil Service Reform Act ("CSRA"), the Court rejected a claim under the Back Pay Act that would have indirectly provided for review of adverse federal personnel action by a court that was not an "appropriate authority" to review that action under CSRA. The Court concluded that Congress intended to withhold such review by failing to provide for it in the CSRA, which it deemed a comprehensive and exhaustive charter of protections and remedies for federal employees. United States v. Fausto (1988).

Following the Court's lead, the circuits have routinely denied federal employees review of adverse agency action under *Bivens,* the Back Pay Act, the Administrative Procedure Act or other statutory remedies, against U.S. agencies or individual federal officers, except to the extent authorized by CSRA. See, e.g., Ayrault v. Pena (7th Cir.1995). Thus a federal employee in a service not covered by Title VII (e.g., the judiciary) has no *Bivens* damages remedy even though he has no other congressionally enacted judicial or administrative procedure for vindicating a claim of unconstitutional race discrimination. See Lee v. Hughes (11th Cir.1998).

In recent years at least 21 states and Puerto Rico have recognized counterparts to *Bivens* claims under state constitutions—17 through an implied cause of action approved by the highest court of the state, and 4 others by statute. See Donoghue and Edelstein, "Life After Brown: The Future of State Constitutional Tort Actions in New York," 42 New York Law School L. Rev. 447 (1998). In employment settings these claims may become impliedly precluded by other remedies as with federal employees' attempts to use *Bivens*. But a state cause of action for employment discrimination gives rise to a property interest that may not be impaired without Fourteenth Amendment due process. Logan v. Zimmerman Brush Co. (1982). And government actions that create "suspect classifications" potentially violate the equal protection standards of the Fifth and Fourteenth Amendments. See National Education Association v. South Carolina (1978); Califano v. Goldfarb (1977). Public employees' First Amendment claims are increasingly constrained by decisions heavily weighting the government employer's interest in efficient management and discipline. See Waters v. Churchill, (1994).

5. SECTION 1985(3)

Section 1985(3) is a purely remedial statute that, like § 1983 but unlike § 1981, creates no substantive rights itself. Great Am. Fed. S & L Ass'n v.

Novotny (1979). Its "deprivation" clause, by far the most frequently litigated, provides a federal cause of action for damages for the redress of conspiracies that have the purpose and result of "depriving either directly or indirectly, any person or class of persons of the equal protection of the laws, or of equal privileges and immunities under the laws...." The Supreme Court has not decided if § 1985(3) supports a prayer for injunctive relief. Bray v. Alexandria Women's Health Clinic (1993).

The conspiracy elements are standard, requiring an agreement by two or more distinct persons or entities to engage in conduct that resulted in the deprivation of the requisite rights, plus some overt act in furtherance of that agreement. In general, § 1985(3) is not violated by discussions, agreements, or actions taken between two or more individuals who serve the same corporate or other entity. Wright v. Illinois Dept. of Children & Family Services (7th Cir.1994).

The question of what rights are protected has proven more difficult. Paving the way for damage actions against purely private actors, the Supreme Court has held that state action is a required element if the particular right plaintiff invokes is itself dependent on state action. Griffin v. Breckenridge (1971). Because the First Amendment prohibits infringements only by government, a § 1985(3) claim against union members for conspiracy to deprive plaintiffs of rights to free speech and association failed for lack of evidence of state involvement. United Brotherhood of Carpenters and Joiners v.

Scott (1983). But since virtually all rights protected by the U.S. Constitution also depend on state action, § 1985(3) reaches only those private conspiracies aimed at interfering with the two constitutional rights that are "protected against private, as well as official, encroachment." These are the Thirteenth Amendment right to be free from involuntary servitude and a limited right to interstate travel. *Bray.*

In *Griffin,* the Court added a distinct claim element that requires the plaintiff to show "some racial, or perhaps otherwise class-based, invidiously discriminatory animus behind the conspirators' action." The "animus" requirement applies to claims alleging government official as well as purely private conspiracies. Aulson v. Blanchard (1st Cir. 1996). Conspiracies directed against groups defined by race or racial advocacy most clearly meet the class-based motivation or animus requirement of § 1985(3). *Griffin.* As under § 1981, however, the kind of "race" qualifying for protection is not always apparent. For example a circuit court has ruled that a target religious group containing both Jewish and non-Jewish members could not constitute a class for § 1985(3) purposes because of its racial diversity. Jews for Jesus, Inc. v. Jewish Community Relations Council of New York, Inc. (2d Cir.1992).

The "perhaps" language in *Griffin* suggested that certain non-racial yet still group-based motivations might also sustain a § 1985(3) claim. But the Court has held that conspiratorial conduct "motivated by economic or commercial animus" is outside the statute's reach. *Carpenters*. At a minimum, the target class is cognizable "only when it is comprised [sic] of a distinctive and identifiable group" whose members could be ascertained "by means of objective criteria." *Aulson*. There is no consensus whether conduct motivated by animus based on politics, gender or disability is actionable.

By analogy to the construction of § 1985(3)'s criminal counterpart, 18 U.S.C.A. § 241, the Court has also insisted that a § 1985(3) conspiracy must have the specific purpose, and not merely the effect, of interfering with a protected right. The defendants' conduct must be "aimed at" that right. So even assuming that women are a class that the statute protects from anti-female animus, the Supreme Court in *Bray* concluded that private anti-abortion protesters targeted women trying to enter a clinic not because the women were members of that class, but because they were seeking abortions. And the constitutional right to an abortion could not support the deprivation clause claim because that right, like most, is protected only against public, not private interference. *Bray*.

In sum, as long as the Court limits the protected target "class" to groups defined by race or the advocacy of racial views, § 1985(3) will seldom be needed when the conspirators include state actors: government officials today rarely conspire on racial grounds. And the statute will provide scant protection against the far more numerous purely private conspiracies, except the few designed to enslave or to infringe the right to interstate travel.

The Court has left open whether conspiratorial deprivation of equal rights protected by federal or state statutes might also trigger § 1985(3) liability. *Carpenters*. But it has set one firm outer limit. Section 1985(3) is ousted if the particular federal statute on which plaintiff relies—for example, Title VII—has its own elaborate remedial and procedural scheme. Great American Fed. S & L Ass'n v. Novotny (1979).

It is not settled whether a public official sued under § 1985(3) may claim a variant of the qualified immunity defense that is available to an individual defendant under § 1983. A decision denying that defense reasoned that the § 1985(3) requirement of intentional, race-based animus already protects defendants from liability for actions taken in good faith; the additional protection of qualified immunity is not necessary to assure that a public official will vigorously discharge the duties of his office. Burrell v. Board of Trustees of Georgia Military College (11th Cir.1992). But see Bisbee v. Bey (10th Cir.1994).

B.   THE EQUAL PAY ACT OF 1963

The Equal Pay Act of 1963, 29 U.S.C.A. § 206(d) ("EPA"), requires "equal pay for equal work" within the same establishment regardless of sex. The concept of "equal work" lies at the heart of the Act. General comparisons between two jobs carrying unequal pay will not suffice to establish that work is "equal"; rather, demonstrating an EPA violation demands specific showings of equivalent skill, effort, and responsibility, as well as performance under similar working conditions. Once an inequality is found, however, it cannot be remedied by reducing the wages of the higher paid member of the other sex.

The EPA contains four affirmative defenses. It permits exceptions to the equal pay for equal work principle when differentials are pursuant to: (1) seniority systems; (2) merit systems; (3) systems which measure earnings by quantity or quality of production (incentive systems); or (4) factors other than sex.

1. EPA COVERAGE, THE PRIMA FACIE CASE AND AFFIRMATIVE DEFENSES

a. Coverage

Why would a plaintiff resort to the Equal Pay Act when Title VII proscribes sex discrimination in *all* terms and conditions of employment, not just for compensation between persons of different genders holding "equal" jobs? For starters, it may be the only game in town. EPA looks primarily to the Fair Labor Standards Act, 29 U.S.C.A. § 209 *et seq.* ("FLSA"), to which it is an amendment, for provisions on coverage, as well as enforcement. In sharp contrast to Title VII, EPA has no coverage threshold defined in terms of the employer's number of employees. Instead, it covers employers of any size, unless the employer is in one of several specifically exempted industries. 29 U.S.C.A. § 213. These industries include certain fishing and agricultural businesses as well as small local newspapers.

An employee not in an exempted industry may assert an FLSA, and therefore an EPA claim if she has some contact with interstate commerce. This contact may be established by satisfying one of two requirements. The first concerns the nature of the work implicated by the plaintiff's claim. If the employee is "engaged in commerce" or produces "goods for commerce," the work is covered, no matter what the employer's size.

An alternative FLSA avenue protects employees who, though not themselves engaged in or producing goods for interstate commerce, work for nonexempt businesses that are. This alternative measure of FLSA coverage extends EPA's protection to persons employed by "enterprises" engaged in commerce or producing goods for commerce. Such enterprises will be deemed to meet the interstate commerce test if they (1) achieved certain sales volumes or (2) were part of certain industries specifically mentioned in FLSA.

A third approach, based on text unique to EPA, arguably reaches more broadly than the FLSA alternatives. It focuses on the relation between other employees' production and interstate commerce, without regard to the commerce involvement of the plaintiff or the defendant employer. The EPA prohibits employers that have "employees subject to" EPA from engaging in unequal pay discrimination against [other] "employees." 29 U.S.C.A. § 206(d)(1). Read literally, the EPA would therefore appear to protect all employees of employers that have at least two employees of different genders who are engaged in or producing goods for commerce, even if those employers are not FLSA "enterprises."

The Act defines an employer as "any person acting directly or indirectly in the interest of an employer in relation to an employee...." 29 U.S.C.A. § 203(d). Notwithstanding this definition, claims against supervisors or managers in their individual as distinct from official capacities are likely to be dismissed because in an individual capacity a defendant lacks control over the plaintiff's terms of employment. See Welch v. Laney (11th Cir.1995).

b. *Equal Work*

The first step in the plaintiff's prima facie case is to establish that the plaintiff performed work equal to that of another of the opposite sex. Job equivalence, as measured by skill, effort, responsibility, and working conditions, need not be precise, only substantial. Corning Glass Works v. Brennan (1974). The issue in *Corning Glass* was whether the employer violated the EPA by paying a higher base wage to male night shift inspectors than it paid to female day shift inspectors. Historically, Corning had paid higher wages to the night inspectors, who were then all male. After the enactment of the EPA, Corning opened both jobs to men and women, but a collective-bargaining agreement perpetuated the differential in favor of the night jobs. The Court defined "working conditions" to refer to a job's "hazards" and "surroundings," but not time of day, which the Court concluded did not render substantially equal working conditions unequal. Accordingly, Corning had prima facie violated the EPA by paying women who worked days less than men who worked nights for equal work.

The circuit courts have similarly disregarded minor differences between jobs to find work "equal." See, e.g., Hein v. Oregon College of Education (9th Cir.1983). But when a plaintiff of one gender is not responsible for tasks important to the enterprise that are assigned to a comparator of the other gender, she does not perform equal work and therefore has no right to equal pay.

c. *Unequal Pay*

Another element of the plaintiff's prima facie case is a showing that the plaintiff is paid less than another of the opposite sex. First, the plaintiff must be paid a lesser "rate" of pay. Second, this rate must be compared with that of an individual of the opposite sex performing substantially similar work.

(1) EQUAL "RATE" OF PAY

Commissions worth less per sale to female than to male employees who provide the same total service to an employer's clientele violate the EPA because they yield women a lesser "rate." Bence v. Detroit Health Corp. (6th Cir.1983).

(2) THE NECESSITY OF A "COMPARATOR" WITHIN A SINGLE "ESTABLISHMENT"

In order to show unequal pay, there must be some comparison between the complaining individual and one of the opposite sex in a substantially similar position. The plaintiff, therefore, must demonstrate that an individual of the opposite sex received greater compensation for substantially the same job. This task is accomplished through the use of a comparator. The comparator may be one who held the job before the plaintiff, who replaced the plaintiff, or who held a substantially similar position contemporaneously with the plaintiff. See Brinkley–Obu v. Hughes Training, Inc. (4th Cir. 1994). Finally, the comparator must also be employed in the same establishment as the plaintiff. These requirements may be subdivided into four components.

First, the comparator may not be hypothetical but rather a specific and better paid individual performing a job of substantially equal skill, effort, and responsibility. EEOC v. Liggett & Myers, Inc. (4th Cir.1982). Where a plaintiff identified her male comparators in general terms as "any men who got any higher salary increases than [the plaintiff] did," the plaintiff failed to carry a prima facie case. Houck v. Virginia Polytechnic Institute and State University (4th Cir.1993).

Second, the comparator must perform a substantially similar job. The court analyzes the job, not the qualification or performance characteristics of individual employees holding the job, and only the skill and qualifications actually needed to perform the job in question are considered. Miranda v. B & B Cash Grocery Store, Inc. (11th Cir.1992). Additionally, the examination rests on the primary, not the incidental or insubstantial job duties. Where the plaintiff performs substantially similar tasks but the comparator also has significant additional primary duties, the prima facie case fails. Mulhall v. Advance Security, Inc. (11th Cir.).

Third, the comparator may be a past, present or future employee in a substantially similar position. There can be a valid comparison between the plaintiff, a former "Vice–President, Administration," and a current "Vice–President, Controller" because financial concerns were essential to both jobs. *Id.* But if the plaintiff cannot establish that the plaintiff's predecessor, successor, or contemporary was paid more for the same responsibilities, the plaintiff has failed to make a prima facie showing. Weiss v. Coca–Cola Bottling Co. of Chicago (7th Cir.1993)

Finally, the comparator must be an employee of the same "establishment" as the plaintiff. The Secretary of Labor has defined "establishment" to mean "a distinct physical place of business rather than ... an entire business or 'enterprise' which may include several separate places of business." 29 C.F.R. § 1620.9(a) (1993). In "unusual circumstances," however, a single establishment can include more than one physical location. 29 C.F.R. § 1620.9(b) (1993).

When there is centralized control and administration, some courts have been willing to find a single EPA establishment despite several physical locations. See, e.g., Brennan v. Goose Creek Consolidated Indep. Sch. Dist. (5th Cir.1975). By contrast, other circuits have restricted the comparison of salaries to employees in one physical location when the local office where plaintiff worked made the ultimate hiring decision and, within a broad range determined by the central office, set specific salaries, Meeks v. Computer Associates International (11th Cir.1994); or where the employer conferred independent personnel decisionmaking authority on managers at the plaintiff's facility. Foster v. Arcata Associates, Inc. (9th Cir.1985).

d. *The Employer's Defenses*

Once a plaintiff has established a prima facie case, the employer bears the burden of producing evidence and persuading that the employment practice fits within one or more of EPA's 4 affirmative defenses. "Unequal pay" for equal work is permitted when the payment is made pursuant to (i) a seniority system, (ii) a merit system; (iii) a system which measures earnings by quantity or quality of production; or (iv) a differential based on any factor other than sex. 29 U.S.C.A. § 206(d)(1).

Affirmative defenses (i)–(iii) are rarely used. These three defenses specifically require a "system." This system need not be formalized or structured, but employees must know about it none-the-less. And a defendant asserting a seniority system affirmative defense must "be able to identify standards for measuring seniority which are systematically applied and observed." Irby v. Bittick (11th Cir.1995). Further, the system must be operated in good faith and not used as a way to maintain sex-based wage differences. The third defense, a system based on quality or quantity of production, has little independent vitality. First, if employees are paid the same "rate" for their work based on production, there is no EPA violation. Second, a quality or quantity system is so closely related to a merit system that it has no separate significance. The majority of litigation in the area of affirmative defenses, therefore, has centered around the rather ambiguous defense (iv), "any factor other than sex."

Examples of "factors other than sex" include salary retention policies, prior salary, and economic benefit to the employer. See, e.g., Kouba v. Allstate Insurance, Co. (9th Cir.1982). Another circuit has allowed reliance on prior salary only when other business considerations—such as the selectee's greater amount of experience in a closely related job—reasonably explain its utilization. *Irby.* A compensator's greater experience in similar positions remains a neutral, nondiscriminatory reason, even if the plaintiff has greater total service. See Lindale v. Tokheim Corp., (7th Cir. 1998). But regardless of other factors, where sex is even a "but for" cause, the EPA is violated. See Peters v. City of Shreveport (5th Cir.1987).

Another factor that has been approved as something "other than sex" is reliance on differential economic benefit to the employer of otherwise equal "male" and "female" jobs. Byrd v. Ronayne (1st Cir.1995) (alternative holding). A clothier could pay its salesmen more than its saleswomen where the men produced greater benefit to the employer because the men's clothing department generated higher profit margins and revenues. But compensation disparities keyed solely to gender-based actuarial differences are not saved by the "other than sex" exception. City of Los Angeles, Department of Water and Power v. Manhart (1978). The Supreme Court has also rejected time of day as an "other than sex" defense. *Corning Glass.*

e. *Retaliation*

The FLSA anti-retaliation provision, applicable by reference to EPA, prohibits retaliation in language more cramped than § 704 of Title VII. By offering protection against reprisal only to those who have "filed any complaint" or "instituted any proceeding," it does not in terms protect those who have made an informal on-the-job protest. But the federal judiciary views access to available avenues of protest of such importance that at least five circuit courts have nevertheless extended such protection to informal protesters. See EEOC v. Romeo Community Schools (6th Cir.1992). But see Lambert v. Genesee Hospital (2d Cir.1993). Consistent with the tradition under FLSA, it has been held that EPA authorizes compensatory and punitive damages for unlawful retaliation. Travis v. Gary Community Mental Health Center, Inc. (7th Cir.1990).

2.   ENFORCEMENT, LIMITATIONS, AND REMEDIES

a.   Enforcement

Although the EEOC has enforcement responsibility and may file civil actions under the EPA, a private plaintiff need not exhaust state or federal administrative remedies before proceeding to court. Under provisions of the FLSA that EPA incorporates by reference, the action may be brought in state or federal court against a private or public employer. 29 U.S.C.A. § 216(b). A suit may be brought under the EPA by an employee or the EEOC. The EPA grants authority to the Secretary of Labor to initiate suit against an employer for monetary damages or injunctive relief. The courts have upheld the constitutionality of a 1978 Presidential transfer of this authority to EEOC. See, e.g., EEOC v. Hernando Bank, Inc. (5th Cir.1984).

While under Title VII the EEOC must try to eliminate an unlawful practice through informal methods of conciliation, the EPA contains no similar provision. The Equal Pay Act, unlike Title VII, has no requirement of filing administrative complaints or awaiting administrative conciliation or determination. County of Washington v. Gunther (1981). Accordingly, courts have found no requirement of prior administrative filing or informal conciliation. See *Hernando Bank.*

An employee may initiate suit seeking monetary damages up until the point the EEOC files a complaint against the employer. If the EEOC files an action, the employee's right to sue or become a party to an action brought by other employees is terminated. The EEOC's suit is deemed to commence from the date a complaint is filed that names EEOC as a party plaintiff, or from the date the EEOC's name is added as a party plaintiff.

Suit may be brought individually or on behalf of a class. As under ADEA, if the suit is brought as a class action, each class member must consent in writing to become a party and the consent must be filed with the court. 29 U.S.C.A. § 216(b). Under either ADEA or EPA, therefore, a class action may not be pursued under Federal Rule of Civil Procedure 23. See Lachapelle v. Owens–Illinois, Inc. (5th Cir.1975).

b. *Limitations*

The FLSA provides a two year statute of limitations for filing an EPA action, three years in the case of a "willful" violation. These statutes of limitations compare favorably from the plaintiff's perspective with the 180-day or 300-day administrative filing deadlines of Title VII, now also made applicable to ADEA.

The three-year limitations period for willful violations is available when an employer knows that, or recklessly disregards whether, its conduct violates the statute. See McLaughlin v. Richland Shoe Co. (1988). Willfulness under the FLSA refers to conduct that is more than merely negligent; yet the requisite willfulness for purposes of limitations may be found not just when the employer believes its conduct violates the statute, but also when the employer was merely indifferent to whether its conduct constituted a violation. Trans World Airlines, Inc. v. Thurston (1985); Walton v. United Consumers Club, Inc. (7th Cir.1986).

c. *Continuing Violations*

The judicially-created "continuing violations" doctrine provides certain plaintiffs an escape from the statute of limitations. The doctrine allows a court to take jurisdiction over a cause of action, or impose liability, for a discrete EPA violation that occurred outside the limitations period. Plaintiffs have invoked the doctrine under both the Equal Pay Act and Title VII, but the courts have afforded it a wider sweep in EPA cases. This is probably because of the nature of the sole EPA violation, which is predicated on unequal compensation, which continues from paycheck to paycheck. Brinkley–Obu v. Hughes Training, Inc. (4th Cir.1994).

Because "each unequal paycheck is considered a separate violation of the Equal Pay Act, a cause of action may be brought for any or all violations occurring within the limitations period...." Gandy v. Sullivan County (6th Cir.1994). The plaintiff took a position at a pay rate below that of her predecessor and was paid unequally for nine years before she filed suit. The defendant argued that the statute tolled three years after the first unequal paycheck. The court concluded that the action was not time-barred as long as at least one discriminatory act occurred within the limitations period. A majority of circuits concur with Gandy that an actionable EPA violation occurs each time an employee receives an "unequal" paycheck, not just when the first such paycheck is issued. See, e.g., Ashley v. Boyle's Famous Corned Beef Co. (8th Cir.1995).

d. *Remedies*

EPA remedies are governed by two provisions of FLSA, 29 U.S.C.A. §§ 216 and 217. These sections authorize recovery not only of unlawfully withheld wages but also of an equal amount denominated "liquidated damages." An employee plaintiff may then recover unlawfully withheld wages, liquidated damages and attorney fees plus costs. Unlawfully withheld wages accrue from no earlier than two years prior to the filing of the complaint and continue until a court order. The accrual period begins three years prior to the filing of a complaint if the employer is found to have acted "willfully."

After the passage of the Portal-to-Portal Act of 1947, the imposition of liquidated damages in FLSA cases became discretionary with the trial judge. 29 U.S.C.A. § 260. She may not award liquidated damages when the employer proves "to the satisfaction of the court" that it acted in good faith and had a reasonable belief that its conduct did not violate FLSA. The burden is on the employer to show that it acted in the sincere and reasonable belief that its conduct was lawful.

In 1974, FLSA was amended to extend the reach of EPA to state and local government employers. The Supreme Court rejected a Tenth Amendment challenge to the power of the federal government to regulate wages and hours of state and local government entities under the FLSA. Garcia v. San Antonio Metropolitan Transit Authority (1985). It is less clear that EPA damage actions may be brought against states in Federal court. The Eleventh Amendment bars such actions unless Congress in the EPA expressly overrode that immunity by a valid exercise of its authority under § 5 of the Fourteenth Amendment. See Seminole Tribe v. Florida, (1996).

3. GENDER–BASED COMPENSATION DISCRIMINATION OUTSIDE THE REACH OF EPA BUT PROHIBITED BY TITLE VII

In *County of Washington v. Gunther,* the plaintiff challenged the employer's practice of intentionally setting the wage scale for female, but not male guards at a level substantially lower than recommended by its survey of outside markets. That decision was actionable, if at all, only under Title VII; EPA was not implicated because the male and female comparator jobs did not involve substantially equal work. Yet whether Title VII applied was doubtful in view of that part of Section 703(h), 42 U.S.C.A. § 2000e–2(h), known as the Bennett Amendment, which removes from Title VII's reach practices "authorized" by EPA. The Supreme Court held, however, that Title VII may regulate an intentionally discriminatory gender-based compensation practice that EPA does not prohibit—as well as the "unequal pay for equal work" claim that EPA does prohibit. In other words, the only compensation practices affirmatively "authorized" by the EPA, and therefore beyond the reach of Title VII by virtue of the Bennett Amendment, are those insulated by EPA's four affirmative defenses. This holding provides a remedy for intentional, gender-based compensation discrimination to a woman who holds a unique position and therefore cannot invoke EPA for lack of a male comparator.

Gunther provides little guidance, however, on key related questions about the scope of Title VII respecting gender-based compensation discrimination. May Title VII ban pay practices not prohibited by EPA where an employer intent to discriminate can be proved only inferentially, a la *McDonnell Douglas/Burdine*? Can Title VII reach compensation practices neutral on their face that have discriminatory gender impact? Or what if the employer has dual intentions, one intentionally discriminatory and another benign, as in *Price Waterhouse,* the landmark Title VII "mixed motives" decision?

4. COMPARABLE WORTH

The comparable worth theory would mandate upward adjustment in the wage rates of all men and women holding jobs traditionally held predominantly by women, even absent wage discrimination between male and female employees whose work is "equal" or evidence of intentional discrimination based on gender. Plaintiffs would prove simply that a "woman's" job was of similar "worth" to the employer as a "man's" job, yet commanded lesser compensation. The revised wage level is supposed to represent a court's or legislature's evaluation of the job's "worth" to the employer.

EPA affords no relief for a comparable worth claim, because by hypothesis the plaintiff and the higher paid employee are performing non-"equal" jobs. The similarity is only in the "worth" of the respective jobs to the employer. The difficulty with a comparable worth challenge under Title VII is that the differences between the comparison jobs preclude the plaintiff from proving that she suffered intentional disparate treatment. Attempts to secure judicial recognition of the comparable worth theory by challenging the employer's pay system as a neutral practice with adverse impact on women have also been conspicuously unsuccessful. See American Federation of State, County, and Municipal Employees v. Washington (9th Cir.1985).

The Supreme Court has not addressed the issue of comparable worth. But in *County of Washington v. Gunther* the Court specifically noted that allowing the intentional disparate treatment claim there did not require it to make its own subjective assessment of the value of the male and female guard jobs.

Comparable worth claims will therefore probably still fail. Even if the plaintiff may base a prima facie case on the adverse impact of the "subjective" pay practice in question, the employer can assert a market-related justification that is likely to be adjudged a matter of business necessity. In the face of the pre–1991 case law that consistently rejected comparable worth claims, the silence of the Civil Rights Act of 1991 on the subject is a significant indication that Congress hews to the relatively narrow yardstick of nondiscrimination, eschewing gender-based minimum standards. Comparable worth has been endorsed by a few state legislatures, but most states continue to reject the notion that market-driven job wage rates equate to discrimination based on gender.

5. CLAIMS COVERED BY TITLE VII AND EPA

Assume a case covered by both statutes, one involving "equal pay for equal work." Why would some plaintiffs resort to the Equal Pay Act, with its narrow proscription of only one kind of sex-based wage discrimination, when Title VII also prohibits other forms of sex-based wage discrimination and sex discrimination affecting other terms and conditions of employment? The answer lies in varying proof requirements and differences in enforcement and remedial schemes.

In an unequal pay for equal work situation, there are three potentially available ways of proving a

Title VII claim. A plaintiff may offer "direct" evidence of gender discriminatory intent, evidence from which such discriminatory intent may be inferred, or evidence that establishes an EPA violation. The federal circuit decisions are divided over which of these proof modes is permissible or indispensable. Some courts require direct or express evidence of discriminatory intent to show an "equal pay" violation of Title VII. See EEOC v. Sears, Roebuck & Co. (7th Cir.1988); Plemer v. Parsons–Gilbane (5th Cir.1983). But see Fallon v. Illinois (7th Cir.1989). For these courts, then, the *Gunther* facts represent the outer limit of Title VII liability for gender-based discrimination in compensation.

On the other hand, several circuits have decided that the *McDonnell Douglas/Burdine* inferential evidence approach may be used to prove a Title VII violation of unequal pay for equal work. See, e.g., Miranda v. B & B Cash Grocery Store, Inc. (11th Cir.1992). These circuits, however, divide over whether the traditional Title VII allocation of burdens of proof, or the very different framework established by the EPA, controls. A slim majority consider Title VII and EPA claims completely independent; these courts require proof for each alleged violation that tracks the distinct elements and burden shifts of each statute. See Meeks v. Computer Associates International (11th Cir.1994). Other circuits, however, hold that a violation of the EPA is ipso facto a violation of Title VII; this means that the Title VII claim requires no independent evidence of intent, direct or indirect. See Korte v.

Diemer (6th Cir.1990). Regulations promulgated by the EEOC support the latter view. 29 C.F.R. § 1620.27(a) (1993).

The difference between these approaches can substantially affect outcome. The prima facie case for an EPA claim is simply that the employer pays different wages to employees of the opposite sex for "equal work"—work requiring substantially equal skill, effort, and responsibility and performed under similar working conditions. Once the plaintiff has made this showing, the defendant bears the burden of establishing one of the affirmative defenses. There is no separate requirement under the EPA that the plaintiff offer evidence of intent to discriminate; in this sense the EPA is a "strict liability" statute. See *Meeks*.

By contrast, the standard, inferential prima facie evidence required to establish a Title VII individual disparate treatment claim begins with a showing that the plaintiff occupies a job similar to that of a higher paid member of the opposite sex. The defendant must then produce evidence of a legitimate nondiscriminatory reason for paying less. If the defendant does so, the plaintiff may prevail only by proving in a variety of ways that the employer intended to discriminate based on gender. *Burdine; McDonnell Douglas*. In sharp contrast to EPA, employer intent is critical, and the Title VII plaintiff throughout the case bears the risk of nonpersuasion on the "ultimate" question of intentional disparate treatment because of sex. *St. Mary's*.

Until the 1991 Civil Rights Act amendments, these different approaches to the required elements of unequal pay for equal work claims under Title VII and EPA had minimal practical importance. The remedies under EPA were more congenial to the plaintiff than the remedies under Title VII, because EPA afforded the possibility of liquidated damages while Title VII remitted the plaintiff to back pay done. So the plaintiff with only an unequal pay work equal work claim usually took the EPA route, which was also easier to establish. But the 1991 amendments expanded the remedies under Title VII to include compensatory and punitive damages for intentional or "disparate treatment" violations; and most EPA violations fit that description, even if no direct evidence of intent is required. In circuits that equate the eased EPA proof standards with the more stringent Title VII standards, the plaintiff can now recover Title VII's potentially more generous remedies (compensation and punitive damages in addition to back and front pay) by carrying the lighter EPA burden.

C. THE AGE DISCRIMINATION IN EMPLOYMENT ACT OF 1967, AS AMENDED ("ADEA")

1. IN GENERAL

Age differs from race, sex, religion and national origin in that it lies on a continuum, and everyone who lives to be 40 crosses into the federally protected category. The universal vulnerability to age discrimination and consequent identification with its victims generated widespread political support for protection. This support found expression in ADEA remedies that, as originally enacted in 1967, were more generous than those afforded by Title VII as originally enacted in 1964. Indeed, in the 1960's Congress trusted juries to consider fairly claims of age discrimination, but not Title VII claims, and at least in part this is a reflection of the universality of aging. Initially, these factors also engendered sympathetic handling of age claims not only by juries but by the federal judiciary as well.

On the other hand, perhaps because of its very universality, there is a greater general willingness to acknowledge that some types of performance decline with advancing age than that work-related capabilities vary by gender, national origin, or race. Age discrimination is therefore seen as a less invidious form of discrimination; protection is seen as needed only from exaggerated, not from statistically supportable stereotypes, from "arbitrary" rather than all discrimination. Age Discrimination in Employment Act, 29 U.S.C.A. § 621, "Statement of Findings and Purpose."

In recent years, these latter attributes have come to the fore in legislative and judicial decisions, lessening or eliminating the previous relative advantage age discrimination plaintiffs enjoyed over their Title VII counterparts. Congress has retained the 20–employee threshold for employer coverage, while Title VII and the Americans with Disabilities Act apply to employers with only 15 or more employees.

The Civil Rights Act of 1991 eased the Title VII plaintiff's burden of proving disparate treatment discrimination, especially for the common case where employer motives are mixed, but made no similar amendment to ADEA. Soon thereafter, the Supreme Court declared that the plaintiff's ultimate burden in an ADEA disparate treatment case is to demonstrate that the employer's reliance on age had a "determinative influence on the outcome"—a requirement more onerous than the Title VII plaintiff's burden, after the 1991 amendments, to show that race, sex, religion or national origin was a "motivating factor." Hazen Paper Co. v. Biggins (1993).

Hazen also puts in doubt whether the disproportionate adverse impact proof mode remains available under ADEA. Moreover, the ADEA defendant who carries the "same-decision" burden apparently still defeats liability altogether; in contrast, the 1991 Civil Rights Act subjects the Title VII defendant who carries that burden to potential liability for declaratory relief and attorneys' fees. Lower federal courts have explicitly permitted employers to defend ADEA claims by relying on the high cost of employing, and the declining productivity of older workers; the similar Title VII BFOQ defense has been in distinctly bad odor since the *Johnson Controls* decision and new § 703(k)(2). Finally, while the 1991 amendments gave the Title VII plaintiff virtual parity with the ADEA plaintiff with respect to a right to trial by jury, the ADEA monetary remedies originally authorized in 1970 (back pay and, for willful violations, an equal additional amount of "liquidated" damages) remain unchanged and have arguably been eclipsed by the more generous compensatory and punitive damages now available under Title VII.

2. COVERAGE

The ADEA prohibits age discrimination against employees or job applicants who are 40 years of age or older. It is therefore clear that the plaintiff must be 40 at the time of the alleged unlawful employment practice. See, e.g., Doyle v. Suffolk County (2d Cir.1986). In view of the principal purposes underlying its enactment, ADEA has also been held not to prohibit "reverse" age discrimination in favor of an older worker. See Hamilton v. Caterpillar, Inc. (7th Cir.1992). But what if the plaintiff compares his treatment to more favorable treatment received by a younger person who is also over 40? The Supreme Court has held that the ADEA plaintiff need not show that she was replaced by someone younger than forty. O'Connor v. Consolidated Coin Caterers Corp. (1996). Prima facie she need only produce evidence from which it may be inferred that the employer relied on the comparator's younger age in making the challenged decision. The Court added, however, that "such an inference cannot be drawn from the replacement of one worker with another worker insignificantly younger."

An over-forty plaintiff need not show prima facie that he was replaced at all if younger, otherwise similarly situated employees were retained when plaintiff was let go and assumed plaintiff's duties after employer decided it could not afford a replacement. Torre v. Casio, Inc. (3d Cir.1994). It has even been held that a claim lies when the employer, after rejecting the plaintiff, hires, promotes or retains an older employee. See Greene v. Safeway Stores, Inc. (10th Cir.1996).

The reverse discrimination issue is whether over-forty employees, although clearly within the group protected from discrimination on the ground that they are too old, state a cognizable claim when they complain that they suffered discrimination because they are too young. The Seventh Circuit rejected an attempt by workers aged 40–50 to assert that a special early retirement program made available only to workers at least 50 years old amounted to unlawful reverse discrimination against the plaintiff class. In effect the court construed the statutory phrase prohibiting discrimination against an employee "because of his age" as a one-way street banning only discrimination against an individual who is older. The court relied on what it took to be Congress' desire in enacting ADEA to protect older persons only from discrimination rooted in the stereotype that ability and productivity diminish with age. *Hamilton.*

ADEA was amended in 1986 to remove the then current upper age limitation, 70, for the vast majority of covered employees. Thus, in general, ADEA prohibits mandatory retirement because of age at any age. The most important surviving exception authorizes the mandatory retirement at age 65 of a highly compensated person "employed in a bona fide executive or a high policy making position" who has an "immediate, nonforfeitable annual retirement benefit" aggregating $44,000. ADEA '12(c)(1), 29 U.S.C.A. § 631(c)(1). But to be "entitled" to that nonforfeitable benefit within the meaning of the exemption, and hence denied protection, it may not suffice that the executive is actually receiving in excess of $44,000. Two circuits have divided on whether payments in the requisite amount must be due and owing at retirement under the terms of a pension, profit-sharing, savings, or deferred compensation plan, or whether an employer may, on an ad hoc basis, purchase the right to discriminate by inflating the plaintiff's post-retirement income to push it over the $44,000 threshold. Compare Passer v. American Chemical Society (D.C.Cir.1991) with Morrissey v. Boston Five Cents Savings Bank (1st Cir.1995).

Until recently, other exceptions permitted the mandatory retirement of tenured college- and university-level professors and law enforcement officers and firefighters. They were subject to involuntary retirement at age 70 or, in the case of public safety officers, younger, at the local governments' discretion. Those exceptions expired December 31, 1993. A 1996 statute re-establishes for at least four years a retirement exemption with respect to the public safety officers, but it does not renew the expired exemption concerning tenured faculty. ADEA § 4(j), 29 U.S.C. § 623(j), as reenacted and amended by the Age Discrimination in Employment Amendments of 1996, Pub.L. 104–208, effective September 30, 1996.

ADEA covers "employers" who have 20 or more employees for each working day in each of 20 weeks in the current or preceding calendar year. As under Title VII, the appellate courts have held that an individual supervisor of the corporate employer is not himself an "employer" liable under ADEA. See, e.g., Birkbeck v. Marvel Lighting Corp. (4th Cir.). It also covers labor unions having 25 members, as well as employment agencies. As of July 1994, the numerical coverage threshold under the 1990 Americans with Disabilities Act has been coextensive with that under Title VII, namely 15 employees; this will mean that fewer persons will be protected from age than from the other major forms of discrimination.

The Older American Act Amendments of 1984 specifically protect U.S. citizens "employed by an employer in a workplace in a foreign country," which covers overseas employees of American and American-dominated corporations. State and local governments were included in the term "employer" by amendments in 1974, a constitutional exercise of Congressional authority under the Commerce Clause. EEOC v. Wyoming (1983). But after Seminole Tribe v. Florida, (1996), suit against a state under ADEA may proceed in Federal court only if ADEA is also a valid exercise of Congressional power under § 5 of the 14th Amendment that expressly abrogates the state's Eleventh Amendment immunity. Two circuits, the Eleventh and the Eighth, have answered this question in the negative, but the 2d, 3d, 7th, 9th and 10th have found an express and valid abrogation. *See* Humenansky v. Regents of the University of Minnesota, (8th Cir.1998). ADEA has been held to constitute the exclusive remedy for age discrimination in government employment. See Zombro v. Baltimore City Police Department (4th Cir.1989).

Elected officers of state and local government are excluded from the "employee" definitions and thus enjoy no protection under Title VII or ADEA. See Title VII § 701(f), 42 U.S.C.A. § 701(f), and ADEA § 11(f), 29 U.S.C.A. § 630(f). Until recently, these definitions also excluded from protection members of such officers' personal staffs, immediate advisors, and other appointees responsible for setting policy, unless they were subject to state or local civil service laws. But the Civil Rights Act of 1991, overturning a Supreme Court decision, generally protects these previously exempt appointees of elected officials by extending to them all "rights" and "protections" of both Title VII and ADEA, together with the "remedies" that would ordinarily be available in actions against state or local government—that is, all but punitive damages. See § 321(a), incorporating § 302(1) (Title VII rights), § 302(2) (ADEA rights), and § 307(h) (Title VII and ADEA remedies). But unlike other state or local government (or private) employees, these newly-covered government appointees do not receive a de novo hearing in state or federal court but are remitted to an adjudicatory hearing before EEOC, subject only to limited judicial review. Sections 321(c) and (d).

Although ADEA does not include the federal government within the definition of "employer," a separate provision requires that personnel actions affecting most federal employees 40 or older shall be made "free from any discrimination based on age." § 15, 29 U.S.C.A. § 633a. Specific provisions in other statutes authorize mandatory separation of federal air traffic controllers and law enforcement officers and firefighters at various specified ages. See 5 U.S.C.A. § 8335; and only civilian members of the military departments are covered. Helm v. California (9th Cir.1983).

EEOC has adjudicatory authority to resolve federal employees' age discrimination complaints. In contrast to federal employee complaints under Title VII, the federal service age discrimination complainant may bypass any process available from his employing agency as well as from EEOC and proceed directly to federal court for a de novo hearing. A complainant making this choice need only give EEOC, within 180 days after the alleged unlawful employment practice, 30 days' notice of its intent to sue. ADEA § 15(c), (d), 29 U.S.C.A. § 633a(c), (d). The federal age discrimination complainant who chooses to initiate administrative review of the challenged decision will be deemed to have exhausted those remedies if the employing agency or EEOC has taken no action on a charge within 180 days of its filing. Alternatively, if the agency or EEOC reaches a decision, the complainant has 90 days

within which to file a judicial action. See Adler v.
Espy (7th Cir.1994).

3. PROOF MODES

ADEA forbids age discrimination in hiring, firing
or classifying employees or job applicants, and in
any other "terms, conditions, or privileges of employment." 29 U.S.C.A. § 623(a)(1). ADEA also prohibits the creation of an age-hostile environment.
Crawford v. Medina General Hospital (6th Cir.
1996). It bans bias in employment advertisements
or referrals.

The prima facie theories of liability under ADEA
parallel those of Title VII, from which its language
was derived. Many cases involve express or direct
evidence, such as statements attributed to management agents that the employer needs "new blood"
or strives to become "young, lean, and mean."
Liability may not be predicated on such statements
when they are merely "stray remarks in the workplace," for example comments uttered by co-employees or low-level supervisors or others divorced
from the decisional process affecting the particular
plaintiff. Even a supervisor's comment that the
plaintiff was an "old fart" did not demonstrate that
the employer's stated reason for not rehiring plaintiff was pretextual, absent a nexus between the
supervisor's state of mind and the employer's reason for its decision. Bolton v. Scrivner, Inc. (10th
Cir.1994).

But statements expressly reflecting preference for youth or animus toward age lose their "stray" character and become actionable when announced by top executives, incorporated into official company planning documents, or uttered by a representative of management with decisionmaking or recommending authority with respect to the plaintiff. See EEOC v. Manville Sales Corp. (5th Cir.1994). And the fact that such comments were made over a long period of time argues for rather than against their admissibility; while any particular comment may be remote in time from the alleged violation, as a whole the comments may show a pattern of age-based animus. Moreover, age-related remarks that can be linked to managers responsible for overseeing the implementation of a layoff are relevant as tending to show that the layoffs themselves were tainted by unlawful motivation. Armbruster v. Unisys Corp. (3d Cir.1994).

The BFOQ defense of § 4(f)(1), applicable to express age-related employment actions, has been limited by the Supreme Court to circumstances where age would prevent virtually all members of the excluded group from performing the job in question because they lack a trait essential to the business. Western Air Lines, Inc. v. Criswell (1985). Presumably, given the cross-pollination of BFOQ principles between decisions under Title VII and ADEA, a BFOQ under ADEA must now meet the even more stringent requirements of *Johnson Controls*. BFOQ is the employer's principal defense to the age-based forced retirement of an individual; § 4(f)(2), after its amendment in 1978, no longer countenances the use of benefit plans to compel retirement at any age. Public Employees Retirement System of Ohio v. Betts (1989).

The most common mode of proof tracks the individual *"McDonnell Douglas"* disparate treatment case of the kind that also predominates under Title VII. See *O'Connor v. Consolidated Coin Caterers Corp.* In such cases employers have enjoyed particular success when the plaintiff's termination can be shown to have taken place as part of a comprehensive, economically motivated reduction in force or "RIF." Because a force reduction is itself a legitimate reason for termination, courts typically require plaintiffs discharged in those circumstances to produce "plus" evidence beyond the prima facie case tending to show that age was a factor in the challenged termination. See, e.g., Hardin v. Hussmann Corp. (8th Cir.1995). One plaintiff carried that burden by offering evidence of two age-related comments by company officials in connection with the transfer of two younger employees into the department from which plaintiff had been downsized. *Hardin.* Another succeeded by showing half-hearted efforts to place him in alternative positions for which he was qualified. The company's statistical evidence tending to show that the organization as a whole was not age-discriminatory failed to conclusively negate the inference plaintiff's evidence raised that he individually had been treated unfavorably because of his age. Cronin v. Aetna Life Insurance Co. (2d Cir.1995).

If a plaintiff makes that showing, the employer must come forward with an age-neutral justification for her discharge—a neutral justification other than simply that the termination took place as part of the reduction in force. Viola v. Philips Medical Systems of North America & North American Philips Corp. (2d Cir.1994). Indeed in one circuit "RIFFed" plaintiffs enjoy an easier burden than the "single-discharge" plaintiff. They need only show that younger employees received more favorable treatment during a RIF, and not that their particular replacements were younger. Collier v. Budd Co. (7th Cir.1995). The inference of discriminatory treatment is not drawn so lightly in a single-discharge case, where there is no assumption that job requirements are fungible unless the single plaintiff's responsibilities are absorbed by others. Gadsby v. Norwalk Furniture Corp. (7th Cir.1995).

The plaintiff must show prima facie that one or more persons significantly younger than herself were retained, while she was dismissed despite having met the employer's legitimate performance expectations. Even then, the employer can avoid liability by offering evidence of a legitimate nondiscriminatory reason for retaining the younger workers, thereby casting on the plaintiff the final burden of demonstrating the pretextual nature of that justification. See King v. General Electric Co. (7th Cir.1992). One potent defense in ADEA actions is that the supervisor who imposed the employment detriment (e.g. firing) on the plaintiff is the same person who hired him, which makes allegations of animus against older people less plausible. Brown v. CSC Logic, Inc. (5th Cir.1996). In such circumstances, the plaintiff must show that this proffered justification is a pretext for age discrimination. Roper v. Peabody Coal Co. (7th Cir. 1995). As under Title VII, the more generalized and subjective the justification, the more vulnerable it is to a finding of "pretext."

The Supreme Court's recent refinement of the Title VII "pretext" concept in *St. Mary's* has recently been adapted to actions under ADEA. Thus even though the employer's stated reason for its conduct is refuted by the evidence, the employer may be absolved of liability if the factfinder determines that the false explanation was a cover for something other than discrimination because of age. See, e.g., Miller v. CIGNA Corp. (3d Cir.1995). ADEA plaintiffs who attempt to show pretext solely by attempting to undermine the employer's stated legitimate reason may anticipate even more exacting scrutiny under the *St. Mary's* standard than Title VII plaintiffs, because the ADEA plaintiff's burden after *Hazen* is to demonstrate that age is not merely a "motivating" but a "determinative" factor in the employer's decision. See, e.g., Rhodes v. Guiberson Oil Tools (5th Cir.1996); *Miller v. CIGNA Corp.* Perhaps because of this complicating consideration, the lower courts are experiencing at least as much difficulty in applying *St. Mary's* to ADEA cases as to actions under Title VII.

4. MIXED MOTIVES IN ADEA DISPARATE TREATMENT CASES

Where the plaintiff's evidence shows lawful as well as unlawful factors for the employer's conduct, ADEA plaintiffs must generally show that age was a determinative factor in the challenged employment decision; the employer must then carry the burden of persuading that it would have taken the same employment action independent of the unlawful component of its aggregate complex of reasons. See, e.g., Rose v. National Cash Register Corp. (6th Cir.). Where there is no employer admission of unlawfulness, and the evidence does not reveal an obviously unlawful motivation, the jury should be charged that the plaintiff must prove age played a "determinative" role in the challenged decision. That requires a showing, where the challenged decision proceeds from more than one motive, that age was a "but-for" cause of the decision; it does not require a showing that the unlawful factor was predominant. *Miller.* Although the "determining" or "determinative" factor requirement frequently appears in the ADEA opinions of the lower federal courts, it has not been squarely endorsed by the Supreme Court. Simpler words recently recommended by the Seventh Circuit for jury instructions on this issue ask "whether age accounts for the decision—in other words, whether the same events would have transpired if the employee had been younger than 40 and everything else had been the same." Gehring v.

Case Corp. (7th Cir.1994). See Umpleby v. Potter & Brumfield, Inc. (7th Cir.1995).

Key amendments made to Title VII made by Section 107 of the Civil Rights Act of 1991 shed light by way of contrast on the proof elements, defenses and remedies under ADEA. That section declares a Title VII unlawful employment practice established when the plaintiff demonstrates that employer reliance on protected group status was a "motivating factor" for "any" employment practice, "even though other factors also motivated the practice." Section 107, adding Title VII § 703(m), 42 U.S.C.A. § 2000e–2(m)(1988). Once plaintiff shows a discriminatory motivating factor, the Title VII defendant employer has the burden of demonstrating by a preponderance of the evidence "that it would have taken the same action in the absence of the impermissible motivating factor." Section 107(b), adding Title VII § 706(g), 42 U.S.C.A. § 2000e–5(g) (1972).

The text of these sections suggest that the Title VII defendant's "same decision" burden is triggered not only by "direct" testimony of discriminatory motive, or substantial evidence that an employer agent, practice or policy treated the plaintiff adversely on a prohibited ground, but also by the more common and less telling *McDonnell Douglas/Burdine* "inferential" evidence that the plaintiff applied, was minimally qualified, and was rejected. Further, the defendant must carry the "same-decision" showing by a preponderance of the evidence. Section 104 (adding subsection 701(m) to Title VII,

42 U.S.C.A. § 2000e(m)). Finally, even if the defendant succeeds with "same-decision" showing, it does not escape liability entirely. Although the employer will not be liable for back or front pay or backward-looking damages, it is still deemed to have committed a law violation remediable by prospective relief and attorneys' fees. Section 107(b)(3) (adding paragraph (2)(B) to § 706(g) of Title VII, 42 U.S.C.A. § 2000e–5(g)).

It is unclear which if any of these important modifications to Title VII mixed-motive cases will ultimately be held to apply to actions under ADEA. Although other parts of the 1991 Act refer directly to ADEA, § 107 does not. If the omission is ultimately regarded as legislative oversight, the ADEA defendant, like the Title VII one, will be forced to carry the same-decision burden regardless of whether the plaintiff established prima facie that age was a "determinative" factor through "direct" evidence or the *McDonnell Douglas* inferential formula. Moreover, the employer who carries the "same-decision" burden will still have violated ADEA and be liable for prospective relief and attorneys' fees. But lower federal courts have instead been giving the 1991 Act a "plain text" reading, thereby treating the absence of any reference to ADEA in § 107 as advertent. Accordingly, they consider ADEA mixed-motive cases to be governed by the pre–1991 Act Title VII regime of the *Price Waterhouse* plurality, as tightened up by concurring Justices White and O'Connor. Under that view the employer does not bear a "same-decision" burden unless the plaintiff's prima facie evidence of age-based motivation is "direct," "substantial," or both. See *Miller v. CIGNA Corp.* In addition, a defendant who does carry that burden will not be exposed to declaratory relief or attorneys' fees as under the amended Title VII, but will escape liability completely.

Of course if the ADEA plaintiff is really required to show prima facie that age was a "determinative" factor in the sense that "but-for" the employer's reliance on age it would not have taken the challenged action, then a "same-decision" defense could serve no sensible function. The employer who carried that defense would be negating exactly what the plaintiff had just proved! That lower courts continue to recognize a same-decision ADEA defense therefore suggests that a "determinative" factor, although more substantial in an employer's calculus than a Title VII "motivating" factor, is nevertheless something less than a "but for" factor.

The individual disparate treatment evidence of age discrimination may be buttressed, as under Title VII, by statistical or anecdotal evidence or both that the employer systemically discriminates on a widespread, routine basis. See EEOC v. Western Electric (4th Cir.1983). But courts have required refined and technically significant statistical evidence and sometimes also anecdotal testimony by multiple individuals before they will conclude that the employer is responsible for a pattern or practice of discrimination.

5.   DOES A "NEUTRAL PRACTICE/AD-
VERSE IMPACT" THEORY SUR-
VIVE UNDER ADEA?

The neutral practice theory derived from the *Griggs v. Duke Power* interpretation of Title VII has until recently been widely recognized to be available to prove claims under ADEA. See, e.g., Abbott v. Federal Forge, Inc. (6th Cir.1990). But the continued utility of neutral practice/adverse impact proof in ADEA actions has been undermined by *Hazen Paper Co. v. Biggins,* a decision limited on its facts to defining age-based disparate treatment. Even if the impact case survives, the plaintiff must show that the employer's practice has significant adverse impact on protected group members vis-a-vis similarly situated employees younger than 40, not on subsets of the over-40 protected group. Lowe v. Commack Union Free School Dist. (2d Cir.1989). And employers have successfully cited cost factors in defending the adverse impact of neutral practices on older workers. One court precluded any use of the disparate impact theory to prove age discrimination resulting from across-the-board, cost-cutting measures implemented by a company in an effort to avoid bankruptcy. Finnegan v. Trans World Airlines, Inc. (7th Cir.1992).

More generally, ADEA complainants face the defense that apparently neutral requirements or benefits limitations that have disproportionate adverse impact on the basis of age are motivated by and are in fact conducive to cost reduction or productive efficiency. Consider, for example, employment compensation geared to years of service, which in turn is usually strongly correlated with age. That employer will incur higher average costs in employing relatively older workers. When the employer then lays off higher-paid employees or those with greater seniority because of the greater cost reductions it thereby achieves, is it unlawfully discriminating because of age? If so, is the form of discrimination express or simply the disparate effect of a neutral practice?

Where the covariance between compensation or seniority and age is overwhelming, most courts, until recently, treated a practice that selects employees for termination or forced early retirement on the basis of higher salary or greater service as a variety of express discrimination. These courts generally followed the EEOC's administrative interpretation which rejects the defense that cost savings is a "reasonable factor other than age" under § 4(f)(1) of the Act. See 29 C.F.R. § 1625.7(f)(1986) and Metz v. Transit Mix, Inc. (7th Cir.1987). But see EEOC v. Chrysler Corp. (6th Cir.1984). Even viewing such practices as neutral, some courts held that cost savings did not amount to a business necessity justifying the resulting adverse impact on protected group members. Leftwich v. Harris–Stowe State College (8th Cir.1983); Geller. Alternatively, they concluded that the defense failed because the employer bypassed available less restrictive means—for example, reducing the salaries of senior workers—to effect the desired savings. See *Metz*.

The Supreme Court may have rendered much of this law obsolete by holding that discrimination on the basis of a factor merely correlating with age— e.g., pension status, years of service or seniority—is not unlawful disparate treatment under the ADEA. *Hazen*. The employer in *Hazen* allegedly fired the plaintiff to prevent his pension benefits from vesting, which the Supreme Court agreed would violate ERISA. But the same conduct, standing alone, does not violate ADEA, the Court concluded, unless a particular employer is dually motivated by the employee's age as well as his pension status, or is shown to have treated pension status as a proxy for age. As guidance for determining whether an employer is motivated by the plaintiff's age, the Court described the "essence of what Congress sought to prohibit in the ADEA" as inaccurate, stigmatizing stereotyping based on the belief that older workers are less productive or efficient. It follows that if an employer fires an employee solely in order to reduce salary costs it is not intentionally discriminating on the basis of age, even if being older substantially correlates with higher compensation. Anderson v. Baxter Healthcare Corp. (7th Cir.1994).

The Court in *Hazen* had no occasion to decide whether employer reliance on years of service or pension status, as distinct from age as such, could violate ADEA as an instance of disparate impact, for no disparate impact claim was made there. It is now more doubtful, however, that the current Court would answer that question affirmatively. The Court continues to view disparate treatment, as distinct from disproportionate adverse impact, as "the essence of what Congress sought to prohibit. . . ." Three justices in *Hazen* alluded to "substantial arguments that it is improper to carry over . . . impact analysis from Title VII to the ADEA." Their logic seems to be that disproportionate adverse impact results because the neutral factor on which an employer relies correlates with age; accordingly, allowing the impact theory would undermine the Court's holding that employer reliance on factors correlated with age is not unlawful disparate treatment.

Long shadows cast by *Hazen* have doomed subsequent disparate impact claims. A school linked salary to work experience in a way that excluded over-40 applicants at 4.2 times the rate of younger applicants. Although the school's years-of-service factor was age-correlated, its salary policy was held "economically defensible and reasonable"; plaintiff therefore had the burden to "demonstrate that the reason given was a pretext for a stereotype-based rationale." EEOC v. Francis W. Parker School (7th Cir.1994). Other circuits have launched more frontal attacks on the ADEA impact claim, relying not just on *Hazen* but on Congress' failure, when it codified the Title VII impact theory in the 1991 Civil Rights Act, to add a parallel provision to the ADEA. See Ellis v. United Airlines, Inc. (10th Cir.).

Even when ADEA disparate impact claims are recognized, they are subject to a defense unavailable to the Title VII defendant.

The provisions of the 1991 Civil Rights Act that restrict the impact defense by tying the employer's justification to the plaintiff's particular job as well as the overall business make no mention of the ADEA. So cost savings remains a defense to ADEA disproportionate adverse impact claims, even though that action is not related to the capability of an individual to perform a particular job. See Jones v. Unisys Corp. (10th Cir.1995).

6. RETALIATION

Section 623(d) of ADEA provides protection against retaliation. Former employees, in particular those who have been discharged, are among the "employees" shielded by § 623(d). *Passer v. American Chemical Society.* Further, the employer need not have affected the terms or conditions of the former employment; withholding letters of recommendation or providing negative information to prospective employers may also constitute forbidden retaliation. *Passer.* The ADEA provision, like § 704, the Title VII counterpart, has been construed to shield a wide range of on-the-job "opposition" in addition to formal participation in ADEA proceedings. See, e.g., Grant v. Hazelett Strip–Casting Corp. (2d Cir.1989).

7. THE OLDER WORKERS BENEFIT PROTECTION ACT

Prior to the 1990 enactment of the Older Workers Benefit Protection Act ("OWBPA"), § 4(f)(2) of the

ADEA exempted employers from liability for "a bona fide employee benefit plan such as retirement, pension, or insurance plan, which is not a subterfuge to evade the purpose of [the ADEA]." 29 U.S.C.A. § 623(f)(2). The EEOC had interpreted this exemption to require a cost justification for any age discriminatory provision in an employee benefit plan. The interpretation required that any reduction in fringe benefits for older employees would be lawful only if the employer's actual cost of providing that benefit was higher for older employees than younger ones and the employer was spending the same amount for its older employees as its younger ones. Thus, an employer was permitted to reduce the health insurance coverage of an older employee only if the premiums for covering the worker were greater than those of covering a younger employee.

The Supreme Court, rejecting the unanimous position of the courts of appeals and the EEOC, gave former section 4(f)(2) an expansive reading. *Public Employees Retirement System of Ohio v. Betts*. First, the Court held that the exemption pertains to plans that regulate any fringe benefit (for example, disability plans) and not just to retirement, pension, or insurance plans. Second, as a matter of law, a plan provision adopted before an employer becomes subject to ADEA cannot be deemed a "subterfuge" to evade the Act's purposes. Third, even a plan provision adopted thereafter will not be considered a subterfuge except in the unlikely event that the plaintiff is able to prove that it was "intended to serve the purpose of discriminating in some non-fringe-benefit aspect of the employment relation," such as discrimination in hiring or compensation.

The OWBPA, enacted October 16, 1990, repeals the § 4(f)(2) exemption, reinstates the EEOC cost justification rule, and declares that employee benefit plans are covered by the ADEA's general prohibition against age discrimination. Specifically, the Act requires that "for each benefit or benefit package, the actual amount of payment made or cost incurred on behalf of an older worker [shall be] no less than that made or incurred on behalf of a younger work."

The OWBPA also expressly permits employers to follow the terms of a bona fide seniority system, provide for the attainment of a specified age as a condition of eligibility for a pension plan, and provide bona fide voluntary early retirement incentive plans. Such a voluntary plan is bona fide if it does not confer more valuable benefits on younger workers.

8. WAIVER OF RIGHTS OR CLAIMS UNDER THE ADEA AFTER OWBPA

Some employers have required employees to sign a release waiving all rights and claims, if any, under the ADEA as a condition to receiving severance benefits. Prior to the enactment of OWBPA, the ADEA did not state whether an employee could release her rights under the ADEA without supervision by the EEOC. Courts of Appeals, however, generally have upheld the validity of private releases so long as a waiver is "knowing and voluntary."

The OWBPA resolves this question by specifically permitting unsupervised releases (those not approved by EEOC), provided that: (1) the waiver is in writing and written in terms likely to be understood by the average individual eligible to participate in the plan (or by the individual herself); (2) the waiver specifically refers to the rights or claims arising under the ADEA; (3) the individual does not waive rights or claims that may arise *after* the waiver is executed (See Adams v. Philip Morris, Inc.) (6th Cir.1995); (4) the individual waives rights or claims only in exchange for additional consideration (that is, consideration in addition to anything of value the individual is already entitled to receive); (5) the individual is advised in writing to consult with an attorney prior to executing the waiver; (6) the individual is given at least 21 days in which to consider the agreement (the individual must be given 45 days if the waiver is requested in connection with an exit incentive or group termination program); (7) the agreement provides for a period of at least seven (7) days following execution to revoke the agreement and does not become effective until this period has expired; and (8) if the waiver is requested as part of an exit incentive or group termination program, the employer must inform the individual in writing (in understandable language) of: (a) any class or group of individuals covered by the program and any eligibility factors and time limits for the program; and (b) the job titles and ages of all individual eligible or selected for the program and those within the same job classification or organization unit not eligible or selected for the program.

Waivers are subject to attack as not "knowing and voluntary." See Griffin v. Kraft General Foods, Inc. (11th Cir.1995). No waiver or settlement of an EEOC or court action is considered "knowing or voluntary" unless the above requirements have been met and the individual is given a "reasonable period" in which to consider the settlement. The OWBPA imposes the burden of proof upon the proponent of the release to prove that the minimum statutory requirements for ADEA releases have been satisfied. And no waiver agreement affects the EEOC's ability to enforce the ADEA or an individual's right to file a charge or participate in an EEOC investigation or proceeding.

The Supreme Court has held that a release which fails to comply with OWBPA requirements does not bar an action under ADEA. The plaintiff's retention of consideration received for a waiver agreement does not ratify the waiver, and the employee need not tender back that consideration as a prerequisite to suit. Oubre v. Entergy Operations, Inc. (1998). EEOC has subsequently issued regulations on waiver of rights and claims under ADEA. 29 C.F.R. Pt. 1625 (1998).

Employer policies that require terminated employees to sign a general release of all claims to be eligible for enhanced severance benefits do not discriminate expressly, even though they may put pressure only on members of the over-40 protected group to waive rights under ADEA. The bundle of accrued claims that an over-40 employee would be required to release would not necessarily be worth more than the bundle released by any particular employee under 40. For example, more of the younger employees may be members of minority groups or women, who as such would be forfeiting distinct protection under other statutes that are part of the waiver package.

9.   ADEA PROCEDURES

EEOC is charged with enforcement of the Act, and ADEA provides criminal penalties for intentional or willful interference with its processes. It investigates claims of age discrimination, attempts conciliation, and has the power to file civil actions. But individual actions are the major means of enforcement, and many ADEA procedures and remedies are borrowed from the Fair Labor Standards Act. See, e.g., EEOC v. Tire Kingdom, Inc. (11th Cir. 1996).

The standards for administrative charge filing under ADEA are more relaxed than those under Title VII. The major superficial similarities are the twin requirements that a complainant file a charge of discrimination (1) with EEOC, within 180 days of an alleged violation, or within 300 days in a deferral state; and (2) with an appropriately empowered state agency, if one exists, which then must be deferred to for a maximum of 60 days or until it dismisses or surrenders jurisdiction. But EEOC itself is given only 60 days of deferral, in contrast to the 180 days specified by Title VII, and plaintiffs may then proceed to federal court without demanding or receiving a "right to sue" letter from that agency. If, however, the plaintiff awaits EEOC's right to sue notice, the action must be commenced, as under Title VII, within 90 days after the plaintiff receives it.

In addition, the Supreme Court has leniently construed the ADEA's apparent requirement that a state filing precede the filing of an ADEA action in federal court. A complainant's failure to file a state agency charge before commencing a federal action is not fatal; the federal court will simply stay its proceedings until a state charge is filed and the state deferral period elapses. Oscar Mayer & Co. v. Evans (1979). For this reason lower courts in ADEA cases have also not followed the approach taken by the Supreme Court's *Mohasco* decision under Title VII, which subtracts the 60-day state deferral period from the 300 EEOC filing deadline and thus effectively requires a state filing by day 240; the 300 days to file with EEOC in ADEA actions remains 300, rather than 240 days. Thelen v. Marc's Big Boy Corp. (7th Cir.1995).

Securities industry and other employees who have agreed individually to arbitrate statutory discrimination claims as a condition of employment have been held precluded by the Federal Arbitration

Act ("FAA") from instituting judicial actions under
ADEA without first exhausting the agreed upon
arbitration procedures. Gilmer v. Interstate/John-
son Lane Corp. (1991). It remains unclear whether
those employees will be precluded from resuming
such stayed lawsuits after the issuance of an adverse arbitration award. Further, it is uncertain
whether the compulsion attaches where the arbitration promise is contained in a collectively bargained
agreement negotiated not by the putative plaintiff
but by her union. See Chapter 19, Section G.4.

Until the Civil Rights Act of 1991, the plaintiff
was required to initiate an ADEA action within the
2- or 3-year limitations period applicable under the
Portal-to-Portal Act. But an amendment made by
the Civil Rights Act of 1991 eliminates the Portal-
to-Portal Act limitations periods. Section 115 instead requires EEOC, when it dismisses or otherwise terminates a proceeding, to notify the charging
party, who then may (and must) bring a private
action against the respondent within 90 days of
receipt of that notice. That amendment was not
made to shorten the statute of limitations on ADEA
claims but rather to preserve them: EEOC had
proven incapable of acting on many age discrimination claims before the former 2- or 3-year statutes
expired. Sperling v. Hoffmann–La Roche, Inc. (3d
Cir.1994). Nevertheless circuit courts, regarding the
new 90-day provision as "procedural," have applied
it to bar claims filed after the effective date of the
1991 Civil Rights Act even on claims accruing be-

fore that date. Garfield v. J.C. Nichols Real Estate (8th Cir.1995).

ADEA may be somewhat more restrictive than Title VII in one procedural respect, although probably largely in form. No ADEA class action may be maintained under Federal Rule 23, which in appropriate circumstances permits class members to be bound without their specific consent. But multiple plaintiffs may join together under Federal Rule 20; and "representative" actions are permitted under ADEA § 7(b), which incorporates by reference § 16(b) of FLSA, 29 U.S.C.A. § 216(b). The class representatives must frame their court complaint so as to notify the employer that it will have to defend an opt-in representative action. *Sperling.* (The Third Circuit has also insisted, as a prerequisite to an ADEA representative action, that the class representatives must have included a similar notice in their administrative charge filed with EEOC. Lusardi v. Lechner (3d Cir.1988)). Section 16(b) accordingly allows a would-be "class member" who has not filed a charge affirmatively to "opt in" the action by giving a written consent to joinder as a party plaintiff. The Supreme Court has authorized district courts to facilitate this process by ordering employers to produce the names and addresses of employees similarly situated to the representative and to issue a consent document approved in form by the court itself. Hoffmann–La Roche, Inc. v. Sperling (1989). And the required degree of similarity between the allegations of the putative joiner and those of the named plaintiff is less than is required for FRCP 20(a) permissive joinder. K–Mart Corp. v. Helton (Ky.1995), cert. denied,   (1996).

Further, paralleling the practice followed under Title VII in the case of true Rule 23 class actions, most circuit courts have adopted a "single-filing" rule that rather liberally permits would-be ADEA representees who have not filed timely charges with EEOC to piggyback on the timely filed charges of their co-joined individual plaintiffs or "representatives." See, e.g., Grayson v. K Mart Corp. (11th Cir.1996); Howlett v. Holiday Inns, Inc. (6th Cir.). But see Whalen v. W.R.Grace & Co. (3d Cir.1995).

10.   ADEA REMEDIES

An individual may be awarded injunctive relief, back wages, statutory "liquidated" damages equal to the amount of back wages, attorney's fees, and costs. 29 U.S.C.A. § 626(b), incorporating by reference the remedies authorized under the Fair Labor Standards Act, 29 U.S.C.A. §§ 216–17. Although, as under Title VII, back pay is routinely available as a remedy for a proven ADEA violation, similar limitations on its scope apply. For example back pay will be denied for the period beginning after an employer eliminates the position from which plaintiff was terminated, provided it has not created a comparable position. Bartek v. Urban Redevelopment Authority of Pittsburgh (3d Cir.1989).

The circuits generally approve front pay as an ADEA remedy that is almost routinely available when needed. See, e.g., McKnight v. General Motors

Corp. (7th Cir.1990). But see Blum v. Witco (3d Cir.1987) and Wells v. New Cherokee Corp. (6th Cir.1995). Its duration extends until the plaintiff fails to make reasonable efforts to secure substantially equivalent employment or until he obtains or is offered such employment. See Dominic v. Consolidated Edison Co. of N.Y., Inc. (2d Cir.1987).

Since the age 70 cap on the class protected by ADEA was removed effective January 1, 1987, it is theoretically possible for front pay to continue indefinitely, or at least for the duration of an employee's lifetime as predicted by a standard mortality table. But an employer's normal retirement age may well serve as a practical cap on the duration of what would otherwise be an astronomical total amount of front pay. Olitsky v. Spencer Gifts, Inc. (5th Cir.1992).

Liquidated damages equal to the compensatory back pay award are available under ADEA in the same circumstances as they are available under the EPA, i.e., when the violation is "willful" within the meaning of the FLSA. This means that the double award is available only if the employer knows that its employment practice violates ADEA or recklessly disregards whether its conduct will violate the Act; it is not enough that the employer knows that the Act is potentially applicable to the practice in question. *Trans World Airlines Inc. v. Thurston,*. Employer conduct must be more than merely voluntary and negligent to constitute a willful violation, but need not involve the kind of egregiousness or malice that most circuits require for punitive damages under Title VII or ADA. The Supreme Court specifically rejects these additional requirements. *Hazen Paper Co. v. Biggins.*

Hazen also made it clear that the *Thurston* definition of willfulness applies to cases concerning alleged ad hoc disparate treatment against individual employees, as well as to alleged disparate treatment resulting from the kind of formal policy at issue in *Thurston*. But the Court also wrote that an employer "who knowingly relies on age" does not "invariably" commit a knowing or reckless violation of the ADEA. This is because the Court's test finds willfulness only when the employer knows that or recklessly disregards whether it is violating the prohibitions of the statute, not simply when it knowingly takes age into account. Specifically, the Court in *Hazen* sought to preserve "two tiers of liability" in ADEA cases by finding liability for back pay whenever an intentional violation is established, but denying liquidated damages even for intentional violations when "an employer incorrectly but in good faith and nonrecklessly" believes that its conduct is not prohibited or is affirmatively authorized by the statute.

Consequently, while conduct constituting a constructive discharge is by its nature serious, aggravated and almost surely intentional, it does not follow that every such violation is willful. Peterson v. Insurance Co. of North America (2d Cir.1994). Some violations, however—unlawful retaliation is an example—may inherently involve knowledge or reckless disregard of the prohibitions of the statute, so liquidated damages should follow as a matter of course from a finding of liability. Compare Edwards v. Board of Regents (11th Cir.1993) with Starceski v. Westinghouse Electric (3d Cir.1995) and Grant v. Hazelett Strip–Casting Corp. (2d Cir.1989).

Although a 1978 amendment clarifies that jury trials are available on liquidated damages claims as well as on claims for lost wages, there are unresolved legal questions about the computation of the liquidated damages award. The major issue is whether the doubling should be based on the full compensatory award, including front pay, replacement of lost pension income, and other fringe benefits or, as one circuit has held, should be limited to the amount of back pay. Compare Bruno v. W.B. Saunders Co. (3d Cir.1989) with Blim v. Western Electric Co. (10th Cir.).

The circuits also disagree whether, when liquidated damages are awarded, the court may additionally award front pay. See Walther v. Lone Star Gas Co. (5th Cir.1992). A similar debate surrounds prejudgment interest. Courts that, despite *Thurston,* view liquidated damages as at least partly compensatory reject prejudgment interest, holding that the plaintiff who receives both would be overcompensated. See McCann v. Texas City Refining, Inc. (5th Cir.1993). Courts that consider liquidated damages as the ADEA's substitute for punitive damages allow prejudgment interest in addition. Starceski; Reichman v. Bonsignore, Brignati and Mazzotta (2d Cir.1987). The latter view is fortified by the Supreme Court's reaffirmation that ADEA liquidated damages are designed to be punitive. Commissioner v. Schleier (1994).

Despite *Hazen's* confirmation that ADEA authorizes "legal remedies," the Civil Rights Act of 1991 gives Title VII plaintiffs alleging disparate treatment important remedies that the circuit courts have uniformly held unavailable under ADEA: compensatory and punitive damages. See Moskowitz v. Trustees of Purdue University (7th Cir.1993). But state law claims authorizing compensatory or punitive damages may often be joined with ADEA claims. See Sanchez v. Puerto Rico Oil Co. (1st Cir.1994).

Accordingly, while it could be said categorically before the 1991 Act that an ADEA plaintiff was remedially better situated than a claimant under Title VII, that is no longer necessarily true. To be awarded more than back and, with luck, front pay, the ADEA plaintiff must prove wilfulness; and even then she is likely to receive an award equal to only back pay doubled, or at best twice the amount of back and front pay combined. By contrast, the Title VII plaintiff, by showing no more than an intentional violation, may now recover not just back and front pay but compensatory damages, although those will be capped in amounts that vary with the size of the defendant's employee complement. Only when she seeks punitive damages must the Title VII plaintiff show something akin to ADEA wilfulness. On the other hand, the 1991 Act caps the sum of compensatory and punitive damages available under Title VII, while there is no absolute cap on the size of ADEA liquidated damages. An ADEA plaintiff who recovers a very large award of back pay, front pay or both may accordingly still find that his liquidated damages exceed the capped amount a Title VII counterpart could recover by way of compensatory and punitive damages.

The 1991 Act denies successful ADEA plaintiffs, unlike their Title VII counterparts, more than a nominal recovery at the statutory rate for the fees of expert witnesses. James v. Sears, Roebuck and Co. (10th Cir.1994). And in contrast to § 706(k) of Title VII, ADEA, per the FLSA, authorizes attorneys' fees only to "plaintiffs," not "prevailing parties." Thus even a prevailing ADEA defendant who can make the extraordinary showing of frivolousness demanded by the Christiansburg Garment interpretation of § 706(k) of Title VII may not be entitled to an award of attorneys' fees from the plaintiff.

D. SEX DISCRIMINATION IN FEDERALLY FUNDED EDUCATION PROGRAMS: TITLE IX

Title IX of the Civil Rights Act of 1964 redresses sex discrimination in employment, as well as in admissions and general educational activities, by federally funded education programs. North Haven Bd. of Educ. v. Bell (1982). Title VI of that Act prohibits discrimination based on race, color, or national origin in federally funded programs or activities. 42 U.S.C.A. §§ 2000d–2000d–4a. But Title VI does not reach employment practices except where a primary objective of the federal assistance is to provide employment. 42 U.S.C.A. § 2000d–3. Accordingly, even though many judicially developed liability and remedy standards are used interchangably in cases under both Titles, discussion here will be limited to Title IX.

Title IX's primary prohibition provides that . . .

No person in the United States shall, on the basis of sex, be excluded from participation in, be denied the benefit of, or be subjected to discrimination under any education program or activity receiving Federal financial assistance. . . . 20 U.S.C.A. § 1681. See also 20 U.S.C.A. § 1684 (prohibiting discrimination because of blindness or severe visual impairment).

Federal assistance includes grants, loans, or contracts other than those of insurance or guaranty. 20 U.S.C.A. § 1682. See 20 U.S.C.A. § 1685 (contracts of insurance or guaranty). One holding of Grove City College v. Bell (1984), that federal assistance funneled directly to students constitutes "assistance" to the students' educational institutions, thus triggering Title IX regulation of programs or of the institution itself, appears undisturbed either by subsequent decisions or by the 1987 Civil Rights Restoration Act discussed immediately below.

1.   COVERED PROGRAMS OR ACTIVITIES

Lower courts had held that discrimination in any Title IX "program or activity" within an institution receiving federal assistance was a violation of Title IX, even if the particular discriminatory program was not the subject of the assistance. But in *Grove City College,* the Supreme Court interpreted the phrase "program or activity" narrowly, holding that Title IX prohibited discrimination only in the particular educational program or activity receiving the federal assistance, not in all the educational programs and activities conducted by the institution receiving such assistance. The Civil Rights Restoration Act of 1987 overturned this holding by defining the "program or activity" covered by Title IX to include "all" of a recipient's operations. 20 U.S.C.A. § 1687.

So where federal aid is extended to any program within a college, university or other public system of elementary, secondary or higher education, the entire institution or system is covered by the prohibitions of Title IX. 42 U.S.C.A. § 1687(2)(B). See Yusuf v. Vassar College (2d Cir.1994). Where a state and local government department (or agency) other than a school receives federal aid for an educational program or activity, and the funds stay within that particular department, only that department is subject to Title IX sanctions; but if the aid is distributed to other departments or agencies, all entities that receive it are covered. 42 U.S.C.A. § 1687(1)(B). Finally, a private corporation that receives aid as a whole or that provides a public service would fall under Title IX; but the entire corporation may not be covered if the federal funds are extended to only a geographically separate facility. 42 U.S.C.A. § 1687(3)(B).

2.   EXEMPTIONS

Title IX redresses sex discrimination in employment by federally funded education institutions. See *North Haven Bd. of Educ.* The Restoration Act exempts entities controlled by religious organizations from Title IX coverage if the application of Title IX's ban on sex discrimination would conflict with the organization's religious tenets. 20 U.S.C.A. § 1687(4).

3.   ELEMENTS OF A PRIVATE ACTION UNDER TITLE IX

The Supreme Court has implied a private right of action under Title IX. Cannon v. University of Chicago (1979). The right of action appears to extend to claims of sex discrimination in employment, for example claims by teachers against school districts. See Preston v. Commonwealth of Va. (4th Cir.1994) The preceding statement must be qualified, however, because a Supreme Court decision holding Title IX applicable to employment practices did not specifically consider whether a violation would give rise to a private right of action. See *North Haven Bd. of Educ. v. Bell.* Thus a debate is emerging in the circuit decisions over whether the existence of a detailed judicial remedy for employment discrimination under Title VII of the 1964 Civil Rights Act (amended as of 1991 to permit compensatory and punitive damages subject to statutory caps) forecloses a judicially implied remedy for employment discrimination under Title IX with respect to gender-discriminatory practices of federally funded education institutions that are actionable under Title VII. Compare Lakoski v. James (5th Cir.1995) with Lipsett v. University of Puerto Rico (1st Cir.1988).

Even if a school district is subject to a private damages action under Title IX for gender-discriminatory employment practices, the scope of such liability is unclear. The Supreme Court has just held in a case involving a teacher's sexual abuse of a student that no damages remedy lies against the education entity unless an official with authority to end the discrimination had actual knowledge of the unlawful discrimination and failed adequately to respond. Gebser v. Lago Vista Ind. Sch. Dist. (1998). Presumably some teachers with gender-based employment discrimination claims could meet this strict standard, but only if the harassment was committed by, or came to the attention of, a principal or other high-ranking administrative official. Liability would be considerably broader, and could more readily reach co-worker harassment of teachers, if the stringent *Gebser* actual knowledge standard is limited to the student-plaintiff context. Then employee plaintiffs might be able to utilize the broader standards of entity liability developed under Title VII.

The administrative regulations promulgated under Title IX, like those under Title VI, prohibit discrimination resulting from facially neutral policies that have gender-discriminatory effect as well as intentional discrimination based on gender. See 34 C.F.R. § 106.21(b)(2). Lower courts have applied the impact principle to Title IX actions when the plaintiff distinctly pleads a violation of the applicable implementing regulations, as distinct from the statute alone. See, e.g., Mabry v. State Bd. of Community Colleges & Occupational Educ. (10th Cir. 1987).

A related uncertain question is whether individual supervisors and managers, as distinct from institutional educational federal funds recipients, are separately subject to Title IX liability. A majority of the few decisions on point hold that they are not. See,e.g., Lipsett v. University of Puerto Rico (1st Cir.1988). But see Mennone v. Gordon (D.Conn. 1995). Creative plaintiffs' counsel have attempted to skirt this obstacle by suing educational officials individually for Title IX violations under the "and laws" branch of § 1983, with mixed success. Compare Seamons v. Snow (10th Cir.1996), with Pfeiffer v. Marion Center Area Sch. Dist. (3d Cir.1990) and *Mennone v. Gordon.*

4.   DAMAGES

The Supreme Court has held that a successful Title IX plaintiff is eligible for all traditional legal and equitable relief that may be appropriate, damages as well as back pay and prospective relief. Franklin v. Gwinnett County Public Schools (1992).

Further, the Civil Rights Remedies Equalization Amendment of 1986 permits federal courts to award retrospective relief under, among other statutes, Titles VI and IX, against a state or state agency, expressly abrogating their Eleventh Amendment immunity. 42 U.S.C.A. § 2000d–7(b). Because *Franklin* concerned intentional discrimination, it is unclear what the effect of its broad language may be on damages in Title IX cases challenging neutral practices.

E. COSTS AND FEES: FEDERAL RULE OF CIVIL PROCEDURE 54(d), THE CIVIL RIGHTS ATTORNEY'S FEES AWARDS ACT, AND FEDERAL RULE 68

1. RECOVERING COSTS OF SUIT: F.R.C.P. 54(D)

Attorney's fees under Title VII or § 1988, the provision authorizing fees for prevailing parties in actions under the Reconstruction Civil Rights Acts, are ordinarily awardable only to prevailing plaintiffs. But either side that prevails is presumptively entitled to *costs* under Fed. R. Civ. P. 54(d). And a losing Title VII plaintiff may be assessed costs even when her claim was not frivolous, unreasonable, or without foundation. Croker v. Boeing Co. (3d Cir. 1981). The awarding of costs lies within the sound discretion of the district court and may be denied where the award would be inequitable. Friedman v. Ganassi (3d Cir.1988).

The "costs" recoverable by any prevailing party are limited, however, to items specified by a separate federal statute, 28 U.S.C.A. § 1920. These include clerk and marshal fees, fees of the court reporters for transcripts "necessarily obtained for use in the case"; printing disbursements and witness fees; specified docket fees; and fees for court-appointed experts and certain interpreters. Most important, "costs" as used in Rule 54(d) do not include the prevailing party's attorneys' fees. This is consistent with the ordinary "American rule," which calls for each side to pay its own lawyer, win or lose, unless there is specific statutory authority for fee "shifting." Title VII and ADEA are such fee-shifting statutes, as discussed immediately below.

2. ATTORNEY'S FEES FOR PREVAILING PARTIES: THE CIVIL RIGHTS ATTORNEY'S FEES AWARDS ACT

The Civil Rights Attorney's Fees Awards Act (the "Act"), a 1976 amendment to 42 U.S.C.A. § 1988, permits a discretionary award of attorney's fees, in a "reasonable" amount, as part of the costs recoverable by "prevailing" parties, other than the United States, in any action or proceeding pursuant to 42 U.S.C.A. §§ 1981, 1982, 1983, 1985, and 1986, as well as Titles VI and IX. The purpose of the award is to enable plaintiffs to attract competent legal counsel. The Act parallels separate statutory authority to award attorney's fees to prevailing parties in actions under the Rehabilitation Act of 1973, 29

U.S.C.A. § 794(a); the Age Discrimination in Employment Act, 29 U.S.C.A. § 626(b) (incorporating standards from the Fair Labor Standards Act, 29 U.S.C.A. § 216(b)) (fees expressly limited to prevailing *plaintiffs*); the Equal Pay Act, 29 U.S.C.A. § 206(d) (also based on the Fair Labor Standards Act, 29 U.S.C.A. § 216(b)); and Title VII, 42 U.S.C.A. § 2000e–5(k). In fact, over a hundred separate statutes allow for court awarded attorney's fees. The principles governing eligibility for and computation of awards are largely interchangeable among these statutes.

Although a plaintiff must receive at least some relief on the merits in order to become a "prevailing party" eligible for fees, success on a "significant issue," even if it is not a "central" one, will suffice. Texas State Teachers Ass'n v. Garland Independent School Dist. (1989). A plaintiff adjudged to be a prevailing party should ordinarily receive a fee award absent "special circumstances," such as the plaintiff's egregious misconduct, Christiansburg Garment Co. v. EEOC (1978), or completely hollow victory.

To achieve success on a "significant issue" and thus "prevail" so as to be eligible for fees, all the plaintiff need obtain is some relief that alters his legal relationship with the defendant and is more than merely technical or *de minimis*. Indeed, even if plaintiff can prove that her lawsuit was the "catalyst" for changes made by the defendant without judicial compulsion or a settlement, and those changes resulted in some significant relief the suit was designed to produce, the plaintiff is eligible for prevailing party status and, in turn attorneys' fees. See Church of Scientology v. City of Clearwater (11th Cir.1993). In general, plaintiff may be considered prevailing so long as the relief eventually obtained is "of the same general type" as the relief originally sought. Lyte v. Sara Lee Corp. (2d Cir. 1991). An injunction requiring a company to correct a racially intimidating work atmosphere, for example, has sufficed as the predicate for a fee award to a plaintiff who lost on most of his individual claims of race discrimination. Ruffin v. Great Dane Trailers (11th Cir.1992). Courts have sometimes resorted to a highly subjective appraisal of plaintiff's original objective in bringing suit. See, e.g., Cady v. City of Chicago (7th Cir.1994).

A finding of a violation under § 1983 may lead to an award of nominal damages where the predicate constitutional violation is "absolute," that is not dependent upon the merits of the plaintiff's substantive assertions or proof of injury resulting from a violation. Carey v. Piphus (1978) (nominal damages available for denial of procedural due process). The Supreme Court has held that a plaintiff technically "prevails" if she recovers only nominal damages, even when substantial damages were sought, "by forcing the defendant to pay an amount of money he otherwise would not pay." But it further held that the amount of a "reasonable" fee award in such a case would usually be nothing, in view of the slight degree of success achieved in the litigation. Farrar v. Hobby (1992).

In Carey the Court held that nominal damages must be available for deprivations of "absolute" rights like procedural due process because of "the importance to organized society that those rights be scrupulously observed...." After *Farrar,* however, plaintiffs suffering little or no actual economic or emotional injury from such a constitutional deprivation will find it more difficult to attract counsel. Of course lower courts may limit Farrar to its facts, where the jury failed to specify the constitutional right violated or find that the defendant's conduct caused the plaintiff's (nominal) damages. Even absent actual damages, an award of nominal damages may permit the § 1983 plaintiff to recover punitive damages for a malicious or aggravated violation of procedural due process. One tactic to evade *Farrar* has been specifically rebuffed. A plaintiff's lawyer first asked for nominal damages at the end of trial, when things looked bleak for his client; the plaintiff, who then recovered $1, was technically prevailing but recovered no fees. Romberg v. Nichols (9th Cir.1995).

But what if the plaintiff seeks only declaratory relief or an injunction from the outset, and he prevails? Has he not then achieved substantial, indeed entire success on the merits? And what if there are multiple claims? A plaintiff's recovery of compensatory damages on less than all of the claims not only makes him technically prevailing but also entitles him to attorneys' fees, although only with respect to the hours reasonably expended in pursuit of the successful claim or claims. See Blum v. Stenson (1984).

Recent decisions struggle to define whether a plaintiff's "primary" goal was recovery of substantial monetary damages or merely injunctive relief to vindicate constitutional rights; if the former, then a "reasonable" fee may be nothing at all where the defendant's conduct is altered but no monetary relief is obtained. Compare Cramblit v. Fikse (6th Cir.1994), with Friend v. Kolodzieczak (9th Cir. 1995).

Because the Court in Farrar mentioned that the plaintiff prevails by obtaining a "consent decree, enforceable judgment or settlement," one circuit concludes that the decision implicitly rejects the catalyst theory. S–1 v. State Bd. of Educ. of North Carolina (4th Cir.). Other circuits, however, continue to embrace the theory, dismissing the quoted phrase as not pertinent to the question in *Farrar*. Zinn by Blankenship v. Shalala (7th Cir.1994); Baumgartner v. Harrisburg Housing Authority (3d Cir.1994).

It has been argued that the *Farrar* limitation, while applicable to all cases under the Reconstruction civil rights acts, should not apply to "mixed-motive" cases under Title VII or the ADA. This is because Section 706(g)(2)(B), added by the 1991 Civil Rights Act, specifically authorizes an award of attorneys' fees even when the employer makes the "same-decision" showing—that is, where the plaintiff has had only partial success. But appellate courts have rejected that argument, observing that the decision to award and the amount of attorney's fees is discretionary under Section 706(g)(2)(B) just as under Section 1988, the provision construed in Farrar. See, e.g., Sheppard v. Riverview Nursing Center (4th Cir.).

Recoverability of fees for services performed in a preliminary administrative proceeding depends in part on whether the proceeding is optional or mandatory. If the state or local administrative proceeding is a prerequisite to a judicial action, as it is under Title VII and ADEA, fees for legal services performed in that hearing can be recovered. New York Gaslight Club, Inc. v. Carey (1980). Fees may also be awarded for successful Title VII or civil rights work performed in state judicial proceedings that are contemplated by the federal statutory scheme, even when no federal action follows. And a prevailing party may also recover, to the degree of her success, fees for services rendered in an unsuccessful judicial action if she ultimately prevails in a subsequent related judicial action. Cabrales v. County of Los Angeles (9th Cir.1991).

If the prior administrative hearing is optional, however, fees are generally not awarded because such a hearing is not considered an "action or proceeding to enforce" civil rights under the language of § 1988. For example, a plaintiff is not required to exhaust his administrative remedies before bringing a § 1983 action, Patsy v. Florida Bd. of Regents (1982); so services performed in administrative proceedings on § 1983 claims are not compensable under § 1988. Webb v. Dyer County Bd. of Education (1985).

Sometimes, however, where the administrative work, while not mandated by statute, is nevertheless "useful and of a type ordinarily necessary to advance the civil rights litigation," fees may be awarded. *Webb.* The Supreme Court applied this exception when it found that administrative proceedings to enforce a consent decree were "crucial to the vindication of [plaintiff's] rights" and accordingly compensable. Pennsylvania v. Delaware Valley Citizens' Council for Clean Air (1986) (*"Delaware I"*). Fees were also awarded to a plaintiff for his attorneys' preclearance work before the United States Justice Department under § 5 of the Voting Rights Act of 1965, where the district court had conditioned plaintiff's remedy on the results of those administrative proceedings. Brooks v. Georgia State Bd. of Elections (11th Cir.1993).

But fees for services performed in optional administrative proceedings are recoverable only if the proceedings are "a part of or followed by" a federal lawsuit on the merits. North Carolina Dept. of Transportation v. Crest Street Community Council (1986). If no judicial action is ever filed, no possibility of recovery exists. At a minimum, then, a plaintiff must file a court complaint. But c.f. Moore v. District of Columbia (D.C.Cir.1990).

Fees may be awarded *pendente lite* when a plaintiff achieves some durable interim relief on the merits, for example an injunction that works some permanent change in the legal relations between the parties. See Hanrahan v. Hampton (1980) More generally, the Supreme Court has approved the award of fees pendente lite to a party who has obtained some relief on the merits at trial or on appeal. Hewitt v. Helms (1987). But plaintiffs do not acquire prevailing party status by virtue of obtaining an injunction pending appeal that merely preserves the status quo, at least in a circuit that determines the propriety of such injunctions principally by balancing the equities concerning the grant or denial of that relief, rather than by weighing the merits. LaRouche v. Kezer (2d Cir.1994). And attorney's fees for preliminary injunctive relief have been denied where the injunction is ultimately reversed on appeal, the party having obtained that injunction then being regarded as not having prevailed. N.A.A.C.P. v. Detroit Police Officers Ass'n (6th Cir.1995).

To calculate the amount of a "reasonable" award of attorney's fees the court must arrive first at a "lodestar" figure that represents a reasonable hourly rate multiplied by the number of hours reasonably expended on matters on which the plaintiff prevailed. Blum v. Stenson; Hensley v. Eckerhart (1983). There is a strong presumption that the lodestar represents a reasonable fee, and any upward or downward adjustments may take into account only those factors not used in arriving at the lodestar. See *Hensley; Delaware I*. Both the reasonable hours and reasonable rates questions are committed to the discretion of the district courts, see, e.g., Zuchel v. City and County of Denver (10th Cir.1993); but elements of legal analysis integral to their decisions are reviewable de novo. Fees sought by the plaintiff that are attributable to attorney time devoted to distinctly unsuccessful claims will be deducted from the overall request. Daniel v. Loveridge (10th Cir.1994). But where a party prevails on only one of multiple legal claims rooted in the same factual nucleus, fees should not be reduced automatically. Instead, so long as the plaintiff has obtained "excellent" relief, he should recover a fully compensatory fee encompassing all hours reasonably expended on the litigation. *See Blum; Hensley.*

Less than "excellent" but still "substantial" relief may warrant a fee reduction in proportion to plaintiff's overall degree of success. *Hensley;* Goos v. National Ass'n of Realtors (D.C.Cir.1996). Fees reasonably incurred in developing an unsuccessful *argument* may be compensable if that argument was in support of a successful claim. Jaffee v. Redmond (7th Cir.1998). By not reducing the fee award simply because the plaintiff fails to prevail on every contention, this approach encourages plaintiff's counsel to advance alternative grounds for relief as authorized by F.R.C.P. 8(e). The lodestar-based fee award need not be proportionate to the amount of damages a plaintiff recovers with respect to a successful issue. Riverside v. Rivera (1986) (upholding attorney's fee award of $245,456 where recovery under federal civil rights statutes was only $13,-300).

Time spent in establishing the prevailing party's entitlement to a fee award under § 1988 is itself compensable. See, e.g., Clark v. City of Los Angeles (9th Cir.1986) (citing cases). But such requests for "fees-on-fees" will be reduced to the degree that the merits "merits fees" award is discounted, as a percentage of merits fees claimed. For example, where plaintiffs recovered 87.2% of the fees claimed for work related to the underlying merits of the action, a reduction of 12.8%, their lodestar award for the fees incurred in petitioning for those fees was also disallowed by 12.8%. The court distinguished a caution by the Supreme Court that fees for work on the merits should not be reduced simply because the trial court failed to reach or rejected alternative legal grounds (as opposed to claims) advanced by a prevailing plaintiff. Thompson v. Gomez (9th Cir. 1995).

Even with respect to claims on which the plaintiff prevailed, fees may not be awarded for hours that are "excessive, redundant, or otherwise unnecessary." *Hensley.* Where EEOC successfully prosecuted a disparate treatment claim on behalf of the plaintiff, who joined the action to assert state law claims on which she did not prevail, a circuit court ruled that she was entitled to attorneys' fees only with respect to the additional contribution, if any, by her attorney to the EEOC's successful efforts. EEOC v. Clear Lake Dodge (5th Cir.1995). But where another court halved the hours for which compensation was requested to account for duplication in services rendered by plaintiff's two counsel, it was an abuse of discretion also to cut the rate of hourly compensation. Carter v. Sedgwick County, Kansas (10th Cir.1994).

The Court in *Blum v. Stenson* held that the lodestar is based on market rates in the relevant community, and therefore fees awardable to nonprofit legal services organizations may not be limited to actual costs. Similarly, fee awards may compensate for the work of law clerks and paralegals, again at market rates. Missouri v. Jenkins (1989). To say that the lodestar rate is based on rates prevailing in the relevant community masks two difficult subissues: which lawyer's rate in a diverse legal community where lawyers of differing experience, special skills, and reputation enjoy different degrees of market power; and which community's rate where a lawyer from one community performs services in another with a significantly different prevailing market average. *Blum* seems to rest on the premise that the appropriate market rate for § 1988 purposes is "the opportunity cost of that time, the income foregone by [the lawyer in] representing this plaintiff." Gusman v. Unisys Corporation (7th Cir.1993). It follows that the established billing rate of the prevailing party's lawyer, in that lawyer's usual working community, deserves significant weight.

The lodestar figure may be augmented to compensate for delay in payment. Risk of delay is compensated "either by basing the award on current rates or by adjusting the fee based on historical rates to reflect its present value." *Missouri v. Jen-*

kins. The Eleventh Amendment does not bar such an adjustment in a Federal court action against a state, because fees constitute an item of "costs" under the language of § 1988, which abrogated Eleventh Amendment immunity.

Additional adjustment factors to the lodestar include the novelty and difficulty of the questions presented, the extent to which the demands of the case preclude other legal employment, the undesirability of the case, awards in similar cases, and the experience, reputation, and ability of the attorneys. These adjustment factors may refine but cannot substitute for the basic multiplication of a reasonable billing rate by the number of hours reasonably expended on successful claims. The Civil Rights Act of 1991 includes expert fees as a part of an attorney's fee award under both § 1988 and Title VII.

Delay in payment should be distinguished from risk of loss or "contingency." A Supreme Court decision has ended a debate among the circuits by flatly precluding a lodestar enhancement for such risk. Burlington v. Dague (1992). Although the underlying claims at issue were brought under modern environmental statutes, the Court's opinion and citations to cases in which fees were sought under § 1988 or Title VII strongly suggest that the holding will apply to fee applications under the latter statutes as well.

What if, as a result of *Dague* or otherwise, a putative plaintiff cannot attract counsel? Title VII Section 706(f)(1)(B), 42 U.S.C.A. § 2000e–5(f)(1)(B), authorizes the court, upon application and under such circumstances as it deems just, to "appoint an attorney" for a complainant and authorize commencement of the action without fees, costs, or security. And what if the court is unable, after diligent effort, to locate a lawyer willing to take the case without up-front compensation? There is authority that § 706(f)(1)(B) may be read to require the coercive appointment of counsel; this reading is partly justified by the fact that the unwilling lawyer may ultimately be compensated by a statutory award of attorneys' fees if his client prevails. See Scott v. Tyson Foods, Inc. (8th Cir.1991).

The Court has held that fee-shifting statutes (§ 1988 in particular) are not violated when prevailing plaintiffs waive their right to such fees in settlement agreements. Evans v. Jeff D. (1986). The Civil Rights Act of 1991 leaves this decision undisturbed.

Section 1988 does not invalidate a contingent fee arrangement providing for payments substantially in excess of the reasonable fee recoverable from the defendant. Venegas v. Mitchell (1990). In other words § 1988 controls only the relationship between the losing defendant and the prevailing plaintiff, not between the plaintiff and plaintiff's own attorney. Venegas thus reinforces a plaintiff's capacity to secure counsel of her choice by upholding the integrity of the private fee agreement. On the other hand, the plaintiff's attorney's fee award under § 1988 may not be limited by a contingent-fee arrangement that calls for a lesser sum than the lodestar. Blanchard v. Bergeron (1989). But see Time Products, Ltd. v. Toy Biz, Inc. (2d Cir.1994).

While a prevailing plaintiff is ordinarily to be awarded attorney's fees in all but special circumstances, the Supreme Court has interpreted § 706(k) to preclude attorney's fees to a prevailing defendant unless the plaintiff's action was "frivolous, unreasonable, or without foundation...." Christiansburg Garment Co. v. EEOC (1978). This appears to mean that a fee award to a prevailing defendant is unwarranted where the plaintiff's claim, although plainly flawed, is colorable, or where plaintiff prevailed on a narrow claim closely related to another on which it failed. LeBlanc–Sternberg v. Fletcher (2d Cir.1998). The plaintiff's failure to establish a prima facie case, the unprecedented nature of a claim, the defendant's offer of a settlement, or the dismissal of an action before trial all figure in determining whether a claim is sufficiently frivolous, unreasonable, or groundless to justify taxing attorney's fees against a plaintiff. If the defendant can show that a plaintiff asserted a claim in subjective bad faith, the case for awarding the defendant his attorney's fees is stronger. But the circumstances warranting fees to a prevailing defendant must be truly exceptional, so much so that a trial court does not abuse its discretion in denying such fees even if no reason is stated for the denial. Maag v. Wessler (9th Cir.1993).

To show the frivolousness, unreasonableness, or groundlessness demanded by *Christiansburg,* the defendant must ordinarily have prevailed on a motion for summary judgment on the merits, Marquart v. Lodge 837, International Association of Machinists and Aerospace Workers (8th Cir.1994), or even on a motion to dismiss for failure to state a claim. But denial of a defendant's summary judgment motion does not necessarily prevent its recovering attorney's fees under the *Christiansburg* standard if plaintiff should have realized, from subsequent pretrial discovery, that his claim was groundless. Flowers v. Jefferson Hospital Ass'n (8th Cir.1995). And the rare prevailing defendant who is eligible for fees under *Christiansburg* may, like the prevailing plaintiff, also recover the reasonable fees and expenses incurred in proceedings to collect the underlying fee award should plaintiff decline to pay it. Vukadinovich v. McCarthy (7th Cir.1995).

Where EEOC is the plaintiff, it is not enough for the defendant seeking attorney's fees to show that EEOC failed to present credible evidence of discrimination. In such a case the defendant has the even more difficult burden of demonstrating that EEOC should have "anticipated at the outset that none of its evidence of discriminatory conduct was credible" or that EEOC unreasonably believed that it had made adequate efforts to conciliate. See EEOC v. Hendrix College (8th Cir.1995).

The strict *Christiansburg* test has been applied to govern the award of attorney's fees against unsuccessful intervenors. The Supreme Court characterized as "particularly welcome" a union's intervention challenging a proposed settlement of a sex discrimination action in order to protect "the legitimate expectations of ... [male] employees innocent of any wrongdoing." Independent Federation of Flight Attendants v. Zipes (1989). The decision held that intervenors would be liable for plaintiffs' costs of defending a settlement only when the intervention is "frivolous, unreasonable, or without foundation...." In effect, then, intervention becomes per se a "special circumstance" that may warrant denial of a fee award to a prevailing plaintiff.

The Equal Access to Justice Act, 28 U.S.C.A. § 2412(d), goes beyond § 1988 and its Title VII counterpart by providing for fee awards to defendants who defeat groundless, but not necessarily frivolous, claims brought by the U.S. government as plaintiff. There is contradictory authority as to whether EAJA is available in actions under statutes (like the Reconstruction Acts, Title VII, and ADEA) that have their own fee-shifting statutes. Compare Nowd v. Rubin (1st Cir.1996), with Escobar Ruiz v. INS (9th Cir.1986).

3. F.R.C.P. 68: THE DENIAL OF POST-OF-FER COSTS AND FEES TO A PLAIN-TIFF WHO REJECTS A DEFENDANT'S OFFER OF JUDGMENT AND OBTAINS A SMALLER OR EQUAL JUDGMENT

Federal Rule 68 authorizes the defendant, at least 10 days before trial, to "offer to allow judgment to be taken against [it] ... for the money or property ... specified in the offer, with costs then accrued." It then provides that, if the offer is not accepted and a judgment obtained by the plaintiff "is not more favorable than the offer, the offeree must pay the costs incurred after the making of the offer." On its face, then, Rule 68 relieves a defendant who makes such an offer that a plaintiff fails timely to accept and that is equaled or exceeded by a final judgment only from what would otherwise be its liability for the "costs" taxable under Federal Rule of Civil Procedure 54(d) in favor of prevailing parties in any federal civil action. Such an offer is valid even when it is conditioned upon acceptance of its terms by all plaintiffs, and a settlement agreement counts as a "judgment" that may trigger the cost-shifting permitted by Rule 68. Lang v. Gates (9th Cir.1994).

Rule 54(d) "costs," however, are relatively minor, as they are universally understood not to include attorney's fees. The real bite of Rule 68 in civil rights and employment discrimination actions results from its interplay with the provisions in Title VII and § 1988 that call for an award of "a reasonable attorney's fee as part of the costs...." Section 706(k) of Title VII; 42 U.S.C.A. § 1988, final sentence. Importing the above quoted language into the word "costs" as it appears in Rule 68, the Supreme Court has held that a defendant's offer meeting the requirements of Rule 68 relieves a losing defendant of liability not only for the ordinary taxable costs of litigation, but also for the plaintiff's post-offer attorney's fees. Marek v. Chesny (1985). The prospect of relief from post-offer fees greatly increases the defendant's incentive to make a Rule 68 offer, and the Civil Rights Act of 1991 leaves *Marek* intact. But Rule 68 cannot be used to force the plaintiff to pay an award of post-offer attorney's fees to a prevailing defendant. EEOC v. Bailey Ford, Inc. (5th Cir.1994). The *Marek* holding has the same effect in actions under any statute that allows fee awards as a part of "costs," including actions under Title VII, EPA, ADA, and ADEA, as well as the Reconstruction Civil Rights Acts.

To meet the requirements of Rule 68 the defendant's offer must include the plaintiff's "costs" up until the time of the offer, including the amount of the plaintiff's attorney's fees then accrued. Accordingly, those fees, together with ordinary costs, must be added to the judgment on the merits to calculate whether the total received by judgment exceeds the offer and thus relieves the defendant of post-offer costs and fees under Rule 68. Scheeler v. Crane Co. (8th Cir.1994).

In another case, the offer promised not only "costs then accrued," as prescribed by Rule 68, but also "reasonable attorney fees as determined by the court." The Ninth Circuit construed this language to authorize a district judge's award of attorney's fees for plaintiffs' counsel's preparation of a fee petition after they accepted the offer. The decision points up the necessity for defendant's counsel to draft tightly worded offers that not only meet Rule 68's strictures but also stay within them. Any waiver of or limitation on attorney's fees in actions under statutes providing for the recovery of fees by prevailing plaintiffs must be "clear and unambiguous." The court indicated that if the defendant had offered only to pay plaintiff's "costs then accrued," the offer would have clearly and unambiguously limited plaintiff's fees to the full extent that *Marek* and Rule 68 permit. Holland v. Roeser (9th Cir. 1994).

The inclusion of attorney's fees in the Rule 68 post-offer "costs" that the plaintiff may be precluded from recovering assumes that the underlying fee statute includes "attorney's fees" within the definition of "costs." That is the case with most fee statutes, including § 1988, its counterpart under ADEA, and the principal Title VII fee provision, Section 706(k). By contrast, since the "mixed-motive" remedies section of Title VII, Section 706(g)(2)(B), refers to "costs" and "attorney's fees" distinctly and separately, attorneys' fees may not be counted as part of the post-offer Rule 68 "costs" a plaintiff is barred from recovering where the entitlement to fees flows only from that section.

F.   DISABILITY   DISCRIMINATION: THE AMERICANS WITH DISABILITIES ACT OF 1990 AND THE REHABILITATION ACT OF 1973

Title I of The Americans With Disabilities Act of 1990 ("ADA") represents the first comprehensive national legislation banning employment discrimination on the basis of physical or mental disability. Like Title VII, ADA prohibits not only intentional or "disparate treatment" discrimination on the part of covered employers—those with 15 or more employees—but also generally applied, facially "neutral" employment tests, practices or standards that have a disproporationate adverse impact on the disabled. The latter may be justified only if the employer shows them to be "job-related and consistent with business necessity." One set of neutral practices—medical inquiries or examinations (other than those testing for the use of illegal drugs)—is specifically outlawed until an offer of employment is made; thereafter, actual employment may be conditioned on the results of medical history questions and examinations, but those must meet the job-relatedness/business necessity requirement, and their results must be held confidential. But while pre-offer inquiries to applicants concerning the existence or severity of a disability are prohibited, employers may ask whether the employee can perform essential job-related functions.

ADA is distinct from standard employment discrimination laws in its affirmative additional requirement that employers provide "qualified" disabled individuals "reasonable accommodation." An individual is "qualified" if, with or without such accommodation, she can perform the "essential" (not all) functions of the job in question. See Deane v. Pocono Medical Center (3d Cir.1998). The employer bears the burden of showing the infeasibility, excessive cost, or other undue hardship involved in providing the accommodation proposed by the disabled employee.

In this respect and others ADA is an outgrowth of § 504 of the Rehabilitation Act of 1973, 29 U.S.C.

§ 701 et seq. ("RHA"), which prohibits federal funds recipients from excluding or discriminating against any "otherwise qualified handicapped individual" in "any program or activity receiving federal financial assistance." The Civil Rights Restoration Act of 1987 overruled *Grove City College* with respect to Section 504, thereby effectively banning discrimination in all the recipient institution's operations, not merely in programs or activities for which federal assistance is granted. RHA Section 504 is enforced by the administrative procedures of Title VI, which may lead to termination of funding or refusal to extend future assistance. In addition, the Supreme Court, without expressly deciding whether Section 504 gives rise to a private right of action, has approved the award of relief in such a case and held that employers violate the statute even if the federal aid they receive is not for the primary purpose of promoting employment. See Consolidated Rail Corp. v. Darrone (1984). By contrast, lower courts have held that there is no private right of action right under Section 503 of the Act, which requires federal government contractors to "take affirmative action to employ and advance in employment qualified handicapped individuals."

In 1974, Congress amended the definition of "handicapped individual" for Section 504 purposes to include not just those with actual physical impairments, "but also those who are regarded as impaired and who, as a result, are substantially limited in a major life activity...." School Board of Nassau County v. Arline (1987). Moreover, a person suffering impairment of major life activities from tuberculosis is considered handicapped even though his disease is contagious. *Id.* But to be eligible for relief, a plaintiff must generally also be "otherwise qualified," or able to perform the "essential functions" of the particular job. And while inability to function may not be inferred simply from the fact of a handicap, a tuberculosis sufferer may not be "otherwise qualified" if his contagion poses "a serious health threat to others."

The ADA, and decisions construing it, adhere for the most part to the RHA model, expanding it to private, state and local government employment. (The ADA excludes from coverage as employers wholly owned United States corporations and tax-exempt private membership clubs.) An employer may require that every employee be qualified to perform the "essential functions" of a job (the phrase is part of the definition of a "qualified person with a disability); but the judgment whether a disabled employee can so perform must take into account feasible reasonable accommodations." So employers can continue to require that all applicants and employees, including those with disabilities, be able, or with reasonable accommodation be enabled, to perform the essential, i.e., non-marginal functions of the job in question. Although applicants for Social Security disability benefits must also be disabled to be eligible, disability within the meaning of that act does not inquire if the applicant could fulfill the functions of a particular job after receiving reasonable accommodation. Accordingly, most circuits have held that application for or receipt of social security benefits will not by itself defeat an ADA claim through the doctrine of judicial estoppel. See decisions summarized in Rascon v. U.S. West Communications, Inc. (10th Cir.1998).

The determination of whether a person is qualified should be made at the time of an employment action, for example, hiring or promotion. The "qualification" of an applicant should not be based on the possibility that the employee or applicant will become incapacitated and unqualified in the future. And the ADA frowns on paternalistic concerns about what would be best for the person with the disability, since these serve to foreclose employment opportunities.

Under the ADA an employer remains free to select the most qualified applicant available and to make decisions based on reasons unrelated to the existence or consequence of a disability. Employment decisions must not have the purpose or effect of subjecting a qualified individual with a disability to discrimination based on that disability. The non-discrimination concept does not prohibit an employer from devising physical or other job criteria or tests for a job so long as the criteria and tests are job-related and consistent with job necessity. Even a nondiscriminating employer, however, must on an applicant's or employee's request determine whether a reasonable accommodation would enable the disabled person to perform the essential functions of the job without imposing an undue hardship on the business.

Title I prohibits discrimination by employers, unions, employment agencies and union-management committees against "any qualified individual with a disability" regarding any term, condition or privilege of employment.

Section 3(2) of the ADA defines "disability" as:

(1) a mental or physical impairment that substantially limits one or more of an individual's "major life activities";

(2) a record of having such an impairment; or

(3) being regarded as having such an impairment. ADA § 3, 42 U.S.C.A. § 12102.

Section 101(8) of the ADA explains that a "qualified" disabled person is "an individual with a disability who with or without reasonable accommodation, can perform the essential functions of the employment position that such individual holds or desires." This prohibition extends to job applications, hiring, advancement, discharge, compensation, training, or other terms of employment. Section 102(a). Job descriptions are considered primary evidence in establishing the scope of essential functions. Section 101(8).

Title I's broad anti-discrimination policy blends the concepts of equal treatment and affirmative support. Thus an employer may not: (1) classify a disabled applicant or employee in a way that adversely affects the opportunities or status of the person; (2) participate in an arrangement with another organization that has the effect of discriminating against the disabled individual; (3) utilize standards, criteria, or methods of administration that have the effect of discriminating on the basis of the disability or perpetuating discrimination by others subject to common administrative control; (4) exclude or deny equal jobs or benefits to an individual because she has a relationship with a disabled individual; (5) use standards or tests that screen out or tend to screen out an individual with disabilities (unless the standard is job-related and consistent with business necessity); (6) use tests whose results reflect the impairment of the individual rather than the skills or aptitude of the test-taker; or (7) fail to make reasonable accommodations to the known physical or mental limitations of an otherwise qualified individual (unless the accommodation would impose undue hardship.) § 102(b).

The ADA does not exclude infected or contagious applicants or employees from its definition of the "qualified individual with a disability" who is entitled to reasonable accommodation. Indeed the Supreme Court has held in a case under another title of ADA assuring access to services in public accommodations that "asymptomatic" human immunodeficiency virus ("HIV") is in general a covered disability because it substantially limits the major life activity of reproduction. Bragdon v. Abbott (1998) Section 103 of ADA does allow employers the defense of showing that such a person poses a "direct threat to the health or safety of other individuals in the workplace" and that his safe performance "cannot be accomplished by reasonable accommodation...."

The Act neither prohibits nor authorizes testing for illegal drugs, although such tests are not considered medical examinations and accordingly may be conducted even prior to a job offer. Employers may ban the use of illegal drugs and alcohol at the workplace and may hold alcoholics and drug users to the same qualifications and job performance standards as other employees, even if unsatisfactory performance is related to alcoholism.

An EEOC "guidance" on the application of ADA and ERISA to health insurance acknowledges that "not all health-related plan distinctions discriminate on the basis of disability." The guidance permits "broad distinctions" applicable to a "multitude of dissimilar conditions." For example, providing lesser benefits "for the treatment of mental/nervous conditions than is provided for the treatment of physical conditions" would pass muster under ADA. But the guidance also asserts that "health-related insurance distinctions that are based on disability may violate the ADA." And it defines a plan provision as "disability-based" if it "singles out a particular disability, (e.g., deafness, AIDS, schizophrenia ... or disability in general....)" Section 501(c) provides that ADA may not be construed to restrict a health care provider from classifying or administering risks unless it does so as a "subterfuge" to evade the purposes of the Act. Relying on the Supreme Court's interpretation of "subterfuge" as used in another statute, circuit courts have held that a disparity between benefits for mental and physical disabilities does not violate ADA. See Ford v. Schering–Plough Corporation (3d Cir.1998); Parker v. Metropolitan Life Ins. Co. (6th Cir.1997); EEOC v. CNA Ins. Companies (7th Cir.1996); Krauel v. Iowa Methodist Med. Ctr. (8th Cir.1996).

For more detail on the judicial elaboration of the terms "disability," "qualified person," "essential functions," "reasonable accommodation," and "undue hardship," as well as treatment of ADA remedies and procedures, see Lewis, Litigating Civil Rights and Employment Discrimination Laws (West 1996 with 1997–98 Supplement), Chapter 15.

CHAPTER 21

MISCELLANEOUS EMPLOYEE PROTECTION LAWS

A. EMPLOYEE RETIREMENT INCOME SECURITY ACT OF 1974 (ERISA)

Congress enacted the Employee Retirement Income Security Act, 29 U.S.C.A. § 1001 et seq., for the purpose of safeguarding employee retirement and pension benefits. The act established minimum standards for employee participation, vesting standards which create nonforfeitable rights, and funding guidelines. Generally speaking, federal laws preempt all state laws and causes of action which relate to ERISA pension or welfare plans, directly or indirectly. Ellenburg v. Brockway, Inc. (9th Cir. 1985). For example, ERISA preempts state tort and contract actions involving ERISA covered plans. See e.g., Jackson v. Martin Marietta Corp. (11th Cir. 1986) (contract); Dependahl v. Falstaff Brewing Corp. (8th Cir.1981) (tort). As a result of preemption, damages in an ERISA proceeding are limited, but attorney's fees are recoverable. Punitives are not allowed. Massachusetts Mut. Life Ins. Co. v. Russell (1985). Investments are regulated, and minimum standards of fiduciary conduct for trustees and administrators are established, with civil and criminal enforcement measures provided.

ERISA plan administrators have a special fiduciary relationship toward plan participants and beneficiaries. Most federal courts of appeal had applied an arbitrary and capricious standard of review to decisions of plan administration denying benefits. However, the Supreme Court in Firestone Tire & Rubber Co. v. Bruch (1989), placed limits on the utilization of this standard of review, and provided for de novo review, unless a plan expressly grants the necessary discretion to an administrator to construe terms and determine benefits. It should be pointed out that if an employer is found to have acted as a fiduciary toward its employees in misleading them about their benefits, recovery becomes much easier. Varity Corp. v. Howe (1996). Payment of pensions has been assured through the Pension Benefit Guaranty Corporation, which administers the termination insurance provisions. The Retiree Benefits Bankruptcy Protection Act of 1988 also affords workers health, disability, and life insurance protection from insolvent businesses.

B. NATIONAL LABOR RELATIONS ACT

The National Labor Relations Act, as amended, primarily governs employer-union relations. The act grants employees important rights to create or become members of unions, to choose representatives and to bargain collectively, and to engage in or refrain from "concerted activities" for mutual aid and protection. This concerted activity protection is afforded non-union employees, and the National Labor Relations Board (NLRB) frequently intervenes to protect non-union employees so long as their activities are related to wage or working conditions. For example, NLRB involvement based upon "concerted activity" could arise in an employment situation if an employee solicited additional employee support for a group health insurance plan. See Edward Blankstein, Inc. v. NLRB (3rd Cir. 1980). For a more complete summary of the various federal legislation regulating unions, management, strikes, boycotts, etc., see D. Leslie, Labor Law in a Nutshell (3d Ed. 1992).

C. LABOR MANAGEMENT RELATIONS ACT

The National Labor Relations Board ("NLRB"), in administering the Labor Management Relations Act ("LMRA"), may encounter unlawful discrimination during union representation campaigns, certifications, fair representation disputes, duty to bargain situations, or other unfair labor practice proceedings. A certified union's duty of fair representation may be enforced by aggrieved black union members or applicants for union membership in private federal damages actions, Steele v. Louisville & Nashville Railroad (1944), and probably in NLRB unfair labor practice proceedings. See Del-Costello v. International Brotherhood of Teamsters (1983). But minority employees are not protected from union discipline when, bypassing their union, they raise employment discrimination grievances directly with an employer. Emporium Capwell Co. v. The Western Addition Community Organization (1975). An employer probably has a duty to bargain over employment discrimination issues, but employer discrimination standing alone will not constitute an unfair labor practice absent a link between the employer's alleged discriminatory conduct and interference with rights conferred by the LMRA. See Jubilee Mfg. Co., (1973), enf'd sub nom. United Steelworkers of America v. NLRB (D.C. Cir.1974).

Although election results may be overturned if either a union or an employer has appealed directly to race hatred during a campaign, a union is not foreclosed from invoking the election procedures of the LMRA because it has a history of racial discrimination. Compare Sewell Mfg. Co., (1962) with Handy Andy, Inc., (1977). Some courts of appeals, however, have found that the NLRB is constitutionally compelled to withhold certification from an illegally discriminating union. See NLRB v. Heavy Lift Serv., Inc. (5th Cir.1979); NLRB v. Mansion House Center Management Corp. (8th Cir.1973). In any event, the Board may revoke a union's certification if it breaches the duty of fair representation by engaging in discriminatory practices.

D. FEDERAL CONSTRUCTION PROJECTS

Two important federal acts protect workers employed on federal construction projects. The Miller

Act contains a performance bond requirement, and the act permits persons supplying labor and materials to sue in federal district court to collect monies owed for unpaid wages or supplies. The Copeland or "Kickback" Act prohibits by criminal penalty any attempt to force or induce workers to pay kickbacks from wages under federal construction contracts.

E.   EXECUTIVE ORDERS

A number of Executive Orders issued under the authority of the President prohibit employment discrimination. These orders usually establish federal policy in a particular area, require affirmative action programs, and specify responsibility for enforcement. No private rights of action are created, and enforcement and implementation are usually left to the executive agency or department involved.

By far the most important for present purposes is Executive Order 11246. As amended, it prohibits employment discrimination by government contractors on grounds of race, religion, sex, or national origin. It also demands that contractors take "affirmative action" by means of "goals" and "timetables" to boost the representation of protected group members in major job categories to levels that reflect the availability of qualified members of the protected group. There is no specific legislative basis for the Order, but lower courts have followed the lead of the Third Circuit in holding that Congress should be "deemed to have granted" the President the "general authority" to so protect federal interests. Contractors Ass'n v. Secretary of Labor (3rd Cir.1971).

Executive Order 11141 prohibits age discrimination by government contractors and subcontractors; Executive Order 11478 prohibits race, color, religion, sex, national origin, handicap, and age discrimination by the federal government. Other executive orders establish coordinated enforcement efforts and special programs for minority and women's enterprises.

F. FOREIGN BOYCOTT LAWS

The Export Administration Act of 1969, as amended, popularly known as the Foreign Boycott Laws, 50 U.S.C.A.App. § 2407, authorizes the President to prohibit the facilitating of discrimination by foreign governments against "any United States person" on the basis of race, religion, sex or national origin. It also expressly prohibits furnishing racial, religious, gender, or national origin information about any "United States person," or any owner, officer, director, or employee of such person. Violations of the Act or regulations promulgated under it can result in criminal penalties.

G. FEDERAL CREDIT LAWS

The Consumer Credit Protection Act, Title III, prohibits the discharge of an employee because of a garnishment for any one indebtedness. The Consumer Credit Protection Act, Title VI (called the

Fair Credit Reporting Act) regulates the use of credit reports for employment purposes. It should be noted that state laws frequently regulate garnishments. Additionally, blacklisting, employer statements and "service letters" relating to former employees are often areas of state regulation. Some states also regulate or prohibit wage assignments.

H. JURY SERVICE

The Jury System Improvement Act of 1968, as amended, protects any employee's job security in the event the employee is called to serve on a federal jury. See Shea v. County of Rockland (1987) (damages are limited to economic losses). A number of states have enacted similar employee protection laws for state jury service.

I. UNJUST DISCHARGES

Traditionally, the employment at-will concept freely allowed the employer or the employee to terminate the employment relationship at any time and for any reason without further obligation. See Adair v. United States (1908). However, recent litigation and legislation concerning wrongful terminations or unjust discharges have dramatically changed this entire area of the law. See generally, Smith v. Atlas Off–Shore Boat Service, Inc. (5th Cir.1981); Mont. Code Ann. §§ 39–2–901, et seq.

The common-law doctrine of employment-at-will has been the subject of rapid revision by state and federal legislation and judicial decision. Federal and state laws concerning unions, civil service employees, and fair employment give certain classes of employees fairly comprehensive protection from certain types of discharges.

The following theories or laws may provide an employee with a remedy for an unjust discharge or wrongful termination: (1) violation of public policy; see Sheets v. Teddy's Frosted Foods, Inc. (1980) (discussion of illegal act and whistleblowing); (2) breach of an implied contract of employment, usually based upon employment handbooks or oral representations; see Toussaint v. Blue Cross & Blue Shield (1980) (handbook); Schipani v. Ford Motor Co. (1981) (oral representations can override written disclaimers); (3) breach of implied covenant of good faith and fair dealing; see Wagenseller v. Scottsdale Memorial Hospital (1985); (4) breach of express employment contract; (5) promissory estoppel; see Grouse v. Group Health Plan, Inc. (1981) (job change in reliance on employment offer that was later revoked); (6) common law tort actions growing out of the discharge, including but not limited to prima facie tort, intentional infliction of emotional distress, fraud, defamation, tortious interference with contract, invasion of privacy; some jurisdictions recognize a separate tort action for the discharge itself, under the headings of wrongful discharge, retaliatory discharge, abusive discharge, or unjust discharge, etc.; and (7) state and federal statutory protections.

A non-exclusive list of federal statutory protections against discharge includes: the Labor Management Relations Act, 29 U.S.C.A. § 141 et seq.; Age Discrimination in Employment Act, 29 U.S.C.A. § 621 et seq.; Rehabilitation Act of 1973, 29 U.S.C.A. §§ 701, 796i; Equal Pay Act, 29 U.S.C.A. § 206(d); Civil Rights Act of 1964, 42 U.S.C.A. § 2000e–17; Civil Rights Act of 1866, 42 U.S.C.A. § 1981; Civil Rights Act of 1871, 42 U.S.C.A. § 1983; Alcohol Abuse and Alcoholism Prevention Treatment and Rehabilitation Program for Government and Other Employees Act, 42 U.S.C.A. § 290 dd; Vietnam Era Veterans' Readjustment Assistance Act of 1974, 38 U.S.C.A. § 2011 et seq.; Occupational Safety and Health Act, 29 U.S.C.A. § 660; Mine Safety and Health Act, 30 U.S.C.A. § 815; Railroad Safety Act, 45 U.S.C.A. § 441; Longshore and Harbor Workers' Compensation Act, 33 U.S.C.A. § 948; Selective Service Act, 38 U.S.C.A. § 2021; Vocational Rehabilitation Act, 29 U.S.C.A. § 793; Energy Reorganization Act, 45 U.S.C.A. § 5851; Consumer Protection Act, 15 U.S.C.A. § 1674; Employee Polygraph Protection Act, 29 U.S.C.A. § 2001 et seq.; Whistleblower Protection Act of 1989, 5 U.S.C.A. §§ 1213–1222, 2302; Bankruptcy Act, 11 U.S.C.A. § 525(b); Clean Air Act, 42 U.S.C.A. § 7622; Toxic Substances Control Act, 15 U.S.C.A. § 2622; Federal Water Pollution Control Act, 33 U.S.C.A. § 1367; Solid Waste Disposal Act, 42 U.S.C.A. § 6971; Comprehensive Environmental Response, Compensation and Liability Act, 42 U.S.C.A. § 9610; Civil Service Reform Act, 5

U.S.C.A. § 2303; Fair Labor Standards Act, 29 U.S.C.A. § 215(a)(3); Migrant and Seasonal Agricultural Worker Protection Act, 29 U.S.C.A. § 1855; Trade Act of 1974, 19 U.S.C.A. § 2394; Worker Adjustment and Retraining Notification Act, 29 U.S.C.A. § 2101; and the Employee Retirement Income Security Act of 1974, 29 U.S.C.A. §§ 1140, 1141. In a similar fashion, but in a less comprehensive manner, many states have begun to enact protections against discharge.

Traditionally, state unjust discharge actions that involve claims by union employees covered by a collective bargaining agreement, may be the subject of preemption under § 301 of the Labor Management Relations Act, 29 U.S.C.A. § 185 et seq. However, state tort claims, independent of the collective bargaining agreement, are not subject to preemption. Lingle v. Norge Div. of Magic Chef, Inc. (1988).

J. DRUGS IN THE WORKPLACE

Public and private sector drug testing of employees has generated increased litigation and legislation in recent years. This area of the law involves sensitive issues of employee privacy versus employer concern for safety and health. For example, Congress passed the Drug Free Workplace Act of 1988, 41 U.S.C.A. § 701 et seq., to force most federal contractors to establish, supervise, and maintain an employee drug program designed to eliminate the use of drugs in the workplace. See also Skinner v. Railway Labor Executives' Ass'n. (1989); National Treasury Employees Union v. Von Raab (1989).

The National Labor Relations Board views drug testing as a mandatory subject of bargaining when union represented employees are involved. Johnson–Bateman Co. (1989).

K.   POLYGRAPHS

For the most part, the Employee Polygraph Protection Act of 1988, 29 U.S.C.A. § 2001, prohibits the use of polygraphs by employers with regard to job applicants or employees. Limited exceptions are made for some government contractors, some providers of security services, some drug industries, and some instances involving employee crime. The act is administered by the Secretary of Labor, and employees are given a private right of action.

L.   NOTICE OF PLANT CLOSINGS

Most lay-offs or plant closings by employers with 100 or more employees are subject to the notice requirements of the Worker Adjustment and Retraining Notification Act of 1988, 29 U.S.C.A. § 2101. Employers must give 60 days notice to the employees' union or to the employees in the absence of a union, prior to such actions. Failure to comply with the act can result in employer liability for backpay and benefits to employees, and the imposition of fines. Enforcement actions are to be brought in federal district court.

M. MIGRANT FARM WORKERS

The Migrant and Seasonal Agricultural Worker Protection Act, 29 U.S.C.A. § 1801 et seq., attempts to regulate migrant and seasonal farm labor by requiring farm labor contractor registration; by regulating workers safety, housing, and transportation; and by requiring employers to keep certain records. Enforcement provisions include a private right of action for act violations. See Barrett v. Adams Fruit Co. (11th Cir.1989) (act preempts exclusive remedy provision of Florida's workers' compensation law).

N. CONTAGIOUS DISEASES IN THE WORK PLACE

Contagious disease in the workplace, and the increasing number of employees with AIDS (Acquired Immune Deficiency Syndrome), have focused attention on new employer-employee legal issues in recent years.

Of great importance to workers with diseases are medical benefits that are usually protected by the Employee Retirement Income Security Act of 1974, (ERISA) 29 U.S.C.A. § 1140. ERISA protected benefits plans may afford relief from acts of discrimination in connection with discontinuation of health insurance, denial of disability payments or pensions, or forced retirements.

It should also be noted that the Occupational Safety and Health Act, (OSHA) 29 U.S.C.A. § 651 et seq., imposes duties upon employers to provide safe workplaces free from recognized hazards, which can include contagious and other diseases.

An employer who discloses that a worker has a contagious disease may face common law claims for invasion of privacy. Also, states that have adopted fair employment practices laws in the handicap area may offer workers an additional remedy for discrimination. Finally, an employer could face state tort liability for any intentional exposure of workers to contagious diseases. See Chapters 3, 8, supra. Furthermore, the employer could be liable for third-party harm by way of negligent hiring and retention of workers with contagious diseases.

O.   FAMILY AND MEDICAL LEAVE

The Family and Medical Leave Act of 1993, 29 U.S.C.A. §§ 2601, et seq., requires covered employers to grant up to 12 weeks of unpaid job protected leave to eligible employees for certain family and medical reasons. Leave must be provided for: child care after births or adoptions; care of a spouse, child, or parent with a serious health condition; and any serious health condition of the employee that prevents job performance.

P.   VIOLENCE AGAINST WOMEN

The Violence Against Women Act of 1994, 42 U.S.C.A. § 13981, provides a civil rights cause of action for violent crimes with a gender motive. This Act is aimed at individual defendants; however, liability might be imposed upon employers for the acts of their employees. See generally, Doe v. Hartz (N.D.Iowa 1997).

Q. UNIFORMED SERVICES PERSONNEL

No federal anti-discrimination laws have been enacted by Congress to protect homosexuals and lesbians from discrimination; however, there has been a federal effort to assist such individuals in the non-disclosure of their preferences upon entry into the military. See Pub. L. 103–160, approved Nov. 30, 1993, 107 Stat. 1670.

*

INDEX

References are to Pages

ATTORNEYS
See also, Attorney's Fees
As employee vs. independent contractor, 51
Workers' compensation coverage of, 51

ATTORNEY'S FEES AND COSTS
Civil Rights Acts, Reconstruction, 458
Civil Rights Attorney's Fees Awards Act and amendment, 459
Denial of, under Federal Rule of Civil Procedure 68, 474–477
Federal Rule of Civil Procedure 54(d), 458–459, 474–477
Federal Rule of Civil Procedure 68, 474–477
Fee shifting statutes and waiver, 471
"Lodestar" figure, 466–467, 469–470
Pendente lite, awarded, 465–466
Reasonable award, 466–467
Social security insurance programs, 186
Statutes providing for, 459–460

BLACK LUNG (PNEUMOCONIOSIS) BENEFITS LEGISLATION
Generally, 22, 167–172
Benefits, death and disability, 169–171
Black Lung Benefits Act, 22, 167
Black Lung Benefits Amendments of 1981, 22, 167
Black Lung Benefits Reform Act of 1977, 22, 167–168
Black Lung Benefits Revenue Act of 1981, 22, 167
Black Lung Benefits Review Act of 1977, 22, 167
Black Lung Disability Trust Fund, 168
Claims administration and procedures, 168–169, 171
Coal miners, 167
Consolidated Omnibus Budget Reconciliation Act of 1985, 22, 167
Constitutionality, 167
Eligibility, 169–171
Federal Coal Mine Health and Safety Act of 1969, 22
Federal Mine Safety Act of 1997, 172
History, 167–169
Income maintenance program, 22
Scope, 167–169
Special statutory coverage, 81, 84

BOILER INSPECTION ACTS
Absolute and mandatory duties, 15
Federal Employers' Liability Act, 15

BORROWED EMPLOYEE
See, Loaned Employees

DEATH ON THE HIGH SEAS ACT
See also, Seamen
Generally, 17
Twilight Zone, 17

DEFENSES
See also, Tort Liability of Employer
Employer's defenses to compensation claim
Violation of orders and rules, 75–76
Safety rules, regulations, and statutes, 75–76
Willful misconduct of employee, 75–76

DISABILITY
See also, Disability Insurance, Schedule Injuries, "Second Injury" Problem, Social Security Insurance Programs, Wages
Generally, 98–102
Auto insurance and workers' compensation, 131–132
Black Lung Benefits Legislation, 169–171
Categories of
Disfigurement, 101–102
Permanent partial, 100
Permanent total, 101
Temporary partial, 99
Temporary total, 99–100
Death after disability, 105–106
Longshore and Harbor Workers' Compensation Act, 21
Military personnel, 13–14
Nature of, economic rather than physical, 100
Odd lot doctrine, 101
Supplemental Security Income, 185
Unemployment compensation disability benefits, 148–149
War Hazards Compensation Act, 21
Workers' compensation and auto insurance, 131–132

DISABILITY INSURANCE
See, Social Security Insurance Programs

DISASTER UNEMPLOYMENT ASSISTANCE
Unemployment compensation, 147

DISCHARGE, UNJUST
See, Unjust Discharges

DISCRIMINATION
See, Job Anti-discrimination Legislation

DISEASE
Common vs. occupational, 82–83
Pneumonia, 82–83

DISFIGUREMENT
Generally, 101–102
Burns, 102
Scars, 102
Statutes authorizing compensation for, 102

DOMESTIC EMPLOYEES
As casual employees, 44
Defined, 44
Minimum number of employees exception, 44
Workers' compensation coverage of, 44

DRUGS IN THE WORKPLACE
Drug Free Workplace Act of 1988, 495
Drug testing, 495–496
Employee privacy vs. employer concern for safety and health, 495
National Labor Relations Board, 496

DUAL CAPACITY DOCTRINE
Corporate officer, 47
Employee participation in enterprise, 47–48
Employers, 35, 37–38
Executives, 47
Partners, 47–48
Physicians, 37–38

DUAL EMPLOYMENT
Concurrent employers, 54–55
Successive employers, 55–56

DURING COURSE OF EMPLOYMENT
See, In the Course of Employment

ECONOMIC APPRAISAL
Social and economic policies of workers' compensation, 30–31

EDUCATION AMENDMENTS
See, Title IX–Sex Discrimination in Education Programs

ELECTION
Constitutional theories of workers' compensation, 24–25
Of coverage, 24
Presumptive coverage, 25